Nordic Elite Sport

Svein S. Andersen & Lars Tore Ronglan

Nordic Elite Sport

Same ambitions — different tracks

UNIVERSITETSFORLAGET

© Universitetsforlaget 2012

ISBN 978-82-15-01939-0 (Norway)
ISBN 978-91-47-09772-2 (Sweden)
ISBN 978-87-630-0245-5 (Denmark)

Distribution:

Norway
Universitetsforlaget AS
P.O. Box 508 Sentrum
NO-0105 Oslo
www.universitetsforlaget.no

Denmark
DBK, Mimersvej 4
DK-4600 Køge, Denmark
Tel +45 3269 7788
Fax +45 3269 7789

Sweden
Liber AB
Kalendegatan 26
205 10 Malmö
Tel. +46 40 25 86 00
www.liber.se
Kundtjänst +46 8 690 93 30

North America
International Specialized Book Services
920 NE 58th Ave., Suite 300
Portland, OR 97213, USA
Tel +1 800 944 6190
Fax +1 503 280 8832
E-mail: orders@isbs.com

Rest of the World
Marston Book Services, P.O. Box 269
Abingdon, Oxfordshire, OX14 4YN, UK
Tel +44 (0) 1235 465500, fax +44 (0) 1235 465555
E-mail: client.orders@marston.co.uk

All rights reserved. No part of this publication may be reproduced or used in any form or by any means – graphic, electronic or mechanical including photocopying, recording, taping or information storage or retrieval systems – without permission in writing from Universitetsforlaget at www.universitetsforlaget.no

Cover design: Nina Lykke
Prepress: Rusaanes Bokproduksjon AS
Typeset: Minion Pro 10,5/13,5
Printed in Norway by AIT Otta AS

Preface

Very little research exists on organization and leadership of elite sports in the Nordic countries. This book is both an attempt to start filling this gap and to stimulate further research in the area.

The project was initiated in 2009. We are grateful for support from *Centre for training and performance* (CTP) at the Norwegian School of Sport Sciences. 14 researchers from the four Nordic countries have contributed. The book consists of individual contributions, but it has also been a real collaborative effort. In this sense it is more than a scientific anthology. In two extensive workshops the contributors have discussed preliminary versions and attempted to develop a shared format for the presentation of the case studies. In addition the editors have carried out independent research in all four countries, to strengthen the common threads and the comparative perspective. The two editors have contributed equally to the introductory and the final comparative chapters. The editorial process has been an equal partnership. We also have benefitted from criticisms and comments from a number of colleagues as well as key actors within the sport organizations. This book is a research contribution, but hopefully it can also be of use for students as well as practitioners in the field.

Oslo, October 2011

Svein S. Andersen and *Lars Tore Ronglan*

Table of content

Preface 5

Part I What the book is about 9

1 Elite sports in Nordic countries: perspectives and challenges ... 11
   Svein S. Andersen and Lars Tore Ronglan

Part II The emergence of modern elite sport systems 25

2 Elite sport development in Norway – a radical transformation .. 27
   Matti Goksøyr and Dag Vidar Hanstad

3 The institutionalization of Team Denmark 43
   Jørn Hansen

4 The Swedish elite sport system – or the lack of it? 62
   Johan R. Norberg and Paul Sjöblom

5 Finnish elite sport – from class-based tensions to pluralist complexity 83
   Jari Lämsä

Part III Success stories 107

6 The Swedish 'golf and tennis miracle' – two paralell stories 109
   Johnny Wijk

7   Norwegian women's handball – organizing for sustainable success 131
    Lars Tore Ronglan

8   Lions on the Ice: the success story of Finnish ice hockey 152
    Jari Lämsä

9   The revival of Danish track cycling......................... 168
    Klaus Nielsen and Aage Hoffmann

Part IV Perspectives and priorities in national elite sports 191

10 Swedish elite sport: contested terrain...................... 193
    Paul Sjöblom and Josef Fahlén

11 The anatomy of elite sports organization in Finland 209
    Jarmo Mäkinen

12 Danish elite sport and Team Denmark: new trends?........... 224
    Rasmus K. Storm

13 Olympiatoppen in the Norwegian sports cluster 237
    Svein S. Andersen

Part V Same ambition – different tracks........................ 257

14 A comparative perspective on Nordic elite sport: filling a gap... 259
    Svein S. Andersen and Lars Tore Ronglan

Reference list... 285

Presentation of authors 302

Index 304

PART I

What the book is about

1

Elite sports in Nordic countries: perspectives and challenges

Svein S. Andersen and Lars Tore Ronglan

Studies of politics, welfare states and social issues often emphasize the commonalities that constitute a Nordic model. In the domain of elite sport, commonalities exist, but the differences are more striking. Not only are there differences among national elite sport systems, they also often run counter to dominant patterns of political and societal organizations within each country. Sweden, known for its ability to adapt to international challenges, has over the last decades had the most stable overall structures within the domain of sport. Finland has perhaps the strongest tradition for centralization of authority, but in this period, the elite sport system has become increasingly fragmented. In contrast, Norway with the strongest tradition for decentralization and egalitarianism has developed the most centralized elite sport system. In Denmark, where the state has been most reluctant to intervene in economy and society, we find a state institution for elite sport supported by special legislation. In the other countries the state keeps an arm's length distance.

This book explores how such differences have come about, and how they influence the way challenges of modern elite sport are dealt with within the different countries. Of course, there are variations within each country with respect to how different sports are organized and pursue excellence. To illustrate this, we have included a section that illustrates four cases of sustained success stories. The focus of the book is on how elite sport is dealt with within the overall organization of sports, how Nordic countries consistently do well in certain sports, and how special efforts relating to professionalization of elite training and development are organized. A comparison of the Nordic countries will illuminate similarities as well as differences in the four countries: Denmark, Finland, Norway and Sweden.

Why take a closer look at elite sport systems?

In a number of areas, the Nordic countries have been subject to intense comparative research. This is for instance the case for welfare state studies. However, there are no systematic comparative studies of elite sports in the Nordic countries. Recently, *Sport in Society* (2010) published a special edition on sport in the Scandinavian countries. Scandinavia comprises three of the Nordic countries; Denmark, Sweden and Norway. The articles in the edition highlighted some characteristics associated with Scandinavian sport in general, such as the way sport is organized as voluntary organizations (Ibsen & Seippel 2010), the extent to which sport policies reflect the broader Scandinavian welfare policies (Bergsgard & Norberg 2010), and how sports for children are emphasized and organized according to specific criteria (Støckel, Strandbu, Solenes, Jørgensen & Fransson 2010). Even though these issues are related to the organization and workings of elite sport in these countries, elite sport development as such was not specifically discussed.

In the Nordic countries, even within-country studies of elite sports are remarkably few. A couple of studies have discussed the organization of elite sport in Norway (Augestad, Bergsgard & Hansen 2006; Steen-Johnsen & Hanstad 2008), Sweden (Sjoblom & Fahlen 2010), and Denmark (Storm & Nielsen 2010) respectively. One main finding of these studies is that, due to increasing international competition, processes of professionalization and standardization are going on. However, studies of the relationships between the actors constituting the elite sport systems, and the core processes supporting performance development, are still lacking. Particularly, there is an absence of systematic comparisons between the four Nordic countries. These shortcomings in the existing research literature are the point of departure for this book.

The aim of the book is to look into and compare the national elite sport systems, and to dive deeper into some specific success stories in each country. It should be noted that one major sport in all the Nordic countries, namely football, is not specifically dealt with. There are two main reasons for this. First, male elite football is the most commercialized and professionalized sport also in this region of the world. Consequently, professional football constitutes a quite autonomous field in relation to the national elite sport organizations in general. Second, football is the only sport that has already been subject to several Scandinavian studies, both within-country studies (Billing, Frantzen & Peterson 2004; Carlsson 2009; Eliasson 2009; Norberg 2009) and studies with a Scandinavian perspective (Andersson & Carlsson 2009; Gammelsæter 2009).

Success in elite sport can be defined in different ways. A simple way is to measure success purely as results achieved in major international competitions like the Olympic Games and World Championships. Based on this criterion alone, Nordic countries are quite successful in elite sport. However, the field of competitive sport is differentiated. International popularity and prestige, as well as ideas about what kind of sports really 'count', differ widely. Thus, the understanding of success in elite sport should also include national perspectives on what kind of sports are most important in the specific country. Moreover, one could argue that international medals in themselves represent no societal value; it is the societal importance of the medals (e.g. influence on mass sport, national identity, etc.) that make 'success' valuable for a country. Bairner (2010: 740) concluded that a valuable aspect of Nordic elite sports is the strong links between sport and community, and that 'elite performers retain close ties to their roots'.

Success depends on many different factors. We do not attempt to provide a detailed explanation of variations in results among Nordic countries. We focus on the organizational models of elite sports within the different countries and in different sports. However, such models of organization are likely to have a major impact on overall results in international competitions. They are intended to support efforts to develop world class performance. Despite similar ambitions, the Nordic countries have pursued quite different strategies in this respect. National elite sport systems vary considerably with respect to degree of centralization and coordination. Not only do such differences demonstrate significant national variations within a general international trend towards increased rationalization and professionalization of elite sports (Houlihan & Green 2008); the national elite sport systems also develop with a surprising autonomy from general political and societal models of organization in the wider societies. The causes and consequences of such differences are some of the issues to be explored in this book.

In contrast to quantitative studies that are built around rough structural indicators (De Bosscher, Bingham, Shibli, van Bottenburg & De Knop 2008), we try to capture the more detailed structures as well as intentions and processes behind national efforts in elite sports, both at the national level and at the level of specific sports. The development and effects of organizational models are discussed within an institutional perspective. Organizational models are not simply tools designed to deal with specific challenges related to competitiveness in international sports. Strategies reflect underlying struggles over legitimate values and interests, as well as the instrumentality and efficiency of different types of arrangements (March & Olsen 1989). The role of such factors is clearly expressed in the empirical chapters of the book. In the final comparative chapter we will more explicitly draw upon such a conceptual framework.

A major contribution of this book is that it demonstrates the importance of the organizational level in explaining variations in national achievements. Overall tendencies towards isomorphism can go hand in hand with significant differences on this level, even among countries that in a comparative context may be described as most equal cases. Such differences also influence how national developments are conceptualized and analysed by national researchers that have contributed to the book. Both the structure and the content reflect different national self-understandings. Hence, the chapters echo the significance of political processes (Denmark), conflicting organizational perspectives (Sweden), fragmentation (Finland), and networking processes (Norway) in understanding the development and workings of the national systems. This creates special challenges for the final comparative analysis.

Before we enter a more detailed discussion, we will briefly describe how the Nordic countries have performed internationally, in specific sports and generally as reflected in the Olympic results.

Nordic countries – international results

The Nordic countries are in many respects quite similar. They have small populations and comparable social, economic and political systems. They are among the wealthiest countries in the world, with strong welfare states and a strong emphasis on egalitarian values. Social democratic values were the context for investments in infrastructure for mass sports in the post-Second World War period (Goksøyr, Andersen & Asdal 1996). However, this does not mean that modern elite sports have no role to play in these societies. Compared to their size they all do well, and often better than could be expected, in international sports.

As previously mentioned, success can be measured in different ways. Some non-Olympic sports (e.g. golf and tennis) have high prestige and are widespread throughout the world. These sports have been important and remarkably successful in Sweden during the last decades, as will be described in chapter 6. For some professionalized Olympic sports, the major contests are not the Olympic Games. This is the case for football and road cycling, which have a strong tradition in Denmark. Both Sweden and Denmark have done quite well in football, while Denmark and to some extent Norway have achieved good results in cycling. Measured in active members, spectator interest and money, football is the most popular sport in all Nordic countries, while ice hockey comes close in both Sweden and particularly Finland. Also in ice hockey, other tournaments like the World Championships and the play-offs in the US National Hockey League are as prestigious as the Olympic tournament, if not more so.

Nevertheless, given that the Olympic Games is the most prestigious contest in many sports, elite sport organizations in nations worldwide put a major effort into succeeding in the Olympic sports. The Olympic Games also cover a wide variety of sports. Therefore, the simple statistics in the figures below points to the overall national competitiveness of elite sports (Andersen, 2009).

In summer sports, Denmark, Finland and Sweden have all historically done much better than Norway. Finland, Norway and Sweden have strong traditions in winter sports. Due to natural conditions, winter sports have a very weak position in Denmark. Figures 1 and 2 show the Olympic medals won by Norway, Sweden, Finland and Denmark (in summer sports) from 1952–2010.

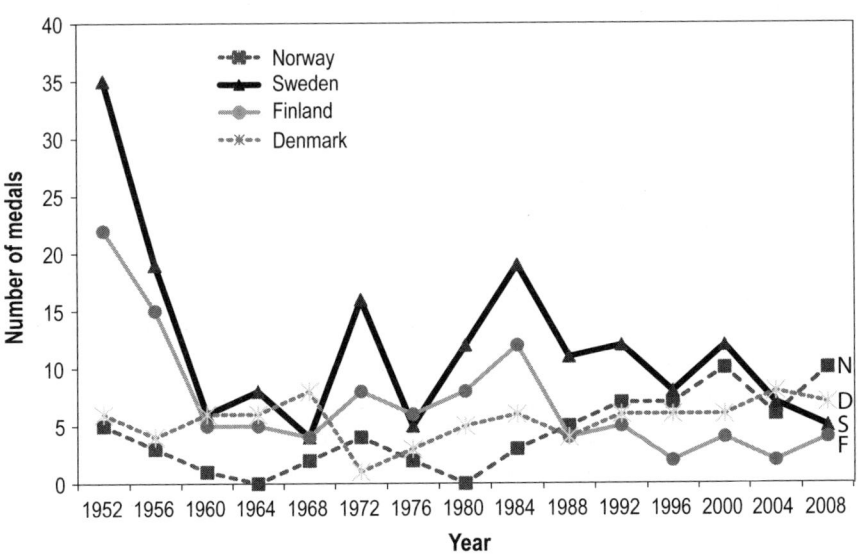

Figure 1.1: Summer Olympics – comparing four countries

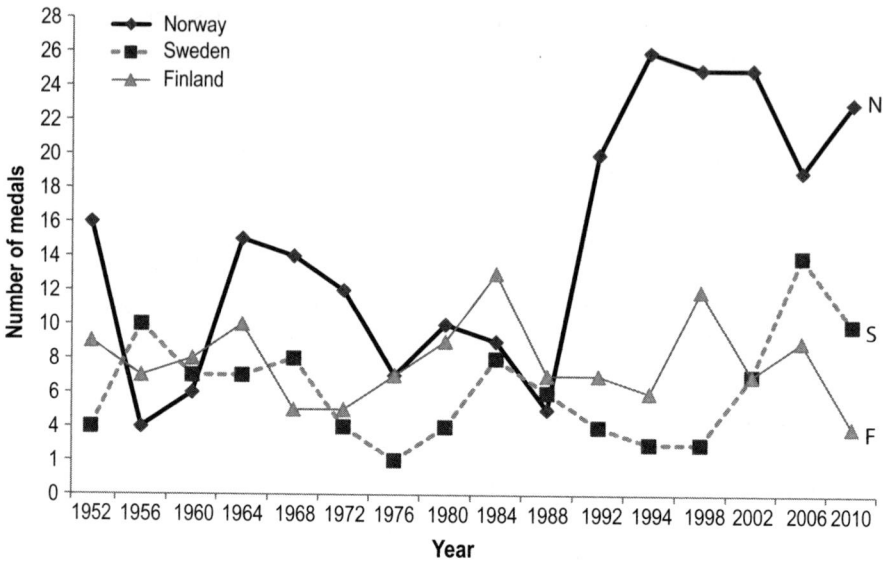

Figure 1.2: Winter Olympics – comparing three countries

There is a significant shift in favour of Norway after 1988, both in the Summer and Winter Olympics. In summer sports, where Norway historically has been much less successful than its neighbours, it has managed to reach about the same level. The average number of Olympic medals has risen from 2.5 to 8. Denmark has been able to keep the same level, while Sweden and Finland have lost ground. In winter sports, Norway has managed to establish a significantly higher level of success than Sweden and Finland. The average number of medals has risen by a factor of 2.3. However, as pointed out, these comparisons do not give a complete picture of elite sport success in the Nordic countries, as it is limited to Olympic medals.

Norway, Sweden and Finland have equally strong traditions in winter sports, while Sweden, Finland and Denmark historically have done better than Norway in the Summer Olympics. With the exception of Denmark in winter sports, natural conditions are much the same. Investment in elite sports in all four countries has increased considerably over the last 20 years. The exact numbers are hard to identify. Augestad and Bergsgard (2007: 280–81) argue that the total spending on elite sports in Norway is a little less than in Denmark. Sweden and Finland, on the other hand, have spent less, particularly on the central level. Significantly, the most striking difference seems to be related to the differences between models for elite sports development.

Elite sports – convergence and divergence

Research on the development of international elite sport systems has given support to the argument that elite sport organizations in Western countries have become more and more similar during the last two decades (Augestad, Bergsgard & Hansen 2006; Green & Oakley 2001; Houlihan & Green 2008; Oakley & Green 2001). Citing Andersen and Eliassen (1993), the authors rightly point out that important determinants of public policy are found in the supranational policy network, rather than in domestic policy alone (Houlihan & Green 2008: 9). To some extent this captures a broad trend of convergence.

Convergence can be defined as alignment with elements in an institutional environment so that there is a lessening of variance around some central dimensions (DiMaggio & Powell 1983). Common elements of national elite sport systems include construction of elite facilities, support for 'full-time' athletes, the provision of coaching, sports science and sports medicine support service; and a hierarchy of competition opportunities centred on preparation for international sports (Bosscher et al. 2006; Houlihan & Green 2008). In this sense, also the Nordic countries have become more similar over the last decades. Such a tendency is not surprising, given the nature of international elite sport.

Elite sport is characterized by intense competitive pressures. Convergence stems from the attempt to apply general blueprints, or templates, or to imitate successful prototypes. Blueprints or templates are general models that are used for comparing or evaluating practices. This line of argument emphasizes how cognitive models, reflecting general ideas about rationality, come to be viewed as appropriate, attractive or necessary institutional recipes in a field of action (Meyer & Rowan 1977). Prototypes are specific representations of such models to be imitated by those organizations that seek to improve competitiveness. Both templates and prototypes may trigger reorientation, reforms and changes across national systems (Wedlin 2007).

Studies of modern elite sport show how the basic elements of the general and abstract model of modern elite sport have been integrated in national elite sport systems in developed countries. Such tendencies reflect macro-institutional processes at the level of the international systems, but also attempts to imitate others that are perceived as particularly successful (Houlihan & Green 2008). This trend towards convergence does not imply that national elite sport in various countries or within specific sport organizes or pursues key elements in modern elite sport in very similar ways. How general ideas, cognitive models and norms in the international environment are exploited, depends on characteristics of the local national context (Thornton & Occasio 2008).

Such local adaptations are typical for all national elite sport systems. As Augestad et al. (2006: 310) have pointed out: 'Even if we find that the various nations have developed a system of comprehensive expertise to serve their national sports teams, a closer examination of the systems will uncover many differences: roles, interaction between roles, patterns of interaction between experts and athletes, decision-making systems, treatment of performers, patterns of influence, ways of thinking, and so on.' As this book will clearly demonstrate, increased convergence on a general level goes hand in hand with remarkable and growing divergence between Nordic elite sport systems.

The development in the Nordic countries is consistent with a growing body of general research over the last decades that emphasizes not only how ideas travel, but also how local actors actively interpret, edit and use them in local contexts (Røvik 2007) Alignment with general models may vary for different reasons; such as available resources, degree of conflict over what is needed and what can be done, or conflicting demands from the wider context about appropriate solutions (Kraatz & Block 2008). Such factors also point to the importance of institutional entrepreneurship, and this concept seems particularly useful when looking at the development of elite sport systems in the Nordic countries over the last decades.

We do not attempt to explain historical developments. However, the ideas about different types and conditions for institutional entrepreneurship is a useful frame for organizing key elements in the stories about why and how the Nordic countries have pursued quite different models of elite sport. Institutional entrepreneurship refers to activities of actors who have an interest in particular institutional arrangements and how to leverage resources to create new ones (Maguire, Hardy & Lawrence 2004: 657). The ability of entrepreneurs to successfully influence institutional arrangements depends on a number of factors, related to their position in the organizational field as well as field conditions (Hardy & Maguire 2008).

As our empirical discussions will show, entrepreneurs may vary with respect to centrality. It is often argued that core actors may have more resources, but fewer incentives for change. Peripheral actors, on the other hand, may be more likely to want change, but their capacity to achieve it is limited. Viewed in isolation, such constellations point to institutional inertia. However, central actors may have more information about new opportunities and alternatives. At the same time, uncertainty about future success or the experience of a crisis may undermine the position of core actors. This may provide opportunities for peripheral actors. The result may be new alliances that can effectively influence the development of the field, but in some cases no one is able to establish sufficient control to enforce a new order.

Nordic development: common challenges, different responses

The argument about convergence implies that countries not only face many of the same challenges, but they also share some general ideas about how to deal with these challenges. The divergence argument emphasizes how local institutional contexts create opportunities and limitations in respect to what are seen as the critical issues and how to deal with them. In the Nordic countries some of these contextual factors are shared, while others differ. Nordic sports have traditionally been, and still are, dominated by voluntary organizations. In contrast to other parts of the world, neither commercial sport activities nor university-based sport activities have played a major role (Ibsen & Seippel 2010). The voluntary activities within local sport clubs form the basis of the overall sports culture in all the Nordic countries. However, there has always been a tension between the broad sport organizations and the Olympic Committees that have emphasized a more narrow set of values related to competitiveness (Goksøyr 2011; Sjöblom & Fahlén 2010).

Organized Nordic sport reflects a broad movement that developed in parallel to the strong welfare states in these countries. Both the welfare state and the sports movement were deeply rooted in social egalitarian values. Before the Second World War, societal politics cut across the functional principle relating to individual sports in all four countries. Typically one sport had one association for 'workers' and one for the 'upper classes'. In Finland this remained the basic arrangement until the early 1990s. In Denmark, Norway and Sweden, as in other Western European countries, societal politics lost out to the functional principle of sports in the 1950s. A common trait in all countries during the 1960s and 1970s was the emphasis on elite sports as amateurism. Elite sports were part of mass sports.

Consequently, even if there were some differences between the Nordic countries, they shared a set of values and institutions that came to influence how the challenges of modern elite sport were defined. Modern elite sport, from the late 1970s and onwards, implied increased focus on competitiveness and national prestige. Such changes reinforced some traditional tensions and introduced controversial new issues. One traditional challenge was the tension between elites and amateurism on the one hand, and the values of the broad mass movement on the other. The increased emphasis on international competitiveness also threatened the basic values related to play, health and the good life: values that were also central to the welfare state. Sole emphasis on competitiveness and results created a number of ethical dilemmas. Increased pressure for commercialization also threatened the role and position of the voluntary sport organizations. Indirectly this raised the question of a new state role, as both the provider of resources and organizer of effective elite sport arrangements.

Despite such common concerns, responses in Nordic countries differed with respect to which actors played a key role, strategies pursued, preferred models of organization, and also with respect to when reforms and changes took place:

In Denmark, debates about reforms started already in the late 1970s. This led to an Elite Sport Law in 1984 and the creation of an elite sport institution, DANTOP, later Team Denmark. In this process, and in the changes that followed, civil servants and party politicians played a key role. A major concern was to ensure that elite sport was taken care of within a welfare state framework.

In Norway, in contrast, initiatives for organizational reforms came from leaders within the broad sport movement and the Olympic Committee. As in Denmark there was a concern for the situation of elite athletes, but with a stronger emphasis on how to improve international competitiveness. The elite sport organization, Olympiatoppen, was established in 1988 as an instrument for both the sports confederation and the Olympic Committee. The state's role remained mainly a provider of resources.

These changes in Denmark and Norway were paralleled by a closer cooperation, and eventually a merger between the national sports confederation and the Olympic Committees in the mid-1990s. However, the conditions for this merger were quite different. In Norway, the position of the national Olympic Committee was strong, in Denmark it was weak. The centralization of special elite sport efforts in both Denmark and Norway supplemented and modified the traditional segmented structure. Nevertheless, individual sports federations still had the main responsibility for developments within their sports. In retrospect, one could perhaps say that both these countries were proactive. They early established institutional arrangements designed to manage challenges, including tensions and controversies, that later became more intense.

In contrast, Sweden has largely dealt with challenges arising from the development of modern elite sport within the traditional organizational structure. This structure emphasizes the autonomy of individual sport federations and clear division of roles and responsibilities between the sports confederation on the one hand, and the national Olympic Committee on the other. Finland has had both a more complex structure and undergone major changes during the last decades. Nevertheless, like in Sweden, Finnish sport has not been able to establish one centralized elite sport body.

In Sweden there have been major changes in how elite sport has been dealt with on a daily basis. However, the relationships between the national sports confederation (RF) and the Olympic Committee (SOK) have been characterized by disagreement and open conflict about organizational solutions and priorities. Although covering and supporting all sports, RF is torn between elite and mass sport priorities. On the other hand, the Olympic Committee, based on strict priorities, provides direct support to federations, clubs, athletes and teams; but only in Olympic sports. Despite the general understanding that this may not be the best way to support national elite sport developments, an alternative cooperative solution seems distant.

Finland kept the main structure of overall sports that reflected societal cleavages from the pre-Second World War era until the mid-1990s. In the years that followed, Finland went through major changes, but in a direction quite different from the other three Nordic countries. There has been a unification of competing confederations reflecting longstanding societal political cleavages. However, the current confederation, TUC, established in the mid-1990s, is weak in terms of authority and operational responsibilities. It mainly provides services for individual sports associations. The overall tendency is towards more autonomy for increasingly specialized independent sports associations that include both competitive and recreational activities. The national Olympic Committee is independent and has a limited role in ongoing elite developments.

National elite sport systems: how to explore and compare?

The focus of this book is national elite sport systems: specifically, how they came about, how they relate to successes in individual sports, and how they differ in terms of centralization, responsibilities and roles, and how this influences the capacity for successful elite sport development.

The first question is: what is covered by the concept of an elite sport system? A wide definition of the concept might include all actors and relationships influencing elite sport, including a number of factors outside the domain of sport. A narrow definition would focus simply on sport organizations with a sole responsibility and focus on elite sport, like the central elite sport organizations in Denmark and Norway and the Olympic Committees in Sweden and Finland. Our point of departure is that we need to look beyond the designated sport organizations, because Nordic elite sport is not separated from the broader sports movement. However, we will limit ourselves to organizations within the sports domain. In the Nordic countries the sports domain is dominated by a relatively small set of voluntary organizations, with a limited direct role for state agencies, school, universities and independent sport research institutes. Given other research questions or other research settings, the boundaries might have been drawn differently.

Before we move on, we need to clarify what we mean by the concept of 'system'. First, our use of the concept is not normative in the sense that it implies an integrated, well-functioning arrangement. Second, systems are not necessarily stable structures; they will often contain elements of dynamics and change. A system perspective directs our attention to the nature of actors, relationships and processes, where interdependencies, intensity of interaction, mechanisms for decision-making and aggregation of individual actions may vary considerably. In this way it serves as an organizing framework (Buckley 1967; Burns, Flam & De Man 2000).

In terms of our overall design, the book focuses on elite sport within a set of countries that represent 'most similar systems' (Meckstroth 1975; Gerring 2007). On a general level, these countries are similar with respect to size, geographical region, societal and political institutions, and welfare state arrangements. As already pointed out, in the domain of sport they share a basic model emphasizing a broad voluntary sports movement, sports for all, and the utilitarian values of sport participation. The sports domain is dominated by one or a few organizations that incorporate regional levels and local clubs. These similar characteristics are the context of the divergent paths that are explored and compared in this book.

The authors of the different chapters are specialists on their own national systems. They possess rich knowledge and have used a variety of methods to provide the data underlying the chapters. Written sources like historical material, results statistics and policy documents are combined with interviews with key informants to enrich the information of each case. The stories they tell are quite different not only in terms of what has happened, but also in terms of what kind of actors and processes they emphasize. The latter reflects both differences in national self-understanding as well as what have been the contingent issues, controversies and priorities. These differences are in themselves quite illuminating for understanding the particularities of elite sport in the different countries.

The editors have written the chapters on the Norwegian system. In addition we also have a comparative ambition. The different emphasis and nature of national contributions raise the question of how and in what ways comparison can be made. How can we distinguish between different realities and different perceptions of realities? To what extent are overall similarities and differences representative of real variation between these countries? To handle such questions, the editors have carried out independent cross-national research, through literature reviews and interviews with key informants. We draw upon the conceptual framework from institutional theory presented above to identify dimensions for systematic comparisons.

A recurring question is why some countries perform better than others in international elite sports. For some countries, the answer is obvious. They have a much greater population and thereby more talents, better natural conditions, more resources for research and development, and better facilities. In this book we explore and compare 'most similar systems'. Such a design goes a long way to control for these most popular explanatory variables. It allows us to take a closer look at the organizational factors and processes that are likely to have an impact on results. As pointed out, this level of analysis has received little attention in the literature.

A comprehensive study which aims to capture why some nations perform particularly well in major sports events, is the 'Sport Policy Factors Leading to International Sporting Success' (SPLISS) study (De Bosscher et al. 2008; De Bosscher, de Knop & van Bottenburg 2009). It compares six European countries of different size, exploiting three levels of analysis: the macro-level (population and GDP), meso-level (factors determined by sport policies and politics), and micro-level (factors that influence the success of the individual athlete). The study is based on an econometric approach, where degree of success is measured as the ratio between various explanatory factors and the number of medals in major competitions.

The contributions in this book illustrate that such studies have a number of limitations. Viewing GDP per capita as an indicator of economic resources available for elite development may not only be inaccurate, but misleading. The Norwegian GDP per capita has grown much more than in the other Nordic countries over the last 30 years. However, the most important improvements in Norwegian Olympic results came from 1988 to the early 1990s. During this period the level and growth in GDP per capita was about the same in Norway, Sweden and Denmark, with only Finland lagging somewhat behind. The key to increased spending in Norway was related to the 1994 Olympics. Later, Norwegian GDP per capita increased significantly compared to the neighbouring countries. However, the budget for elite sport in Norway has stagnated, and in some years decreased. Although results vary, there seems to be no significant differences in total elite sport spending among the four countries over the past decade.

In international elite sports there are small margins that distinguish between the best. Small differences in preparation, systematic development work, and learning and sharing of experiences may have major consequences for results. However, creating organizations that can support such processes cannot simply be designed according to a blueprint. Both in successful individual sports and in national systems of elite sport development, there are important factors that facilitate and constrain specific organizational solutions. What works in one setting may not work in another. It is important, therefore, to view elite sport organizations as outcomes of complex institutionalization processes reflecting historical contingencies, societal developments and entrepreneurial efforts. This is consistent with the institutional framework that we have introduced and which will serve as the analytical framework for the concluding comparative discussion.

The structure of the book

The rest of the book is divided into four principal parts. Part II covers the *emergence of modern elite sport systems* (chapters 2–5). These four chapters deal with the historical development in each of the Nordic countries, focusing particularly on elite versus mass sport, critical decisions about organizational structures and resources, and important controversies and dilemmas inherent in the national elite sport systems. Part III: *Success stories* (chapters 6–9), discusses conditions for and vital processes underlying sustainable success in Swedish tennis and golf, Norwegian women's handball, Finnish men's ice hockey and Danish track cycling. The cases illustrate that there are many different roads to excellence. Part IV: *Perspectives and priorities in national elite sports* (chapters 10–13) illustrates similarities and differences between the national systems. Building on the historical development presented in part II, this section goes further into policy issues, controversies and the actual working of the elite sport systems. Part V: *Same ambition – different tracks* (chapter 14), presents systematic comparisons based on the previous parts. This chapter highlights how the historical development, success in particular sports and current elite sport systems represent significant and sometimes surprising variations within a general broad trend of convergence.

PART II

The emergence of modern elite sport systems

Introduction

This part focuses on the development of modern elite sport within the Nordic countries over the last decades. The countries have a common point of departure. This includes social democratic values, a strong welfare state and sport organized as a broad voluntary movement. They face many of the same challenges, but responses differ with respect to key actors, the timing and nature of change processes and outcomes. In some ways all countries follow a broad international trend towards professionalization, increased application of scientific knowledge, investments in infrastructure and training facilities.

However, within this broad trend, the four countries have become more and more different in the ways elite sport is organized and supported by the state and wider society. What we observe are complex institutionalization processes reflecting local conditions, but also active entrepreneurship that sometimes succeeds and often fails. One central issue concerns the relationship between mass and elite sport. Another is how the broad voluntary sports movement should deal with professionalization, commercialization and the role of the state.

In Norway (chapter 2) key actors within the sports movements in the early 1980s initiated changes that later led to a transformation of the elite sport system. They introduced a new perspective on elite athletes, within the sport and in the wider society, with a strong emphasis on requirements for international success. Chapter 3 on Denmark illustrates a parallel, but quite different, process dominated by party politics and civil servants. It is a story of how elite sport was integrated into a welfare perspective, modifying the role of international competitiveness.

Sweden (chapter 4) differs from the other two by neither being an alliance between different sports organizations, nor being an external, politically driven process. The overall institutional structure remains remarkably stable. The search for a new model to accommodate the needs of modern elite sport has been blocked by lasting tensions between the sports confederation and the national Olympic Committee. In Finland (chapter 5) class-based cleavages within the sports movement lasted to the mid-1990s. The fall of the communist block led to a reorientation, which eventually led to weakening of central sport confederations and sport federations and a trend towards fragmentation.

2

Elite sport development in Norway — a radical transformation

Matti Goksøyr and Dag Vidar Hanstad

Norway has been a relatively successful nation in overall Olympic history, especially when it comes to winter sports. However, from the 1990s, the country has experienced even more victories and greater sporting success than ever before. Since 1992, Norway has been one of the top nations at the Winter Olympics, with more gold medals than any other nation through history. In the same period, Norwegian athletes have also performed better than before in other sports, including summer sports.

The main object of this chapter is to look more closely at the elite sports system that has enabled or helped these things to happen. We will first discuss the historical context from which an elite sports system could make its way and develop. While reflecting and interacting with the wider social and political context, the development of the modern elite sport system from the late 1980s results from entrepreneurial efforts within the sports movement. A key concern has been to define elite sport in a way that co-exists with values of mass sport and an egalitarian tradition. When presenting the resulting system, we will highlight cultural influences, power struggles and sports political controversies. We will also look at additional challenges which the system already meets and might also have to confront in the future.

Our key sources of information were document analysis and analysis of media texts. The systematic review of documents included articles in scientific journals, sport policy documents from the Norwegian Olympic and Paralympic Committee and Confederation of Sports, the Ministry of Culture, and media coverage. Both authors have detailed knowledge of Norwegian sport (e.g. Goksøyr 2010; Goksøyr & Hanstad 2005; Hanstad 2002).

Development after the Second World War

From the start of organized sport in Norway, elite sport had to struggle for its legitimacy. Ideological currents emphasized that sport (and especially its Norwegian parallel 'idrett') should mean something more than just competitions and victories. It was held that genuine sport, in line with this ideology, should have deeper purposes, outside of sport itself, like the strengthening of the nation through improving its physical military capacities and/or improving popular health. Such utilitarian ideas were hegemonic in long periods, especially during times of political controversies (Tønnesson 1986).

The Norwegian Sports Confederation, in its varying forms, often had to adapt to this. Could elite sport provide a purpose outside of itself? During the Second World War, the utilitarian branch of Norwegian sport had proven its worth by unselfishly closing down its competitions and activities, to go into a five-year sports boycott of the German and Nazi authorities, and contribute both to the civil and partly military resistance. Hence, for a period after the war, what could be called utilitarian ideas held a strong position. Thus the influential architect Frode Rinnan, who was a principal sports facilities constructor favored by the Norwegian state, could say in 1948: 'Continental Europe's elegant football factories and palaces of ice with its squads of well-paid gladiators are unfamiliar ideas with us' (Goksøyr, Andersen & Asdal 1996: 121). Or to put it bluntly: the ideas were unknown and we had no desire to know them.

In this ideological context, elite sport in Norway had two channels: it could either work through the different specialized sports federations, including clubs at the local level, or every fourth year it could operate through the Olympic movement. There was also another ingredient in this, for the lack of an elite sports system meant that the performers had considerable freedom, especially in individual sports, to plan and perform their own training and careers. The sports federations to a certain degree administered their own elite sport and participation in international championships. But as Norwegian sport at this time was strictly amateur-based, federations had to adjust to the general rules of the sports confederation, e.g. concerning how an amateur should be defined.

The Olympic connection came to life every fourth year when the national

Olympic Committee was brought into existence. The Norwegian Olympic Committee, hence, was very much an ad hoc organization. However, it was also a compromise between ideologies: between the Olympism of the IOC and the claimed democratic ideals of Norwegian sport. Seen from Norway, the IOC's main legitimacy, regardless of their idealistic assertions, was that they ruled the world's most prestigious sports gathering. However, the IOC was not a democratic organization. Therefore the Norwegian Olympic Committee had to be associated with the Norwegian Confederation of Sports (NIF). Until 1965 the NOK was actually elected at the NIF assembly, as it was identical with the board of the NIF (Tønnesson 1986: 185). This was not in line with the IOC's requirement that national Olympic Committees be independent from both governments and national sports confederations.

The struggle over the Norwegian Olympic Committee and its organizational affiliations was for a long while an unsolved challenge to Norwegian sport. In 1953 a proposal to separate the NOK from the NIF was voted down. In line with enthusiastic moods from historical struggles over the introduction of parliamentarism in Norway, sports leaders would exclaim 'All power to this hall' (Tønnesson 1986: 186) – meaning that the democratically elected spokesmen and spokeswomen of sport should govern all sport, including Olympic elite sport. However, in 1965 these arguments were rejected.

The NOK, on paper, became an independent organization. Nevertheless, it was subjugated to the laws of the sports confederation, to which it also had to deliver its report and accounts. According to the historian Stein Tønnesson, the change of policy in 1965 was related to the lack of success at the 1964 Tokyo Olympics at which Norway, for the first time since 1932, won no medals (best performance: fifth place in men's gymnastics). Improving conditions for Olympic participation and performance was one of the intentions of the new organization of 1965. This structure was in effect until the new restructuring of the 1990s (1996).

In the early postwar era then, elite sport in Norway could be characterized as existing in an environment dominated by values such as amateurism, voluntarism and mass sports. Although there were heroes in sports, their existence and their legitimacy came from the fact that each was 'a sportsman' among many others, with the same values and virtues as the others. Hence Norwegian skiers in the 1930s and skaters in the 1950s could be celebrated as popular heroes (heroes by and for the people). They were popular in a double meaning of the word.

Heroes and elite sports in other words existed in a sports environment where the gap between elite and regular sport was much less spectacular than today. This was an important characteristic of Norwegian sport, although it was not a condition particular to Norway. Elite sportsmen trained in club environments and mostly used normal sports equipment. Even if warnings against 'star worshipping' arose now and then, the coherence and unity of the sports movement, whether it was elite, regular or mass sports, was unquestionable. 'Sport' was seen as one unit. The term 'mass sport' was not to be defined until the 1960s. Instead there was the regular sport for adults, which in reality was the 'normal' sport in the days before children and women, from the 1960s, were welcomed into organized sports.

1952: The Olympics is coming to Norway

The organizing of the Olympic Winter Games in Oslo 1952 illustrated how elite sports could be integrated into the amateur, voluntary and mass sport-dominated Norwegian sporting life. This event gathered support from all sides of Norwegian sports, also the most utilitarian ('hygienic') side (Petersen 1952). This was demonstrated by the actions of Rolf Hofmo, former leader of the workers' sports movement and a renowned critic of the privileges of sports stars. In 1952 he was vice-president in the Norwegian Confederation of Sport and head of the state office for youth and sport (Slagstad 1998). Hofmo, very much a propagator of healthy 'sports for all', went into the Oslo Olympic Organizing Committee as its vice-president and as head of the facilities section.

When asked how working for the Olympics related to his general view on sport, Hofmo answered that the Olympics were a golden opportunity to build sports facilities and a sporting infrastructure from which all Norwegian sport would benefit (Goksøyr et al. 1996). By 'Norwegian sport' he meant 'normal' sport for regular participants. The Olympic venues were in other words to be used by 'all' sportspeople after the games. This proved to be true for most of the facilities, even if the ski jumping hill, Holmenkollen, never became a hill for regular skiers. It was only used once a year, but that is another story. Hence, the link between elite sports and the rest of sport was one of the main legitimating factors for having the Olympics in Oslo.

Nevertheless, the fact that the Olympics came to Norway introduced ways of thinking that influenced how Norwegian sport could work towards elite sports. One thing was that it actually opened up for more women's top level sport than conservative Norwegian sports officials had ever imagined or aspired to. Another influence was on the facilities. From 1952, Norwegian authorities had to acknowledge that new sports facilities should be constructed to so-called international standards. This meant that the international sports federations were the ones who decided the standards of Norwegian swimming halls, volleyball courts, etc. Today this does not seem too outrageous, but it was not an obvious and self-evident idea just after the Second World War (Goksøyr et al. 1996).

However, when Norwegian sports officials accepted things like these, it was under the self-evident condition that the sports movement in Norway should be governed by the virtues of amateurism and voluntarism. In this climate, which continued to exist for many decades after the war, elite sport gradually established itself, while the utilitarian sports ideology (Olstad 1987; Tønnesson 1986) slowly lost its foothold.

The period 1952–1970: Change processes outside sport
In this period, socio-economic development heavily influenced the framework of sport. The postwar reconstruction had taken its toll on sports. It was for example by no means obvious that public or state money should be spent on sport during times when there were more basic needs, and when there was rationing of several goods. However, a gradual economic development led to increasing material and economic prosperity. It also made possible longer holidays and more leisure time. Saturday became a normal day off for most occupations around 1970. As people looked to fill the growing amount of spare time, the introduction of television from 1960, in particular, paved the way for an increasing interest in top level sports.

Still, the organization of elite sports was not changed. It was mostly up to the athletes themselves, and their clubs, how and how much they should train, with the possible exception of football, where coaching and trainer courses had been established. For almost 20 years, the success of the 1952 games was not repeated. The occasional heroes turned up in the traditional winter sports, some also in track and field athletics. The middle distance runner Audun Boysen and the javelin thrower Egil Danielsen were among the few to achieve international success, but this was mainly due to personal ambitions or stimulating club environments. Among sports leaders, frustrations and feelings developed that more could, and should, be done with regards to Norwegian elite sports.

From the 1970s: growing understanding and acceptance of top level sports
Scepticism towards elite sport still prevailed. In a White Paper (Stortingsmelding) on Culture in 1973 a section on sport was included for the first time. It was written by Hans B. Skaset, former board member of the NIF and later Chairman of both the Athletics Association and the NIF. It stated: 'A centrally

directed sports culture which generally emphasizes one-dimensional, extreme performance standards, will hardly encourage other than passive support for sport as an entertainment phenomenon.' Central bodies within sports organizations were also criticized for concentrating too much on elite culture.

Skaset later said that his draft was printed without the politicians seeing any reason to make any changes. However, in some sports circles his ideas were not welcome, and Skaset was heavily criticized. 'My point was to tell what was about to happen. We stood before a development towards elite sport, particularly internationally. I absolutely felt there was reason to point to the unfortunate sides' (Hanstad 2002: 156). Despite this controversy, he was elected as vice-president in the NIF later the same year.

During the 1970s a more offensive thinking emerged, both in relation to mass sport and elite sport. One important phrase in the White Paper on Culture of 1973 claimed that 'sports for all' should be a goal for state policies on sport, and then gave the logically evident, but also politically laden formulation in a follow-up White Paper the same year: 'Also the winners belong to "all"' (St.meld nr.8 [1973–74], St.meld nr. 52 [1973–74]).

This formulation became an important governmental statement legitimating elite sports. It was a way of connecting the 'sport for all' ideal with support for top level sport. It was the first such statement of its kind, and it opened up state intervention in the field of elite sports. Later in the 1970s this was followed up with state scholarships to top level athletes. From 1978, the Norwegian national budget contained funding for such grants. While the rest of the support for sports came from the distribution of the football pools, support for elite sports came through the national budget. It is interesting to note the rationale behind this. Some of the arguments for such measures claimed that this was a way to counter what was seen as a growing commercialization of Norwegian sports.

In the early 1970s, the National Olympic Committee (NOK) initiated discussions with the NIF on the reorganization of elite sport. The NOK's concern was the lack of continuity in the investment (not only financial) in elite sport and the lack of coordination between the different national sports federations regarding resources and competence (Augestad & Bergsgard 2007). As a consequence, a council for coaches and leaders was established in 1974. In 1976 the council changed its name to the Consultant Group for Elite Sport. One of the proposals was to establish a top sport centre (Augestad & Bergsgard 2007).

A similar proposal was submitted by a new group established in 1978, now called the Top Sport Committee, under the leadership of the NOK's chairman (Jan Gulbrandsen). It wrote in its report that such a unit should be led by a chief consultant for elite sport (NIF 1979). The proposal was met with resistance from the NIF because of fears that the sports federations and the NOK would move away from the sports movement in which mass sport was a core value. In 1980 the general assembly voted down the proposal and instead created another committee.

Although the NIF Board did not follow up the recommendation for an elite sport unit, Augestad et al. (2007) in their research project on the Olympic Top Sports Program (hereafter Olympiatoppen) concluded that the recommendations from the Top Sport Committee in 1979 contained all the essential elements in what ended up as such a unit, namely the Project 88. The fact that all these things were happening in the 1970s must be seen as an effect of the increasing importance and seriousness of sports in modern nation states. The process might be called intensification and is certainly related to the professionalization of sports that was taking place simultaneously. The concept of intensification has been developed by Lindroth (1998), building on Heinilä's totalization concept (Heinilä 1984), and is characterized by three central stages; performance focusing, result optimization and resource mobilization. This development expanded in the next decade.

The emergence of an elite sports system
As pointed out in the previous section, some initiatives to coordinate elite sport were taken in the 1970s (Tønnesson 1986; Hanstad 2002). Developments in international elite sport, it was argued, made it impossible for Norwegian athletes to perform well without long-term and well-planned preparations (NIF 1973). This was a trend which had started in the Eastern Bloc and transferred into the West because of the great success in the former Soviet Union and the GDR in this period.

Green and Oakley (2001) point to the increasing similarities between countries in the West and to the putative emergence of a uniform (global) model of elite sport development. Other authors state that, more than ever before, they are based around a single model of elite sports development with only slight variations (Bergsgard, Houlihan, Mangseth, Nødland, & Rommetvedt 2007; Green & Houlihan 2005; de Bosscher, de Knop, & van Bottenburg 2009). The elite sport system in Norway was initiated as an attempt to be more similar to the other nations in the East and West but, as presented elsewhere in this book, the Norwegian model also differed from most others in important ways.

In 1984, as a consequence of a poor performance in the Olympic Games in Sarajevo (Winter) and Los Angeles (Summer), the NIF and NOK decided to establish a central elite sport unit. The overall objective was that Project 88, in cooperation with the federations, should work to raise the level of Norwegian elite sport so that more athletes could compete on a world-class level (NIF/NOK 1988). The first executive director, Thor Ole Rimejorde, told the newspaper *Aftenposten* how athletes could reach this goal:

> First, we get access to more money. Moreover, we hope through such a project to exploit the resources more efficiently. We have good coaches, leaders and athletes. By making conditions more conducive for them, we should also get better results. We hope to launch negotiations with key organizations such as LO (employee organization), NAF (employer organization), schools and the military (Kirkebøen 1984: 48)

This quote is an illustration of Project 88's main focus: the athlete. For the next few years this was expressed in key slogans such as 'the athlete in the centre' and 'the 24 hour athlete'. Rimejorde developed a philosophy built around the athlete. The aim was that the athlete would be given a holistic development. The executive director emphasized the development of the whole person; covering the physiological, intellectual and social capacities. In his opinion too much attention had until then been paid to endurance and strength (Hanstad 2002).

Another objective of Project 88 was to create conditions that allowed the top athletes to live a normal life and have a guaranteed minimum of security for what happens after their careers are over. 'We will try to create understanding for top athletes' situation, so that for example, they do not have to take the exam at school in the middle of the most hectic season' (Kirkebøen 1984). Such a system entailed that elite sport careers could be combined with education, military service and eventually a profession.

Quality of life was – and is – a keyword. Many elements were important: privacy, education, recreation, exercise, and diet. With this in place, one could, according to Project 88, focus on creating optimal results. It had to be a long-term project. It was estimated that 10,000–12,000 hours of training were needed for an athlete as the basis to perform at peak. This required training almost 365 days a year, sometimes several times a day, for many years. The development of a system that could provide the necessary support for athletes engaged in such efforts came gradually:

> We experienced at first that some athletes and coaches did not understand what was required. They made demands on us, which was both important and correct. But the basic premise is to make demands on themselves [...]. Not everyone understood the consequences of calling themselves athletes. At present, however, it is fully accepted that there must be training and commitment (Hanstad 2002: 30).

All in all, 63 athletes: 23 women and 40 men, were the first to be part of Project 88 in 1985. These athletes received scholarships with a basic amount of euros 3,250 (6,750 in 2010 value) and a supplement of up to euros 4,125 (8,625 in 2010 value). Later 24 scholarships were awarded in a less prioritized group, while 10 different teams came under the umbrella. This was followed by new extensions, and in the course of the year, the number of individual athletes reached 105, while 13 teams and 5 development groups were in the project.

The Norwegian model

When Project 88 was incorporated, it was called 'The Norwegian model'. The model emphasized how expertise and insight could be exploited across sports through cooperation between the federations. There was an understanding that there were great benefits in learning from each other's experiences. A transparent elite sport system meant that both positive and negative experiences were quickly recognised. Top-level sports should be characterized by those involved being curious and humble. There was no requirement that Project 88 was to have any form of central control. Each association appointed a contact person who attended the regular meetings and made sure that the cooperation was good.

Patience was a key word for Rimejorde. He was never in doubt that the project would succeed in the long term.

> I said in 1986 that our work would be a failure if at the beginning of the 1990s we had failed to make significant progress. To assess the project before this time would mean that we did not know what it was all about. (Hanstad 2002: 31)

The objective of the project was nevertheless the Olympic Winter Games in Calgary in 1988 and the Summer Olympics in Seoul later the same year. Calgary was a disappointment. Despite the special elite sport effort, Norway did not win a single gold medal, something that had never happened since the Winter Games were introduced in 1924. It was a failure, something Norwegian newspapers were of course acutely aware of. Already two days before the closing ceremony, *Dagbladet* carried a story with the headline 'Fiasco to millions'. The weak performance was, according to the newspaper, the reason that the main sponsor withdrew. 'A myriad of disappointments', wrote the news agency *Norsk Telegrambyrå*, while *Verdens Gang* wrote about the 'Coach Massacre' which would follow the Olympics.

The commentator Arvid Eriksen wrote that sacking coaches would hardly solve the problem. He called instead for an elite culture, and thus an elite sport body. In his opinion the project had failed to gain acceptance among the federations. This was confirmed by others. According to a Ph.D. dissertation by Gotvassli (2005), Project 88 was considered a service organization and an economic and technical catalyst by the federations. One of those responsible for the project, the Vice Chairman of the NOK, Arne Myhrvold, told *Aftenposten* that the widespread democracy in Norwegian sport slowed the work on elite sport: 'I think it is important that the parent bodies (NOK and NIF) must be involved in steering the work for the sports federations. We need a lot more centralized focus on athletes who have the capacity to compete well in the Olympics' (Taalesen 1988: 23).

Those responsible for the project saw some light at the end of the tunnel. There were some talented athletes on their way and the NOK, the NIF and a majority of the specialised sports federations saw the necessity to work together. But how should the future project be organized? The three alternatives were: (1) a foundation, (1) a cooperation with the NOK, and (3) a cooperation with the NIF and NOK (Stensbøl 2010). The last model was chosen to create an elite sports organization called Olympiatoppen.

Olympiatoppen: 'The best of what's best in the federations'

Olympiatoppen was established with overall responsibility for elite sport in Norway (Augestad, Bergsgard & Hansen 2006). It offered financial support and strengthened cooperation across different sports. 'We are the best of the best in the federations' was a key slogan (Hanstad 2006b). Something that seems to be unique in the Norwegian system was the competence flow. Norway is a small country with a population of a little less than five million, with limited human and economic resources for elite sport. Working together and learning from each other across sports were considered critical to achieve competitive advantages.

Olympiatoppen was an extension of Project 88, but contained some new elements. The athletes were still at the heart of the new organization, but it increasingly also focused on strengthening competence among leaders and trainers. A growing economy also generated more funds for the elite sport unit through sponsorships. Olympiatoppen was now in a position to make financial support to the federations conditional on certain policies and practices.

Olympiatoppen was professionalized in different ways. The politically elected leaders of the federations had no longer any final say when athletes were selected for participation in the Olympics. The federations sent a recommendation which was considered by a committee led by the head of Olympiatoppen. Olympiatoppen also intervened in the federations' way of organizing their participation in international championships. It was no longer to be the responsibility of politicians and administrators to be a part of or select the support personnel. Such functions became a natural part of the coaching job. Its responsibilities included granting scholarships to talented performers in all Olympic sports, providing medical support to all national teams, and operating the well-equipped national training centre.

Olympiatoppen used significant resources to apply and develop new competences. In some sports, Norwegian athletes obtained a significant advantage, as for example at ski-preparation and altitude training. For decades, mistakes had been made regarding high altitude training. But a joint project with Olympiatoppen and the Norwegian Ski Association generated knowledge regarding altitude level, duration of training camps and intensity of training, etc. Similarly, Olympiatoppen had a systematic approach to improving ski preparation, in particular in cross-country. Such improvements also provided advantages in biathlon. This illustrates an advantage of having one central unit for elite sports. It is not necessary for each team or federation to have their own specialists in various fields.

After the establishment of Olympiatoppen, Norway improved its performance in international sport (Andersen 2009); most clearly in Olympic winter sports, but also in the Summer Olympics and some sports with international prestige such as athletics and football. In 1994 and 1998, Norway qualified for the FIFA World Cup finals. In the 1994 European Championships in athletics, Norway won six medals, including three gold medals.

Olympiatoppen is often cited as a main reason for these improvements. New ways of organizing and leading elite sport efforts benefitted from better sponsor contracts and more money to invest in elite sport. The decision by the International Olympic Committee (IOC) to host the 1994 Winter Olympics in Lillehammer was an important context for this. As shown above, hosting the 1952 games led to a boom in sport performance. It happened again in 1994. This is the case for almost all host nations (Andersen 2009; Hanstad 2006a).

The Lillehammer Winter Games changed the power balance in Norwegian sport. In addition to facilities for elite sport, the National Olympic Committee received 23 million euros to prepare for the games (formally as a compensation for the government's use of the Olympic symbols). These huge revenues greatly increased the power of the NOK. The NOK used the money to give enormous funds to the national sports federations, and got paid back when the NIF and NOK for the first time elected a common president a few months after the Olympics. Throughout the 1990s, with the Lillehammer Games as a catalyst, elite sport in Norway emerged as an arena for business. Not only did major companies sign significant sponsorship deals, but sport was also used for relationship building.

Corporate executives met in the sporting setting and they engaged in the federations. Before the General Assembly of the NIF in 1990, the industry leaders Jens P. Heyerdahl and Karl Glad had been mentioned as presidential candidates (a former minister was elected), while another industry leader, Gerhard Heiberg, was proposed by the Athletics Association and later the Ski Federation. He had already taken the job as head of the organizing committee for the Lillehammer Olympics. This trend intensified in the following years. Big capitalists like Kjell Inge Røkke, John Fredriksen and Atle Brynestad became owners of football clubs, while a number of other business people spent millions on football shares.

Funding

Olympiatoppen has grown since the start, not least financially. In the second full year of operation, 1990, the budget was almost 2 million euros (about 3.0 million euros in 2010 value). Just under 7 per cent went to the administration, which consisted of two people. The major item of expenditure, 73 per cent, was support for the athletes and teams, in line with the spirit of being a catalyst. In 2001, the budget increased to almost 10 million euros (12.1 million euros in 2010 value), while reaching 14 million euros in 2010.

Olympiatoppen is financed partly by sponsors but mainly by the surplus from the Norwegian National Lottery (Norsk Tipping) and allocated by the government through the Department of Sports in the Ministry of Culture, without specifying who will manage it. The requirement is that the money will secure the foundation for an ethical and professionally qualified elite sport environment, in addition to ensuring funding for sports which are less able to attract commercial sponsorship.

In effect, the NIF Board can in principle decide that Olympiatoppen will have everything – or nothing, if they would rather that each federation should be allocated the money. Obviously Olympiatoppen wants control. All the state money to elite sport goes to Olympiatoppen. In 2009 it represented 90 per cent of the budget. OLT then distributes funds to the federations, based on a contract on collaboration. If a sports federation doesn't want to cooperate with Olympiatoppen, it will not get any financial support. The criteria for receiving funds from OLT are: (1) the federation has to document results, and (2) poor federations receive more money than federations with commercial associations.

The system for funding elite sport was introduced after the Lillehammer Games in 1994. Two years after the games, in which Olympiatoppen received 16.3 million euros (24 million euros in 2010 value) from the government, the top sport unit ran out of funding. The solution was to enter into dialogue with the government. Hans B. Skaset, then General Director for the Department for Sport in the Ministry of Culture, later said about the assessment by the government:

> (Norwegian elite sport) was established with international prestige, and we looked for a solution to continue the development. We were very sceptical to the idea that elite sport would be too dependent on sponsorship. That would mean that only the most attractive sports could survive. So we had to create a scheme where the elite sport was assured a fixed share of public funds each year (Hanstad 2002:158)

After a long process, it was decided to allocate basic funding for elite sports, which was in place for the first time in 2000. Despite dissatisfaction in some federations, it has not been suggested that the practice should be changed.

Controversies and challenges

The Norwegian model of sport is based on three interdependent ideas: sport for all is the goal of the public sport policy; it is a governmental responsibility to reach this goal; and it is believed it can be best realized by a division of labour between public and voluntary bodies. On the one hand, public organizations at different levels (state, county and municipality) provide facilities and subsidize the sport organization while, on the other hand, the NIF-system implements the activities. With only one national umbrella organization for sport, and with a mutual dependency and the division of labour sketched above, the NIF has a monopoly of public funding of sport and has historically fulfilled the role as 'Norwegian sport' (Hanstad & Skille 2010).

Since the establishment of the Department of Sport Policy (DSP) in 1946, an egalitarian ideology has dominated the distribution of the public sector's economic subsidies for sport. For example, and as a major way of spending the state money, the DSP has ensured that facilities are available throughout rurally dominated Norway, to make sport more accessible for everyone. The provision of facilities has traditionally been a responsibility of the local clubs, in cooperation with the municipalities. Today, the NIF is responsible for all sports delivery, focusing on both elite and mass sport participation. Under the NIF umbrella, there are 56 sport federations responsible for the provision of particular sports in Norway, and for the international contact, and 19 district associations.

The relationship between Olympiatoppen, the NIF and the sports federations

Olympiatoppen is the elite sport division within the voluntary umbrella organization (NIF). Each federation is still the 'owner' of its sport. Coaches and most of the staff are paid by each sport federation. They undertake talent-development and organize their national teams. In general the relationship between Olympiatoppen and the biggest federations has worked well during the last 20 years, but there have also been some tensions and conflicts.

For many years the leadership in the Norwegian Football Association (NFF) did not collaborate with Olympiatoppen. They did not think that Olympiatoppen had the necessary competence on football. The Ski Association, particularly cross-country skiing, had a problematic relationship with Olympiatoppen during the 1990s and the first part of this decade (2000–2006). A key issue concerned who 'owned' and who should be credited for their success – in particular during the Olympic Games.

The Chairman of the Ski Association, Jan Jensen, admitted that the Olympics were a traumatic experience for him and his federation because they were pushed completely into the background, even if it was their athletes competing for gold. For example, in the 2002 Salt Lake City Games, Jensen's federation won six gold medals, but it was the head of Olympiatoppen who staged the concluding press conferences and received tribute. In 2002 he said:

> Olympiatoppen uses roughly NOK three millions on our athletes, while the Norwegian Ski Association spent 55 million on elite sport. I mean it's obvious that the basis will be with us. I'm not saying that Olympiatoppen has not done much good, but we have to discuss the roles (Hanstad 2002: 178).

During the same year five federations criticized Olympiatoppen heavily in a letter to the NIF. With reference to the overall action plan for Norwegian elite sport, one question was whether the NIF's intention was that Olympiatoppen should take over the operational responsibility for elite top sport. Another question was whether the NIF Board really wanted Olympiatoppen to take responsibility for, assess and define the requirements for achieving objectives in each sport. Using football as an example, it was pointed out that both leaders in the federation and the team management had significant international contacts, including being present at one hundred international games each year:

'NFF know the required standards through these reference points – Olympiatoppen does not.'

The tension between the parties was illustrated by the answer from the NIF:

> If you try to follow the trend internationally by being spectators at matches, and also believe that this provides reference points for evaluating international elite skills, you underestimate the strong general and professional development that occurs in elite sport.

As a consequence of the controversy in 2002, it was decided that each sports federation should sign an agreement with Olympiatoppen. These agreements are mutually binding. Olympiatoppen's responsibility is to conduct quality control of training and contribute to the establishment of a curriculum for the development of young athletes. The federations' responsibility is that coaches have the required professional competence. They must also ensure that training is properly planned and implemented, recorded in Olympiatoppen's training file, and that this tool is actively used.

Another unit under the NIF umbrella is the district associations which have 50 per cent of the votes at the general assembly. Traditionally, representatives from the 19 district associations have put a strong emphasis on mass sport, while representatives from the federations (in particular the big federations like football, ski and handball) have been seen as more elite sport oriented (Hanstad & Skille 2010). This tension has generally been unproblematic, but there are exceptions. During the NIF's General Assembly in 2003, the district associations refused to increase the share of the budget earmarked for elite sport. They also rejected the use of high altitude chambers, and refused to relax the 'Regulations of Children's Sport'.

How should Olympiatoppen be organized?

Olympiatoppen has, since it was established in 1989, been located as a unit within NIF's main organization. From time to time it has been a topic for discussion whether the present arrangement is the best solution. In 2004, a comprehensive process was initiated by the NIF Board. A committee, consisting of members from the sports federations and district associations, had a mandate to evaluate how Olympiatoppen should be organized in the future in order to ensure that those involved in elite sport had the necessary influence on how elite sports are governed and developed. The committee was led by a member of the board. In the first report, delivered in September 2005, an array of models was discussed (NIF 2005). The committee pointed to a new model under the auspices of the NOK as the best solution. This would imply a separate general assembly for Olympiatoppen and the leader of Olympiatoppen reporting directly to the board of the NOK on professional matters.

This proposal was by some viewed as an attempted coup, where the NIF president, the leader of Olympiatoppen, and the large sport federations had formed an alliance (Ulseth 2006). Two main arguments were used against the proposed change: (1) If the leader of Olympiatoppen reported directly to the board, this could create a cleavage between elite and mass sports within the organization; and (2) this, and the proposition to create a general assembly for the Olympiatoppen, was an attempt by the large federations to achieve a stronger influence over Olympiatoppen. The losers would be the district associations, the small federations, and mass sports more generally. The process was thus seen as touching upon the fundamental democratic balance in the NIF. This balance is secured by the equal votes of the federations and the district association in the general assembly (Bergsgard & Rommetvedt 2006).

Eventually, the NIF the board voted for only a minor change (NIF 2006b). A committee of five to seven members would assist the Olympiatoppen leader in the strategic thinking around Olympiatoppen.

Concluding remarks

The position of elite sport in Norway has, as in the rest of the world, changed dramatically during recent decades. A striking fact of the Norwegian development is the significant improvement in international results after the establishment of Olympiatoppen. Norway has strengthened its position compared to the other Nordic countries. Even so, the role of Olympiatoppen has been contested. The smaller sport federations tend to have good, cooperative relations with Olympiatoppen, while the larger bodies like the Norwegian football and the Skiing Association have taken a more critical stance (Augestad et al. 2006). During the last years the collaboration with these federations has been strengthened.

Following the statutes of the NIF, the confederation should be 'one organization', with a unified board for mass, elite and Olympic sports, and one single top executive general secretary (NIF 2006c, § 4–5). Sports federations, teams and athletes are part of an organized network. The role of the Olympiatoppen is to challenge and support efforts in different sports. It serves as a linchpin, amplifying learning processes. However, everyday development is mainly the responsibility of individual sport federations, where contact and exchange with international within-sports expertise is essential.

3

The institutionalization of Team Denmark

Jørn Hansen

This chapter analyses the factors that contributed to the establishment of Team Denmark and ends with an examination of how the establishment of Danish elite sport policy also reflects a gradual changing of the Danish welfare model influenced by a more liberal thinking. In comparative analysis, the Danish welfare model is referred to as 'a Scandinavian model', 'the universal' or 'the institutionalized welfare model', and is epitomised by a large public sector and universal egalitarian and generous welfare provision. The ideals of equality and welfare have also permeated the history of sport in Denmark, where a vigorous movement promoting mass participation emerged early on.

Historically, strong national organizations coalesced around the 'sport for all' concept, forming a close-knit network of federations promoting non-competitive sport (mainly gymnastics). Special educational establishments (folk high schools) provided youngsters with informal training as trainers and organizers, and legislation was passed guaranteeing these organizations, associations and educational establishments significant public sector funding. Elite sport was less accepted than its grassroots equivalent – certain elements of the sporting and political worlds actively opposed elite sport, particularly the supporting of it with public sector funding.

Until the national institution for elite sport, Team Denmark, was set up in the mid-1980s, progress towards providing support for the elite was therefore somewhat haphazard (Ibsen, Hansen & Storm 2010). In this chapter I will first present the historical context for elite sport, as part of a broader sports movement. The major part is about the political values and processes behind the formation and further development of the national elite sport institution, Team Denmark. The discussion reflects that, in contrast to the other Nordic countries, the national organization of elite sport has very much been shaped by party politics and legislation.

The data sources are mainly the discussions in the Danish Parliament (Folketing), interviews with a few key persons in the political process and presentations from books about Danish sports history, in particular Else Trangbæk, Jørn Hansen and Niels Kayser Nielsen (eds.), *Dansk Idrætsliv vol. 2* (1995); and Ivan Løvstrup and Jørn Hansen, *Da eliteidrætten blev stueren – Eliteidræt og idrætspolitik i Danmark* (2002) and the article by Per Jørgensen (2005): 'Danmarks Olympiske Komité – idrætspolitisk magtfaktor eller blot et historisk appendiks'.

The Danish sports organizations and the welfare model for leisure sport during the 1960s

Before we take a closer look at the establishment of Team Denmark, it is appropriate to make a short presentation of sporting organizations as they existed in the period leading up to this.

There were five main organizations in Denmark in 1976: the Sports Confederation of Denmark (DIF), Danish Shooting, Gymnastics and Sports Associations (DDSG&I), Danish Gymnastics and Youth Associations (DDGU), the Danish Federation for Company Sport (DFIF) and the National Olympic Committee (DOK).

The DIF was the largest of the four organizations and was responsible for elite sport and general sport's interests. Since the formation of the DIF in 1896, competition has played the overall role and Danish champions were officially designated in tournaments organized by special federations under the DIF umbrella. Furthermore, individual national teams were also subject to the DIF's special federations, which meant that the DIF was responsible for the majority of Danish sport practitioners' participation in international competitions.

The DIF was an umbrella organization for special federations under it, each representing a series of associations and clubs across the country. The individual clubs were represented in the district federation, which was responsible for the individual sport branch's interests at the regional level. The individual district federations were represented in the branch committee, so that at the regional level there was a forum for safeguarding both the interests of individual sports branches, the district association, and the overall interests of the DIF, the branch committee. The individual district federations reported to the individual special federations, while the branch committees were directly subject to the committee of representatives.

The DDSG&I originated in the Danish Shooting Organization, which was founded in 1861. The ideological basis for the DDSG&I was formulated in 1972 as: 'The organization's aim is to promote the health and happiness of the individual and the community via sport and culture' (Ministeriet for kulturelle anliggender 1974: 45). The goal of practising sport was not to win competitions but to allow the individual to become more aware of health and fitness. The DDSG&I represented popular sport's interests and did not operate any kind of activity related to elite sport.

The organization was split into three parts with shooting, gymnastics and sport sections, a structure that continued from a local level all the way up through the system. The committee of representatives was the decision-making body and was made up of 40 regional associations. The board was the executive power but was accountable to the committee of representatives.

The DDGU was formed in 1903 to bring together into a single organization those individual youth associations inspired by Grundtvig, whose aim it was to promote enlightenment. In 1965 this organization merged with the Danish Gymnastics Associations, a group of gymnastics associations that had left the Danish Shooting Gymnastics and Sports Associations in 1929 in protest against the special status accorded to the shooting organization. The DDGU was now a reality.

The DDGU's aims and objectives state that DDGU's '... purpose, on the basis of voluntary association work in the promotion of sport and other cultural activities, is to promote general education' (Ministeriet for kulturelle anliggender 1974: 53). Like the DDSG&I, at the DDGU it was felt that sport should not be practised for sport's sake. The DDGU did not want to see elite sport-related participation within its organization. On the contrary, the DDGU's work was based on the desire to create what it defined as the whole person.

In terms of organization, the DDGU and the DDSG&I were very similar. The DDGU had a pyramidal structure, such that the highest authority was the annual assembly, where guidelines were laid down. The daily management and select committees were responsible for putting the elected guidelines into practice. At the bottom of the pyramid were individual associations, some of which were grouped in a main branch on a municipal level. On a regional basis, the main branches were grouped in regional associations. The DDSG&I and DDGU merged in 1992 and became the Danish Gymnastics and Sports Associations (DGI).

The DFIF was formed in 1946 with the aim of representing the interests of sports associations that originated directly from companies and workplaces. The DFIF was different from the other main organizations, in that its individual associations had closed memberships. They admitted only employees from those workplaces to which they were associated, along with their spouses. The DFIF's aim was to stimulate interest in sport and exercise as a whole, particularly in the workplace. Thus at the DFIF, there was no pursuit of any kind of elite sport.

In terms of organization, the DFIF was like a mixture of the DDGU and the DDSG&I. On a municipal level, the company associations formed town confederations that took on the responsibility of both sporting and administrative areas. In round numbers there were about 20 federations and 700 town confederations.

The four main organizations formed several councils and committees to represent common interests. The Sports Council (Idrættens Fællesråd) was created in 1967 as a forum for discussion and for solving common practical problems. On a local level, the Sports Council had a counterpart in the Federation of Sports Associations. It was here that the individual associations could register themselves with the main organizations and thus gain greater presence and negotiating powers.

The National Olympic Committee of Denmark (DOK) was founded in 1905. The DOK's task was to orchestrate and realise Denmark's participation in the Olympic Games and to find funding for that purpose. The highest authority within the DOK was the general assembly. It elected seven of the board's nine board members. The last two board members were a representative of the International Olympic Committee in Denmark and the chairman of the DIF. The DIF and DOK merged in 1993 and became the National Olympic Committee and Sports Confederation of Denmark (DIF) (Hansen 1994).

In the 1960s sport in Denmark gradually became a social political issue. Until then, politicians of all hues clearly felt that the practice of sport was beneficial in nature and that funding via the Gambling Act and municipal support for sporting facilities was a good thing. The Leisure Time Education Act, passed in 1968, marked the first attempt by politicians to introduce legislation that had a direct relationship with youth and sports clubs. Leisure came to be seen as a welfare issue and it was important that legislation had a positive effect throughout sport, for example by creating good facilities where the young people could meet in their leisure time, which they had seen increase as the number of working hours progressively decreased down the years. So it was important to support leaders and trainers who worked with youth groups.

Contemporary sport organizations, who today are well-accustomed to receiving public funding, were initially sceptical, thinking the new law would lead to the professionalization of the work of youth clubs, and they protested when the VKR coalition government of the day – made up of Venstre (Liberals), Konservative (Conservatives) and Radikale (Social Liberals) – failed to mention sport in their cultural–political report a year after the law was passed. This meant that the Ministry for Cultural Affairs elected to form a commission in 1970 to analyse the state of sport and its place in society in the future. The commission completed its work in 1974 with the publication of *Betænkningen om idrætten og friluftslivet [White Paper on Sport and Outdoor Activities]* (White Paper no. 709, 1974) (Ibsen 1995: 112–115).

Towards the establishment of Team Denmark in the 1980s

The White Paper generated little discussion when it was published in May 1974 and was not debated in the Danish parliament before 1976. This was due to the paper's vague and imprecise propositions, which were the result of an attempt to disguise disagreements between sporting organizations in a wide range of areas.

The White Paper's conclusion was that the commission did not wish to change sport's existing organizational and funding principles and traditions. Elite sport in Denmark should, therefore, not expect to get better conditions.

> "The commission concludes that the main emphasis must be on sport in general... The commission believes that the public sector should not participate in the financing of what is in effect a professional sport... In principal, at local level the public sector should not favour a local sporting elite, either financially or in terms of facilities (Ministeriet for kulturelle anliggender 1974: 12).

Nor did the commission want to change the way the public sector supported sport. 'The commission regards support via the Gambling Act as an entirely appropriate form of subsidy.' This conclusion was based on three factors. Firstly, a subsidy of this kind would be independent of the state's fiscal policy. Secondly, the subsidy would be regarded as a non-state subsidy, which would make receiving additional state subsidy easier. Lastly, '...financing via the Gambling Act in all probability places more funds at the organizations' disposal' (Ministeriet for kulturelle anliggender 1974: 12).

The contents of the White Paper were in no way revolutionary. Its proposals and subsequent debate resulted in changes to the Gambling Act. Furthermore, responsibility for sport was brought together under the Ministry of Culture, and finally, cooperation was developed in the Sports Council, so that a dialogue between the state and the sports organizations became more formalised.

During the debate in the Danish parliament, individual political spokesmen vied with each other in praising sport's positive effect on the population's general health and mental well-being and on democracy as a whole, although they were very unwilling to become involved in sporting issues. The conservative spokesman at that time, Poul Schlüter, expressed this unwillingness very precisely when he said '...the state and the municipalities must consciously steer clear as much as possible, entrust initiatives and management to those groups in which the people wish to organize themselves, in which they can participate and enjoy their leisure pursuits' (*Folketingstidende* 1975/76, vol. 2, col. 4924).

The paper's greatest effect was indirect in nature. The parliamentary debate forced individual parties to take a position on the political questions of sport. It marked the beginning of greater party–political interest in sport, which led to the majority of political parties devising political programmes for sport. Furthermore, the development of these party political programmes and the increased interest in sport's political questions brought closer discussions between sports organizations, coaches, managers and active participants on the one side and politicians on the other.

The period from 1976, which initiated political interest in sport, to December 1984 when Act no. 643 concerning the promotion of elite sport was passed by the Danish parliament, was a landmark period for Danish elite sport. The situation had changed since the 1976 debate, when all of the representative parties in the Danish parliament had been against the support of elite sport, in favour of a clear majority of those who positively supported the idea of special initiatives for sport during the reading of the bill in 1984. The arguments for this varied from party to party, but what all of them shared in common was their radical change in attitude to elite sport. An example of this was Venstre (the Liberal party). Peter Brixtofte said in the Danish parliament in 1976 that '...Venstre feels that the practice of elite sport is not a task for the state' (*Folketingstidende* 1975/76, vol. 2, col. 4912). This position changed to the point where in 1984 Helge Sander from the same party emphasised the need for spectator attractions and the propaganda value of elite sports in promoting exports '...on an equal footing with members of the Royal Family and ministers' (*Folketingstidende* 1975/76, vol. 2, col. 4791).

Sports failures and responses

The debate around the conditions for elite sport in Denmark really got started at the end of the 70s, when three factors drew attention to the situation for this group of athletes and the value of elite sport. The coach for the Danish national handball team, Leif Mikkelsen, went directly to Culture Minister Niels Matthiasen (Socialdemokratiet – Danish Social Democrats Party) to inform him about the social conditions for his players. The introduction of professional football raised the domestic league and the national team to a new level, which in turn raised the entertainment value to the satisfaction of the public. The gloomy prospects for Danish success at the Moscow Olympics in 1980 raised the question of whether Denmark should accept that it could no longer compete at the international level or whether a subsidy scheme should be put in place before it was too late.

These three factors were decisive in the decision of the minister for culture to get actively involved in the elite sports debate. However, Niels Matthiasen had no immediate intention to break with a tradition of state non-intervention in sports affairs. Against this background he was willing to accommodate elite sport's problems. However, at the same time he made it clear that, if elite sport was to be supported, the sport itself had to lay down certain requirements for that support and officially ask for help from the minister for culture.

By means of a report on the state of elite sport in Denmark, The Danish Olympic Committee (DOK) sought to respond to this demand from the minister for culture. However, the initiative was not underwritten by the entire body of sport, and this in itself meant that this report could not meet the requirements of the minister for culture. The document's main argument for the state support of elite sport was a narrow one, namely that support would improve results. The goal was better results and not necessarily better conditions for elite athletes.

Niels Matthiasen reacted to the DOK's report by amending his requirement for sport. The entire body of sport no longer had to be in agreement; but merely had to put forward a unified application to the minister for culture, requesting him to set up a committee of inquiry. However, this application did not materialise.

The initiative to set up a consultative committee emanated instead from the Danish Ministry of Culture, which broke with the consensus in this area. It has not been possible to clarify the sequence of events concerning the appointment and make-up of the committee on the basis of a variety of independent sources. The Ministry of Culture's civil servant responsible for sport, Claus Bøje, believed that the minister for culture's decision to appoint the committee was based on personal political ambition. Elite sport was a winner in this respect, in that a large part of society was interested in it and at the same time it was a logical choice according to Bøje (Løvstrup & Hansen 2002: 180–186).

The make-up of the committee caused the DIF and DOK to have less influence on the White Paper's development than was expected. Instead, the committee had a series of young, progressive people with a background in welfare state thinking. They managed to change the stated aim of support for elite sport from being narrowly results-orientated to focusing on improved social and financial conditions for the elite athlete. A new institution, DANTOP, was to be created. The committee proposed a structure for DANTOP's management that on the one hand led to state involvement in the institution's management, and on the other made it impossible for the DIF, the DIF's special federations and the DOK to get an absolute majority on the committee of representatives.

The explanation of why the politicians instead of the sport leaders initiated the reform process could be found in the active role of one key public servant in the Danish Ministry of Culture, Claus Bøje. Since 1972 Claus Bøje had been employed in the Danish Ministry of Culture and after 1976, when sport became a subject field in the ministry he was known as the grey eminence in the field of sport politics.

Niels Matthiasen did not have the same insight into the Danish sport system as Claus Bøje, but concerning sport policy, Niels Matthiasen was advised by Bøje. The latter was a former ice hockey player and critical towards the more conservative sports leaders. In the sports system he was known as an 'enfant terrible'. Together with other young sportsmen Claus Bøje founded the Danish Active Group (DAK, Dansk Aktiv Gruppe) in the beginning of the 1970s.

The DAK's aim was to secure more influence for active sportsmen on the decisions in Danish sport (Løvstrup & Hansen 2002: 58–66). Many of the members of the consultative committee in fact came from the Danish Active Group or had close relations with members of this group. In addition, the Danish sports system, consisting of several main organizations all led by volunteers, appeared rather weak facing the Danish Ministry of Culture. This provided opportunities for a clever civil servant in the Danish Ministry of Culture.

Act no. 643 on the promotion of elite sport

The final White Paper on elite sport in Denmark was made public at the beginning of December 1983. When Niels Matthiasen died on 16 February 1980, Lise Østergård, also a Social Democrat, took over the post of minister for culture. On 3 September 1982, the minority Social Democrat government under the leadership of Anker Jørgensen officially stood down, having been in power for only eight months since the last general election. After two rounds of consultations, Poul Schlüter managed to form a minority government consisting of four parties. He appointed Mimi Stilling Jakobsen of the Centrumdemokraterne (Centre Democrats) as the minister for culture. The government was dependent on a very slim majority. In the negotiations for the budget in 1983 it was unable to achieve a majority for its budget proposal. This caused Schlüter to call a general election on 10 January 1984.

The result of the general election did not lead to the formation of a new government. Overall, the governing parities gained 12 seats. The only party in the coalition to suffer a setback were Centrumdemokraterne, who lost 7 seats, though it is worth mentioning that Fremskridtspartiet (the Progress Party), which for a considerable time had supported the government in power, also lost 10 seats. The parliamentary situation in advance of the parliament's reading of the bill on elite sport and eventual initiatives based on *White Paper no. 992* was such that the government could not alone dictate its desired policy. If political intervention in elite sport in Denmark was going to take place, it required both left-wing and right-wing support in parliament.

On 11 April 1984, Mimi Stilling Jakobsen presented her written statement on elite sport in Denmark to the Danish parliament, based on *White Paper no. 992* (*Folketingstidende* 1975/76, vol, 3. col. 4144). Before we reach the parliamentary debate, it is only natural to take a closer look at how sport's main organizations reacted to *White Paper no. 992*.

The reaction of sporting organizations to *White Paper no. 992*

Because the DIF, DDSG&I, DDGU and DFIF had been represented on the consultative committee and were therefore co-signatories of the White Paper, it could be expected that no official criticism of the paper would come from these quarters.

Svend O. Hansen had been the DIF's chairman since 1978. He died on 27 August 1983 and was succeeded by Kai Holm. Kai Holm was hugely in favour of the proposals for improving conditions for sports that were presented in the White Paper. 'Kai Holm had the board behind him, when he declared the Danish Sports Federation's support for the Danish Ministry of Culture's report on elite sport' (Margolinsky 1984). Kai Holm regarded state involvement in any institution formed to represent the interests of elite sport as being positive, because it would partly function as a safeguard against '...the commercial exploitation of elite sport...partly ensure respectable conditions for [elite athletes] – in terms of education, employment and family life' (Holm 1984).

In the DDGU's magazine *Dansk Ungdom og Idræt [Danish Youth and Sport]* the editor pointed out that the White Paper also expressed the desire to have elite sport included in the budget, which would mean getting the same kind of support that could be seen '... in other countries that we don't normally like to compare ourselves with' (Thygesen 1983). Arne Rasmussen, chairman of the DDGU, did not think there was any danger that the creation of talent centres could cause gifted young people to lose contact with their local associations. '...the young will still be able to do a lot of good work in their local association.' Arne Rasmussen also noted that the White Paper estimated that the special federations under the DIF were using approximately 75 per cent of their resources for elite work. On this basis he thought that, as long as DANTOP became a reality and assumed the DIF's former responsibilities for elite sport,'...a not insignificant part of the reason for the DIF's relatively large share of profit from the Gambling Act would disappear' (Rasmussen 1984).

The DDSG&I did not devote much space to the new White Paper. In the organization's magazine *Dansk Idræt [Danish Sport]*, two articles dealt with the committee's work and with the final White Paper. The main theme in both articles was that the proposed subsidy for elite sport should be earmarked '... without this having an effect on sport in the rest of the country' (Jensen 1983; Madsen 1983).

Like the DDSG&I, the DFIF's coverage of the White Paper in *Firmaidræt* was very limited. The magazine settled for an outline of the White Paper's proposals for initiatives for elite sport and concluded its article by referring to where the White Paper could be purchased (*Firmaidræt* 1984).

In conclusion, the reaction of the four organizations to the White Paper was that they accepted its wish to promote participation in elite sport in a way that was socially and financially responsible. This acceptance presupposed that the increased support for elite sport would not have a detrimental influence on support for sport in general. At the same time Arne Rasmussen argued that the DIF should receive a smaller share of funds from the Gambling Act. This can be viewed as the beginning of a more general debate, arising from the changed structure of sport, about how Gambling Act funds should be distributed between organizations through the potential creation of an autonomous organization for the promotion of elite sport.

The statement of the minister for culture about elite sport
Mimi Stilling Jakobsen's written statement was presented to the Danish parliament on 11 April 1984 and its point of departure was *White Paper no. 992*. Jakobsen began by positioning elite sport in the overall perspective of sport and against this background concluded that, 'The public sector should not favour one form of sport over another.' The reason for not valuing elite sport more than general sport or vice versa was that, 'Elite sport will frequently recruit its practitioners from youth sport in general, which conversely will only be inspired by results from elite sport' (*Folketingstidende* 1983/84, vol. 3, col. 4145).

After her introduction, Mimi Stilling Jakobsen went on to give an account of the considerations of the consultative committee as a result of their investigations. In this section of her statement, Jakobsen placed emphasis on the amount of time elite athletes used to practise their sport and on the consequences for their employment and education. With this as a background she concluded that '…a continuation of the conditions so far prevailing for the practice of elite sport will mean that human costs in the educational and social arena will be incurred simply to preserve Denmark's international status within elite sport' (*Folketingstidende* 1983/84, vol. 3, col. 4145).

To sum up Mimi Stilling Jakobsen's written statement to the Danish parliament on 11 April 1984, she adhered closely to the White Paper's analysis of elite sport's conditions and to the proposal to create DANTOP, which the White Paper believed would improve these conditions. Choosing elite sport's objective as one that made participation in elite sport justifiable both socially and economically was also in accordance with the White Paper's objectives for support. Mimi Stilling Jakobsen could genuinely agree with this objective. Furthermore, it is quite possible that the left wing would gain popular support for the view that becoming an elite athlete should be dependent on having talent and not, as had apparently been the case in the past, on having talent and social status. In contrast, the proposal to minimise the public representation in DANTOP was considered as an attempt to accommodate the right wing's traditional desire to limit public intervention in sporting matters.

Mimi Stilling Jakobsen's statement on elite sport laid the foundation for a broad, solid majority for the future bill on elite sport. It could not be expected that the parties would oppose a bill that prevented unreasonable human costs. Additionally, the left wing had made sure any bill would give athletes from disadvantaged social groups the opportunity to practise elite sport. At the same time, the culture minister's proposal to change the make-up of the committee of representatives more or less fulfilled the centre-right parties' long-standing wish for state support without state management.

The culture minister's proposal for a law on the promotion of elite sport

On October 1984, following her statement and subsequent debate in the parliament, Mimi Stilling Jakobsen submitted her government's bill for a law on the promotion of elite sport. The bill differed from the statement on two points.

Firstly, during her statement the minister had expressed the government view that it was incorrect to have the public represented in DANTOP's committee of representatives. The bill was now changed to 'The committee of representatives must not only represent sport, it must also consist of public authority representatives…to ensure a broad social assessment of the development of elite sport.'

Secondly, the minister's statement contained the wish that DANTOP would be financed using funds from the Gambling Act previously earmarked for cultural purposes. In the bill this was changed to 'State subsidy is provided by…transferring 1/19 of the levy…' (*Folketingstidende* 1984/85, vol. 1, col. 69) on betting and the V6 game. The financing of the development of DANTOP should occur by a gradual increase in the transfer by the state of funds from the levy. This meant that in its final complete form DANTOP should receive 3/19 of the levy on gambling and the V6 game.

The two points in the bill that differed from the minister's statement were both within the areas that were universally opposed by the left wing. The financing of DANTOP was now to take place, as proposed in the White Paper, through a gradual lowering of the government tax on gambling and on the V6 game from 19 to 16 per cent. At the same time the state was to be represented on the committee of representatives.

Despite its concessions regarding state representation, the culture minister's bill still differed from the proposal put forward in the White Paper as regards the size and make-up of the committee of representatives. The minister still wanted to change the size of the committee of representatives, so that, instead of the 37 members proposed in the White Paper, there would be 23. Furthermore, the consultative committee's proposal was that the DIF, the DIF's special federations and the DOK together would make up about 27 per cent of the membership of the committee of representatives. The active participants, managers and trainers would make up 32 per cent, while representatives from the public authorities would make up 29 per cent of the membership (Ministeriet for kulturelle anliggender 1983: 169). The remaining 12 per cent was to be made up by representatives of educational institutions, the Sports Research Council and the Danish Association for Sports Medicine.

In the minister's bill the membership of the committee of representatives was changed, so that the DIF, the DIF's special federations and the DOK would together make up 30 per cent of the membership. The active participants, managers and trainers would make up 26 per cent, while representatives from the state should make up 26 per cent of the membership (*Folketingstidende* 1984/85, vol. 1, col. 407-408). The remaining 18 per cent would be made up of members who represented educational institutions, the Sports Research Council and the Danish Association for Sports Medicine.

Mimi Stilling Jakobsen's bill had reduced the size of the group of active participants, managers and trainers and the influence of the state on the committee of representatives. At the same time she had given the DIF and the DOK more influence. It was no secret that she wanted to minimise the influence of the central government on the committee of representatives. She had stated publicly that she would rather see a total absence of central government representation on the committee of representatives. On the other hand, it might seem strange that she did not follow the consultative committee's position regarding the distribution of members between sports organizations, in this case the DIF and the DOK, and the active practitioners, managers and trainers.

Mimi Stilling Jakobsen's change in position was no less strange in that at no point during the debate was the reasonableness of the White Paper's proposal for the membership distribution of the committee of representatives questioned. The change was not caused by any immediate prompting by the other political parties, so the initiative for these political respects were solely attributable to the minister.

The work involved in the actual writing of the act was, according to Claus Bøje, '…an irritating process…' (Løvstrup & Hansen 2002: 180-186). According to Bøje, Mimi Stilling Jakobsen took home review drafts of the bill that had been prepared at the ministry. But it was not the minister herself, however, who read through the drafts. 'However, it was Kai Holm, Bent Agerskov and Preben Kragelund who were given the work of reading' (Løvstrup & Hansen 2002: 188-190). These three gentlemen's interest in ensuring the DIF and DOK gained as much influence as possible in the committee of representatives goes without saying. The explanation for Mimi Stilling Jakobsen apparently being so open to influence from this quarter must, therefore, be considered a result of good lobbying from the DIF.

On the basis of the minister's proposal for legislation on the promotion of elite sport, it can be concluded that to a large extent she accommodated criticism of her statement based on *White Paper no. 992*. She changed the form of financing so that it complied with what the White Paper had proposed. Furthermore, she changed the composition and size of the committee of representatives, so that the central government would be represented in the committee of representatives, though not to the degree that the White Paper had proposed. That there was a change in the balance of power in the committee of representatives between the DIF and DOK on one side and the active practitioners, managers and trainers on the other can be attributed to good lobbying by the DIF.

The reading of the bill and the culture committee's consultation paper
During the parliament's reading of the government bill on the promotion of elite sport, the most important amendment was submitted by a majority in the cultural committee, consisting of Socialdemokratiet, Socialistisk Folkeparti, Det radikale Venstre and Venstresocialisterne. This majority also wanted to change §1 of the bill, in this case point 3 of the paragraph's eight points, which described DANTOP's overall activities.

In §1 point 3, DANTOP's target group was defined. Here the bill proposed that DANTOP should take measures to, '…communicate the training and instruction opportunities for elite athletes…' (*Folketingstidende*, 1984/85, vol. 1, col. 407). Those proposing the change, wanted to add, '…who are over the age of 15.' This addition was made 'for pedagogical, medical and ethical reasons and out of respect for young people's own capacity to judge the consequences of participating in elite sport…' (*Folketingstidende*, 1984/85, vol. 1, col. 166).

This amendment led to an agreement between the government parties and Socialdemokratiet, whereby, in exchange for not voting against the bill, they were allowed to leave their mark on two main points. The final bill that was passed into law sat well with Socialdemokratiet's fundamental thinking.

As regards the size and make-up of the committee of representatives, the Social Democrats had managed to get a Sports Council representative on the committee. They had also ensured more influence for young participants, managers and trainers than for the DIF, the DIF's special federations and the DOK combined. Additionally, their amendment for a minimum age of 15 for elite athletes was passed.

In his closing remarks to the third reading of the bill, Jimmy Stahr from Socialdemokratiet encouraged everyone, '…to vote for the bill for the sake both of sport in general and of elite sport' (*Folketingstidende* 1984/85, vol. 3, col. 3896).

Steen Tinning, Venstresocialisterne, thought the bill was deficient in two aspects, which prevented Venstresocialisterne from giving their approval. Firstly, Tinning did not think that the bill contained a guarantee that the support for elite sport would not compromise sport in general. Secondly, Venstresocialisterne and Socialistisk Folkeparti put forward an amendment, which was to ensure '...the individual athlete's right to freedom of political expression.... It is precisely these two points: the danger of general sport being compromised, and the fact that we did not manage to secure the right to political freedom of expression, that are crucial for VS...' (*Folketingstidende* 1984/85, vol. 3, col. 3905). The proposal did not win support in the Danish parliament.

Ingerlise Kofoed, Socialistisk Folkeparti, gave an account of her party's position on the final bill in a very short contribution. 'We believe some improvements have been made [in relation to the government's bill], we have succeeded in getting some of our amendments through, but we do not believe the bill is good enough' (*Folketingstidende* 1984/85, vol. 3, col. 3900). On this basis, the Socialistisk Folkeparti abstained in the final vote.

Passing of the Bill on the Promotion of Elite Sport

The bill was passed into law on the basis of a compromise between the governing quartet and the Social Democrats. Thus the basis for the creation of an independent institution for the promotion of elite sport was now a reality.

During the Danish parliament's debate on the White Paper and the subsequent bill, all of the parties were in favour of supporting elite sport in Denmark. The general argument for support was that participation in elite sport should be socially and economically justifiable. The White Paper had established the fact that elite athletes spent a surprisingly large amount of time on their sport, which made it difficult for individual practitioners to maintain contact with their social network and difficult for them to have full-time jobs. The last argument was based on the report's findings that people from disadvantaged social groups were underrepresented among elite athletes.

The bill on the promotion of elite sport marked the end of the debate about elite sport. Parliament had given specific support to elite sport and at the same time, for the first time in Denmark's history, individuals selected by the central government were introduced into the management of an independent sporting organization.

At its birth, Team Denmark was neither an association nor a state institution. It was an independent institution, born like a hybrid with a series of built-in contradictions, which the state and sport organizations, had to manage. When it was established, two-thirds of its funding came from the central government, and the Ministry of Culture would appoint two of Team Denmark's board members. However, Team Denmark, as an independent institution, was not subject to direct state control (Løvstrup & Hansen 2002: 118). Initially, the Law on the Promotion of Elite Sport did not lead to the state adopting a more active sports policy. This took place only when the law was revised in 2004.

The National Danish Olympic Committee (DOK), Team Denmark and the Sports Confederation of Danmark (DIF)

The DOK played a role in the institutionalization of elite sport in Denmark, but the establishment of Team Denmark meant that some of the DOK's tasks and responsibilities would soon become superfluous. For years there had been a conflict between the DOK and DIF about which of those two organizations should make important decisions about the pool of talent and the preparation for the Olympic Games.

In 1986, the Chairman of the DIF, Kai Holm announced that the DOK's main task was to select the Danish athletes to the Olympic Games. At the same time, a number of the other issues under the DOK had been taken over by Team Denmark. The following year, the DIF's board decided, with the support of 50 of the 53 special federations, that the DIF should work for a more democratic construction of the IOC and for a merger of the DIF and DOK.

The Chairman of the DOK, Niels Thygesen, was against a merger with the DIF; and his successor from 1988 Ingo Nielsen was of the same opinion. He decided to reduce the influence of the DIF and Team Denmark on the board of the DOK. But this move came too late. This became obvious when Team Denmark stopped the DOK's announcement of eight athletes to the Olympics in Seoul because they were not on the support list of Team Denmark. In this way, the DOK lost one of its most important functions (Jørgensen 2005: 26–28).

In 1993 the DOK and DIF officially merged under the name Danmarks Idræts-Forbund/Danmarks Olympiske Komité (DIF) but in fact the DOK was integrated in the DIF. Thus the new DIF had two key missions: sport for all and elite sport. In the public the merger did not lead to any discussion as it was the general opinion that the DOK had had its day as an independent institution.

Greater state influence – The Elite Sports Act 2004

From a political perspective Team Denmark's work for elite sport was generally considered a success. For a long time the majority of politicians were not particularly concerned about its work. However, in 1999, 15 years after the law came into being, the government of the day along with members from Socialdemokraterne and Radikale Venstre, decided it was necessary to review the 1984 Act to see if 'it adequately met the challenges of the future' (Kulturministeriet 2005: 5). A working group with representatives from sport and central government were to examine the Act, though without seeing entirely eye to eye about the task. When the general election brought a change of government in 2001, the new centre-right government decided to start the committee work afresh in 2002.

The new culture minister, Brian Mikkelsen from Det Konservative Folkeparti, worked closely with the Sports Confederation of Denmark and, in general, sport and especially elite sport had the minister's attention. In 2004, the Danish parliament passed 'Act no. 288 on Elite Sport', which ensured the Sports Confederation of Denmark and the Danish Ministry of Culture greater influence on the composition of Team Denmark's board. According to paragraph 2 of the law, Team Denmark should be managed by a board of eight members, appointed by the minister of culture. Four of the members should be appointed by the minister of culture and the other four members appointed by the Sports Confederation of Denmark. The act continued to insist that Team Denmark should develop elite sport in a way that was socially and economically justifiable. However, at the same time there was broad agreement on abolishing the 15-year age limit for granting support. It no longer made any sense if Danish elite sport was going to be successful in international competition.

Team Denmark was still an independent institution, but via the Danish Ministry of Culture, central government had ensured better control of the institution, which was now subject to the law on public management, and at the same time the Danish Ministry of Culture had to approve Team Denmark's regulations, budget and annual report (Kulturministeriet, Lov nr. 288).

Danish elite sport policy – from keep at arm's length to hands-on regulation. Toward a more liberal welfare state?

The creation of the law on elite sport in 1984 and its revision in 2004 shows how the attitudes of most politicians in the Danish parliament changed over a period of thirty years, to the benefit of elite sport. A range of politicians gradually became better informed about sport. At the same time a significant historical change in mentality occurred in Denmark, one that was not solely related to the world of sport or unique to the Danish society.

Attitudes in the 1970s were very much influenced by anti-authoritarian thinking deriving from the so-called youth revolution, and looking back at the 1970s we have to say that it was the period when the idea of equality for all embodied by the Danish welfare project reached its culmination. All young people should have equal opportunities to make their mark in society; social inheritance should be broken. Everyone should have the right to receive benefits from the public and sport should be for all. In accordance with this, Denmark signed the European charter on 'sport for all' in 1972 and this subsequently became the overall goal of sport policy (Korsgaard & Børsting 2002). The combination of the anti-authoritarian ideas of youth revolt and welfare state thinking about equality led to a distancing from competition and elite concepts. As a consequence, the majority of politicians found it completely natural to support 'sport for all', while simultaneously distancing themselves from elite sport. In fact, among public opinion formers at that time there was also a widespread scepticism about competition in sport and the 'disciplined sports' as a whole (Hansen 1995: 106).

When, therefore, during the 1976 Danish parliamentary debate the majority of the politicians showed particular interest in sport for all and did not want to 'provide funds that were aimed at an elite', they were acting in accordance with attitudes in general in Danish society of the 1970s.

The Danish welfare model gradually changed in the 1980s. As in the rest of Western Europe, new liberal thinking had become widespread in line with a differentiation of the population. The middle class became the dominant political factor in Danish society and the concept of social equality was pushed into the background. Instead, career processes in which people were paid according to effort and merit became the dominant ideal. Yuppies at the start of the 1980s occupied a role in the media that had previously been taken by hippies in the first half of the 1970s.

In general, historical changes in mentality tend to happen over a long period of time and rarely take hold in a pure form. There are elements from preceding attitudes that carry on in changed form, which explains why the Danish parliament could hardly be said simply to surrender to the delights of elite sport. The link to the 1970s welfare project lay in the formulation of the aim that participation in elite sport should be made socially and economically justifiable. Even the construction of Team Denmark had to guarantee that anyone with the talent and the desire to make an extraordinary effort in training, without regard to income, could make it to the top of their sporting discipline. Instead of maintaining elite sport at arm's length, the construction of Team Denmark in principle gave people the chance to ensure socially and economically justifiable ways of regulating the participation in elite sport at the highest levels.

Confirmation that the change in attitudes outlined above became a reality can be found in the fact that the government led by the Social Democrats at the start of the 1990s continued a policy, which aimed among other things to introduce a differentiated wages policy that would promote opportunities for the middle classes to follow a career in either the private or the public sector. When the centre-right government was elected in 2001, with Anders Fogh Rasmussen as Prime Minister, it drove this policy home. Elite sport became stronger than ever before. The minister for culture immediately expressed his principled support both for voluntary sport in general and specifically for elite sport, and for the first time elite sport was written into the Government Bill. The following was written about elite sport:

> Danish elite sport's potential for making its mark internationally must be strengthened. Through an ethical, socially and economically justifiable development of elite sport, Team Denmark in close cooperation with the voluntary organizations, must be ensured the opportunities to provide elite athletes with the optimal conditions (Regeringsgrundlaget 2001).

With these observations and with the 2004 Act on Elite Sport, the process that had started with the 1984 Act on Promotion Elite Sport was completed. Elite sport had become respectable and from now on would be sitting at the high table. This was a development that fitted snugly with Anders Fogh Rasmussen's thinking that individual human beings should have more freedom and the system should give way to the individual. Or as he formulated it in his accession speech in 2001: 'We must renew Danish society, so that it is natural to reward those who set ambitious goals and achieve them' (*Information* 5 December 2001: 4). In the first decade of the new century this became a way of thinking that applies both to elite sport and to life in general.

4

The Swedish elite sport system – or the lack of it?

Johan R. Norberg and Paul Sjöblom

A historical sketch of Swedish elite sport performances will inevitably lead to the conclusion that the glory days of Sweden took place as far back as the first half of the twentieth century. Competitive sports gained an early footing in Sweden, so that already by the turn of the last century the country had established a relatively extensive international sport exchange with quite impressive results. This is not least apparent in the Olympics Statistics. In the 1912 Stockholm Olympics, Sweden became the best nation by aggregate points, followed by a second place in Antwerp 1920. Even though competition hardened with top sport nations like the USA, Britain, France and Germany, Sweden remained among the best five countries in every Olympic game until 1952 (Sylwén & Karlsson 2008). Athletics especially was a prime Swedish sport. Out of a total of 37 international athletics competitions in 1919–1939 – preferably against the neighbouring Nordic countries, Germany, Italy and Hungary – Sweden won as many as 29 victories (*Nordisk familjeboks sportlexikon* 1940). Further examples of Swedish sports performances are internationally successful elite sportsmen like Harry Persson, the boxer; Arne Borg, the swimmer; and Gunder Hägg, the middle-distance runner.

The period following the Second World War has not been as successful.

The explanation is not that Swedish athletes have performed worse, but that competitiveness has increased (Storm & Nielsen 2010). Still, there have been great moments in sport in recent decades as well. Football won a silver medal in the 1958 and a bronze medal in the 1994 World Cup. Other memorable events and athletes include the boxer Ingemar 'Ingo' Johansson's World Heavyweight Championship in 1959, Björn Borg's five Wimbledon victories in tennis 1976–1980, Annika Sörenstam, the golf phenomenon, Jan-Ove Waldner, the table-tennis player, as well as a large number of alpine skiers headed by Ingemar Stenmark, Pernilla Wiberg and Anja Pärson.

Successes in sport are a result of many factors – ranging from individual abilities and talents to overarching structural and institutional conditions in both sports and society. This chapter focuses on the latter. The aim is to outline the Swedish elite sport system, i.e. the organizational structure, conditions and characteristics of elite sports. This is by no means a simple task. The first problem is lack of information. Swedish elite sports are in many ways an unploughed field of research. A second problem is the actual term elite sport *system,* which indicates a well-reasoned and coherent national strategy for conducting and developing elite sports. This is hardly an adequate description of Swedish conditions. The thesis in this article is rather that elite sports have always held a weak position in Swedish sport. In addition, the financial conditions differ widely between sports. So, even though both federations and athletes spend a great deal of time, effort and resources on elite activities, it is doubtful whether these strategies and conditions deserve being characterized as parts of a uniform 'system'.

The chapter starts with a discussion about general characteristics of the organization, ideology and societal position of Swedish sport, with special focus on elite sports. This is followed by an outline of the historical growth of the Swedish elite sport system. Finally, a number of current controversies and challenges to Swedish elite sports policy are discussed.

The Swedish sports model in between state, market and civil society

Sport as a cultural phenomenon reflects its historical and societal context. A great many characteristics of Swedish sport are intimately associated with specific features in the development of Swedish society and welfare policy. To begin with, Sweden has a long tradition of big, uniform citizen associations, so-called *popular movements*. The first of these, the nonconformist, temperance and labour movements, emerged in the nineteenth century and played an important role in the democratization of Sweden. During the following century, the cooperation between the state and popular movements grew closer, which contributed to a welfare system in Sweden, characterized by dialogue, consensus and an ability to compromise (Lundkvist 1979; Micheletti 1994). Even today the popular movement tradition forms a dominating element in Swedish civil society. Modern studies have demonstrated that more than 90 per cent of the adult Swedish population (16–84 years) are members of at least one voluntary association. Furthermore, every fourth individual has some voluntary commission of trust (Lundström & Wijkström 1995).

A second feature concerns the specific structure of Swedish welfare policy. In international comparisons Sweden – together with the other Nordic countries – is held forth as representing a *social democratic welfare regime* stamped by equality, general security systems and far-reaching state commitments to citizens' well-being and high standard of living. Further characteristics are that the production of welfare primarily takes place under public auspices – at least in the core areas of welfare policy – and that the financing of the generous transfer systems and the comprehensive public sector presupposes high tax revenues and an active labour market policy striving towards full employment (Esping-Andersen 1990; Bergsgard & Norberg 2010).

Both of these features are reflected in the Swedish sports model. Organizationally as well as ideologically, voluntarily organized sport is strongly anchored in the Swedish popular movement tradition. In addition, the activities have for long been integrated into the welfare policy through extensive support from state and municipalities. Both aspects are basic to Swedish sport and important starting points for understanding the structure and conditions of elite sports.

Sport movement organizational structure

Since 1903, voluntarily organized sport in Sweden has been gathered into *the Swedish Sports Confederation* (Sveriges riksidrottsförbund, RF). It consists of 3.2 million members in over 20,000 *local sports clubs* and 7,000 *corporation clubs*. These clubs are in turn organized according to two major principles, one based on the sports activities they practise, the other on geographical location. The sport-specific organization consists of 70 national and relatively independent special *sports federations* (SF), i.e. national independent organizations responsible for specific sports. The geographical organization is, correspondingly, made up of 21 *district federations* (DF) whose task is to support regional sporting life. Most of the local clubs also belong to a so-called *special district federation* (SDF). This is the prolonged arm of the special sport federations at the regional level. The RF's highest decision-making body is the joint *RF Assembly*, which congregates every second year. Between the assembly meetings the activities are conducted by the *RF Executive Committee* (RS) with its office (SOU 2008: 59).

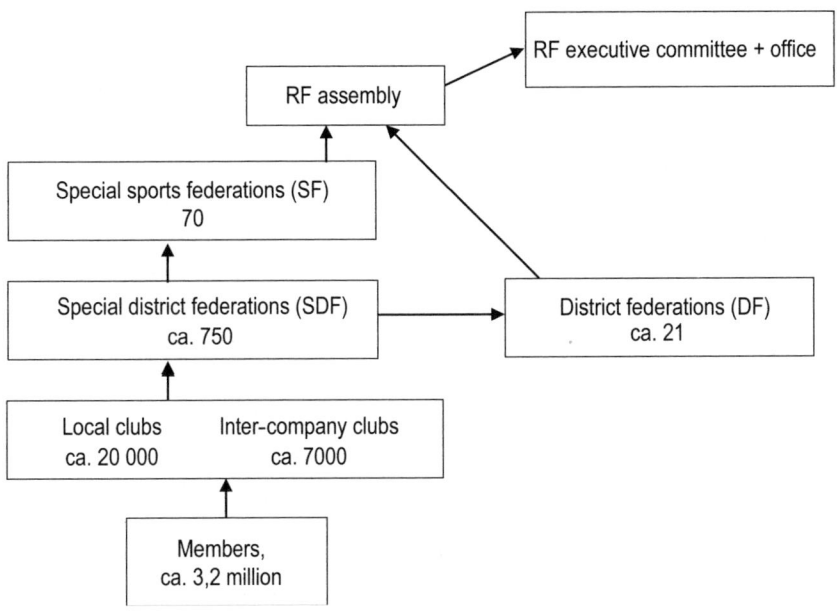

Figure 4.1: The organizational structure of the Swedish Sports Confederation (RF)

Alongside the RF there are two national support organizations. The first is *SISU Idrottsutbildarna*, a study organization where the members are the RF's special sports federations plus another six organizations, the Volunteer Shooters' Movement among others. The primary task of SISU is to support education activities at the local level in the form of state-supported study circles. In addition, SISU comprises a College of Sport and a publishing company. The second support organization is *Sweden's Olympic Committee* (SOK). SOK is the highest authority for issues concerning the Olympic Games in Sweden and consists of the 35 SFs for Olympic sports. The committee's primary task is to organize and implement Swedish participation in the Olympic Games and in European Youth Olympic Festivals (EYOF), including talent development.

Elite sports within the framework of the Swedish sports model

An account of the organizational structure of Swedish elite sports must start with the special sports federations and the local sports clubs. Every SF has the main responsibility for its specific sport. This responsibility includes administrative and representative functions, such as handling rules and regulations, coordinating national leagues, deciding on club membership, contacts with international federations, etc. In addition, the federations are responsible for preparing and conducting national team activities. In this way the SFs form the natural starting point for all Swedish elite sports, both by controlling the institutional frames of each sport and by organizing and developing the best athletes for competitions at the international level.

The local sports clubs are where young talents are discovered and developed. It is also through the clubs that athletes get the chance to participate in national leagues and championships. Furthermore, it is mainly within the framework of local clubs that the training of elite athletes and teams takes place. A great deal of the real competence for organizing and developing sports talents is thus located at the lowest level of the sports movement's organizational structure – with the local clubs and their leaders.

For support functions, the RF plays an important part. Financially, the confederation's elite support is dominated by the so-called basic funding allocated to all SFs. This is a general subsidy, which can be used, for instance, to finance the federations' national teams and elite development. The subsidy amounted in 2009 to 25 million euros and is distributed among the RF's 70 member federations on the basis of their size and activity level. The RF also gives grants to the international work of the federations. Furthermore, in January 2009 the government set aside a total of 20 million euros for a temporary special elite sports programme.

In addition to subsidies, the SFs receive an offer to be part of the RF's special *elite support program*. The national centre is located at the Bosön sports venue north of Stockholm and includes, for instance, national team and coaching education, network meetings and help to special sports federations for drawing up development plans for elite athletes. At regional and local levels there are nine *regional elite sport centres* (Reg EIC), whose activities include physiological and mental support, career counselling and education work.

For sports included in the Olympic programme, the SOK performs an important support function. The committee's elite support was introduced in 1998 through a joint investment from the state and the private sponsors. The support – which in 2009 amounted to 5.7 million euros – consists of financial grants as well as competence support and counselling. The support is based on strict priorities, to create optimal conditions for a limited number of elite athletes regardless of the commercial strength of the sport in question (SOU 2008: 59: 324). By the end of 2009, 149 elite athletes and five teams were included in the programme (Sweden's Olympic Committee 2010).

Responsible for Swedish participation in the Paralympics is *The Swedish Sports Organization for the Disabled* while *The Swedish Deaf Sports Federation* has the responsibility for Swedish participation in the Deaflympics.

A further element in Swedish support to elite sports concerns the chances of young people to combine elite sporting with studies. This has been made possible by so-called *idrottsgymnasier* ('sports upper secondary schools'), i.e. schools where successful youngsters going in for elite sporting can develop their particular sport and simultaneously go through upper secondary school education. In Sweden such schools exist at the national, regional and local levels. The RF is responsible for national activities – so-called national sports upper secondary schools – involving in 2009 ca. 1,300 students distributed among 37 sports and 49 locations. Regional and local activities are organized for students in each area and are usually structured in collaboration between the municipalities concerned and local or regional associations.

For tertiary studies, elite athletes may apply for the RF *elite sports scholarships*. Such a scholarship amounts to ca. 4,000 euros and was in the 2009–2010 academic year granted to 53 elite athletes.

Ideological aspects on the position of elite sports in the Swedish sport model

Ideologically, the popular movement perspective is also broadly anchored in Swedish sport. In the *Sport Wants* document, the RF summarizes the joint vision and fundamental views of the sports movement. The starting point is not sports performances or competition results. On the contrary, a broad social perspective predominates, focusing on voluntary commitment, public health and everybody's right to participate in sports on their own terms (Riksidrottsförbundet 2009a). Consequently, elite sports keep a fairly low profile in the document. Once elite issues are discussed, they are fraught with ambivalence. Of course, there are positive arguments, for example that victories in international championships create a positive image of Sweden and strengthen the national spirit of community. Furthermore, successful athletes may form 'important positive models for children and young people and valuable representatives of our country'. Nevertheless, it is pointed out that elite efforts must not be set in at too early an age, or cause social maladjustment. Some formulations indicate an ambition to modify the image of elite sports. Elite sports make up a fairly small part of competitive sport in absolute terms, and far from all elite athletes collect big incomes via sponsoring and market revenues. Swedish elite sports is characterized by the opposite, rather – that a great many national teams, athletes and leaders manage to keep up a high international standard in spite of acting on a voluntary basis.

One could of course discuss to what extent the members of the sports movement in practice share the broad popular movement ideology that permeates *Sport Wants*. Besides, there are counter images, like the SFs' own annual reports, which tend to focus much more on pure sports events, like national team activities, etc. (SOU 2008: 59: 282–285). Still, this does not take away the effect of the Swedish sports movement always having followed the tradition of seeking societal legitimacy in broad popular movement aspects, which has resulted in the fairly low ideological profile of elite sports.

The sports movement's revenues via civil society, state and market

A third measure of the conditions and position of Swedish elite sports is to compare sports movement revenues from the state, the market and civil society. Not surprisingly, the largest support comes from *civil society*, chiefly through voluntary work. By RF calculations, the economic value of the movement's close to 700,000 voluntary sports leaders amounts to ca. 2.5 billion euros a year. Add to this the direct financial support from members in the form of membership and training fees as well as revenues achieved by the clubs themselves by competition and entertainment arrangements, lottery sales, etc. According to the RF's own data, these self-generated incomes (including membership fees) constitute nearly 70 per cent of an average club's total revenues – voluntary work not included (Riksidrottsförbundet 2005).

Support from the *public sector* is both direct in the form of grants and indirect via tax relief and subsidized facility costs. The overarching state motives derive from welfare policy, with the emphasis on promoting physical activity and meaningful leisure among children and young people. The state (national) support amounted in 2009 to ca. 170 million euros. About 50 million euros was allocated to the RF and its member federations, while the remaining funding was primarily granted to local associations (Government proposition 2009/2010: 1). The municipal (local) support to sports amounts to ca. 350 million euros annually, including about 100 million in grants, e.g. activity support, funding for leader education or for covering various facility costs. The rest consists of subsidies like free access to public sports facilities or subsidized rent or other costs for municipal equipment and materials (SOU 2008: 59: 184–185).

Finally, commercial revenues still form a modest source of income for a great many sports associations. According to RF, advertising and sponsoring the RF, advertising and sponsoring only make up seven per cent of the total incomes of a local sports club (Riksidrottsförbundet 2005:18). Even at federation level market revenues are often small – at least compared to state contributions. However, these are assessments made at an aggregate level. For individual associations the situation may seem quite different. An elite club in football with incomes from large sponsoring contracts, player-sales and public revenues cannot compare with a judo club whose sole incomes consist of membership fees, local activity support and scratch card sales. The same goes for many of the SFs, some of which receive big market proceeds, while others finance their work mostly via state subsidies and voluntary commitment. The Swedish Football Association, for example, accounted in 2008 for incomes of ca. 50 million euros (Svenska fotbollförbundet 2009) followed by the federations for golf and skiing, respectively, with turnover levels of ca. 9 million euros each. Among small federations with few resources may be mentioned water skiing, casting and field hockey. All of these had in 2008 a turnover of less than 150,000 euros, most of it (62–77 per cent) in the form of state funding (Riksidrottsförbundet 2010: 52).

The development of modern elite sports in Sweden
A late and slow professionalization process

The development of the Swedish elite sport system is intimately connected with the *professionalization* of the sports movement. The concept is much debated in Swedish sports research but often used to describe a process where voluntary club-sports have gradually adopted the form of a rational and result-oriented profession of paid employees. As Peterson (1989, 1993) has shown in several studies of Swedish football, this is a multi-faceted process ranging from ideological shifts in the view of sports to far-reaching changes within the financial, organizational, social and cognitive framework of its activities. Furthermore, actual sports practice is affected, for example by systematic training techniques and other measures for maximizing sports successes.

There is little research on the professionalization of Swedish elite sports. The main impression is, however, that this process began late and has been rather slow. There are several reasons for this. One factor that is often mentioned is the strong *popular movement tradition* in the sports movement. Another is the so-called *amateur regulations,* i.e. the prohibition for both athletes and leaders on receiving payment for participating in sports events (Wikberg 2005). A third factor is that the professionalization of elite sports was restricted by the *tangible ambivalence of those in political power to elite sports as a cultural phenomenon*. Such factors are also present in the other Nordic countries where professionalization developed earlier and went further after the 1970s. However, the dynamics of such factors may have worked differently in Sweden due to the strong position of elite sport in the first half of the twentieth century.

The amateur ideal did not prevent clubs and athletes from developing a professional attitude to sport and talent development, but it reinforced the idealistic character of the movement by restricting the possibilities of paid work and economic compensation for elite athletes and coaches (Andersson 2002). Also, several early one-off state subsidies aimed explicitly at supporting elite sports activities. In 1908, for example, the government granted permission for a special sports lottery with the aim to finance the 1912 Olympic Games in Stockholm (Lindroth 1974). However, state support to elite sports was for a long time a controversial issue. In early parliamentary sports debates, politicians often questioned the entire use of elite sport, referring to competition hysterics and unsound professionalism. It was mainly the importance of sport for public health and youth fostering that motivated the creation of regular state funding in 1913 (Norberg 2004).

As in the other Nordic countries, elite sports were not looked upon as respectable within a social democratic welfare policy characterized by ideals of breadth and equality rather than elitism and ranking. This created a discrepancy between rhetoric and practice, with public support to sports motivated by the breadth of sport, whereas state authorities did not prevent sports federations from utilizing part of their support for elite-oriented activities.

Hence, it is doubtful whether one can talk about systematically organized principles for elite sports and talent development in Swedish sport up to the 1950s. For many elite athletes, the possibility of going in wholeheartedly for elite sports was prevented by the prevalent amateur rules. Besides, the federations' and clubs' economic resources were often small and the quality of facilities uneven, as was the supply of qualified coaches and training methods. Therefore, many of the good sports results that were achieved in the first half of the twentieth century were rather due to the good sports environments of some clubs combined with the unique talents and individual efforts of specific athletes. To illustrate this, one may refer to the way Gunder Hägg, the middle-distance runner, described in his memoirs how he largely developed his own training methods, which included field running in three-foot deep snow. Others like Arne Borg, the swimmer, held forth stubbornness and competitive instinct rather than swimming technique as the driving force behind his innumerable records and championships (Andersson & Karlsson 2002).

The post-war period and the breakthrough of the professionalization process

In the period after the Second World War a number of far-reaching transformation processes took place, resulting in new conditions for the professionalization of sports.

The first factor was *the expansion of public support*. By the late 1930s, state support to sport had increased strongly as the government financing of sports was temporarily tied to the surplus of AB Tipstjänst, a newly established gambling company (Norberg 2004). After the war the municipalities took over. The years 1955–1965, in particular, entailed regular *municipalisation* of sport, since the chief responsibility and maintenance of many sports grounds and other facilities, were successively taken over by municipal bodies. This resulted in a shift of balance in public support to sports with the municipalities now adopting the government's former role as the sport movement's main benefactor (Sjöblom 2006; Norberg 2002a).

Even at the state level new subsidies were added. The background was a number of policy reforms focusing on young people's leisure activities. The RF received, for example, new means to employ *sports consultants*, i.e. regional employees to help and develop local clubs. Furthermore, new money was granted for educational courses and leader education as well as special grants for local activity support (Norberg 2004).

Swedish Association of Local Authorities together with the special sports federations worked out norms for facilities adapted for competitions. In parallel, more and more municipal 'competition subsidies' were established. Besides, special efforts for certain junior and A teams were given more space at the expense of regular child and broad activities (Sjöblom 2006).

In the mid-1950s the Swedish Football Association also started arranging special 'elite camps' for boys between 14 and 16 years old. The following decade saw a strong increase in elite-oriented child and youth competitions in sports such as athletics, skiing, tennis, swimming and ice hockey (Hjelm 2000; Patriksson 1990).

The public sector's increased interest in sport culminated in the 1970 parliament 'Sport for All' decision. Ideologically, the decision marked the definite inclusion of sport into Swedish welfare policy. In addition, financial possibilities were now created for a strong improvement of the activities and infrastructure of the whole sports movement. The efforts included anything from increased funding for sports facilities, improved leader education, special grants for sports for the disabled and for sports research as well as a considerably increased organization support (SOU 1969: 29).

A second important condition for the professionalization of the sports movement was the *successive abolishment of the amateur rules*. Even though most members in the early Swedish sports movement defended the principle that sport should not be practised for money, there is no doubt that the amateur issue with time developed into a protracted problem. The rules were often vague and hard to interpret. Besides, it was far from unusual that athletes were offered payment on the sly, which both undermined the legitimacy of the amateur doctrine and led to exacerbating law cases and media scandals. Nor could the amateur rules in the long run prevent individual athletes from taking the step into an entirely professional sports career.

The formal abolishment of the amateur rules took place successively. The first step was taken in 1948 when the RF replaced them by general rules of competition which did not include any amateur definition. In 1967 even these general rules were abolished with the consequence that the whole issue of reimbursement for athletes was referred to the individual special sports federations (Wikberg 2005).

Market adaptation and the expansion of clubs and federations

In the early 1970s, Swedish sport was thus faced with a new situation. Public support had grown considerably in the last decade, and this had created good conditions for expansion and quality improvements. The abolishment of the amateur rules had also provided new possibilities for the sports movement to approach the market sector.

Peterson (1989) has analysed the professionalization of elite football in the 1970s and 1980s through the Halmstad BK club. The result showed how quickly the club developed in the decade that followed, from a traditional voluntarily run football club anchored in the working class to a modern, middle-class-based company. At the organizational level professionalization took the form of extended administration, more paid work and by the members of the board taken from industry rather than through recruiting former players and leaders. Economically, the turnover of the club grew fast, chiefly through sponsors and other market revenues. Even the actual football game changed with the employment of a new English coach. The transformation of Halmstad BK was crowned by two Swedish Championship gold medals in the second half of the 1970s.

Fahlén (2006) has pointed to a similar professionalization process in Swedish ice hockey during the same period. Fahlén emphasizes the influence from professional American ice hockey in that many good Swedish players were recruited to the NHL. However, the ideals and values of professional American ice hockey successively geared Swedish ice hockey in a more professional and commercial direction.

The sports movement's central organizations were also professionalized. Increased funding enabled both the RF and its member federations to develop their administrations. The result showed, not least in 1976 with the establishment of *Idrottens hus* ('The House of Sports') at Farsta outside Stockholm – in premises housing both the RF office and a majority of the SFs (Norberg 2002b).

Sports research and sports education
Also sports research went through an expansive phase. *Idrottens forskningsråd* (IFR – 'The Swedish Sports Research Council') was formed in 1970 with the task of distributing means for sports research, arranging scholarly conferences and ensuring that the results of sports research would also benefit the sports movement. In 1988, *Centrum för idrottsforskning* (CIF – 'the Swedish National Centre for Research in Sports') was established and with its broad representation of sports researchers from various disciplines and universities, the CIF soon took over IFR's role and tasks in Swedish sports research (Åkesson 2010).

In the field of education, measures were taken to make it easier for young athletes to combine elite sports efforts with upper secondary school studies. The result was Riksidrottsgymnasier (National Sports Upper Secondary Schools), where talented young athletes were offered good conditions for developing their special sport within the framework of an upper secondary school programme (Uebel 2006). For tertiary-level studies, the RF managed in the 1980s to work out a cooperation agreement with the university sector offering a reduced course of study for elite athletes. At the same time scholarships were established for youngsters wishing to combine elite training with university studies. Besides university studies special *sports platoons* were created. These enabled promising elite athletes extra training within the framework of their military service during the period 1967–2004.

Vigorous efforts were also made within the sports movement to develop its education activities. In the special sports federations, step-by-step education was introduced to develop their coaches and instructors. In 1978 the sports movement's own people's high school was established at the RF sports venue at Bosön just outside Stockholm. This was followed in 1985 by *SISU Idrottsutbildarna*, a study organization with a variety of courses ranging from training education to nutrition and organizational studies (Wallin 2003).

Finally, sports education was also introduced at the university level. In addition to traditional physical education teaching, which had existed in Sweden since the nineteenth century, new courses and programmes were added in order to professionalize club sports. The first breakthrough occurred in the 1980s with education in sports pedagogy and coaching education. After the turn of the millennium, subjects like sports science, sports management, coaching and leadership were added (Åkesson 2010).

Central efforts to support elite sports and talent development

The professionalization of Swedish sport that began in the 1970s did not immediately result in new central efforts to strengthen the conditions of elite sports. Except for national sports upper secondary schools, the RF stuck to the principle that elite sport and talent development were the responsibility of the SFs. Thus, the federations had to finance their elite activities within the framework of traditional organization funding or by other means. Even the SOK's efforts were limited to preparations for the Olympic Games by minor scholarships to athletes or some federation support.

However, the decentralization of Swedish elite sports began to feel problematic. Not least the SOK questioned why many of the small federations neither cooperated nor learnt from each other in elite sports issues. Therefore, in the mid-1980s, more systematic cooperation and knowledge transfer between different sports was launched, for example, by special national team manager meetings (Reinebo 2010).

At about the same time, the first strategy document, 'Elite Sports in Sweden', was compiled by the RF's Elite Sports Council containing a joint ideology for elite sports development in the country (Eriksson 2006).

The need to develop Swedish elite sports also led to increased cooperation between the RF and the SOK. This began in 1989 with the first agreement and followed in 1992 by a *Centre for Performance Development* (CPU), with the aim of promoting the development of elite sports by cooperative projects between athletes, leaders and researchers. Within the framework of the CPU, investments were made in nine regional elite sports centres (Reg-EIC), with the purpose of supporting regional elite sports through educating and developing both athletes and coaches. In 1995 Bosön obtained the special position of a national elite sports centre (EIC) (Wallin, 2003).

The late 1990s saw the definite breakthrough of publicly financed elite efforts. Typically enough, the explanation is to be found in two sporting failures. The first failure concerned winter sports. The Olympic Games at Albertville in 1992 and Lillehammer in 1994 had produced mediocre results, with only one Swedish gold medal at each and just a few silver and bronze medals. The second failure was Stockholm's application to arrange the Olympic Summer Games in 2004. For this purpose the SOK had managed to recruit a number of major sponsors who were willing to provide resources to raise the performance level of the Swedish Olympic team. After that the government, too, had offered to contribute further means for the planned talent investment. These efforts were, however, shelved when the IOC in September 1997 announced that Athens was to host the summer games. This disappointment was followed by a third disaster in the Nagano winter games in 1998. In spite of favourable conditions – including, not least, a national ice hockey team containing a large number of NHL pros – the only results this time were two silver medals in skiing and a bronze medal in curling.

Together these disappointments led to a crisis awareness, which enabled the SOK to get both industry and government to back up yet another joint elite effort. The government's proposal was to offer the SOK one million euros annually for elite development over a six-year period (1998–2004) on the precondition that sponsors contributed an equal sum. Furthermore – and as a clear expression of the Social Democratic government's ambivalent attitude to elite sports – the very word 'elite' was not to be used. The decision to create a special elite sport program had far-reaching consequences. On an overarching sports policy level it meant a breakthrough for the principle that state support can also be used directly to strengthen the international competitiveness of Swedish elite sports. In addition, the SOK was able to implement a comprehensive development programme called 'Olympic Offensive'. In accordance with the government's request, the costs were distributed between sponsor-financed 'top support' for already established athletes and a publicly financed 'talent support' for promising recruits (Reinebo 2010; Wallin 2003).

After the turn of the millennium, the state has further recognized elite sports as an independent area worth public support per se. In 2008 the government ordinance on state funding to sports activities was supplemented with the objective that the support should also strengthen athletes' international competitiveness. This was followed in 2009 by the launching of a special joint federation means-tested elite campaign of altogether 20 million euros on top of the traditional appropriation.

Controversies and challenges in Swedish elite sports

In Sweden, elite sports have been eagerly discussed in recent years. The discussion has been multi-faceted, ranging from exorbitant performance demands within child sports to special tax relief for elite athletes. The main themes of the debate are summarized below.

Early specialization in child and youth sports

In September 2007 the Swedish press presented the planned elite efforts of Boo FF, a football club, within their child and youth activities. The idea was to offer a limited number of particularly talented children (from the age of nine upwards) the chance of extra football training by professional coaches as well as media training, mental counselling and special nutrition and health education. Even though this talent programme was far from unique, it drew great attention from the media as well as severe criticism. Karin Mattsson, president of the RF, expressed her displeasure, pointing out that children's sporting activities should be guided by play rather than performance and that no selection should occur at such a young age. Furthermore, Lena Adelsohn Liljeroth, minister for sports, was critical and called in the representatives of a number of major sports in Sweden to a discussion about elite efforts within child sports. There were also parents in Boo FF who deplored the planned elite efforts, arguing, for instance, that the narrow elite thinking of the club created unsound demands on the children and that the efforts would lead to higher fees, which could not be afforded by all families (*Svenska Dagbladet* 2007a, 2007b).

The criticism against Boo FF's elite programme reflects an often debated theme in Swedish child and youth sports. Are activities designed according to the logic of competitive sports or are they based on the needs of children? Is sport adapted to the children or is it the young who must adapt to the demands of adult sports? The problems are far from unique to Swedish circumstances. In the end, it is a matter of pitting two kinds of logic against one another: focusing on results, performance and ranking in competitive sports against the ideals of equality and variety within association democracy, where everybody should have the chance to feel that they participate and develop according to their own possibilities and interests (SOU 2008: 59).

The RF management has been long aware of the problems related to talent development in child and youth sports. The *Sport Wants* programme (2009a) includes clear guidelines for how sports clubs should handle the tension between competition fostering and club fostering. The chief message is to split activities into age groups and ambition levels. In *child sports* (0–12 years), competitions should be subordinated to play and the young should compete against themselves rather than being compared to others. In *youth sports* (13–20 years), one should make a start with 'a natural differentiation between various sports ambition levels', where some will choose to go in for serious elite training whereas others will prefer sporting activities at a lower level of ambition. Both in youth and adult sports (above the age of 20), one should, however, be able to choose between elite and broad sports.

The structure of sports for children has also attracted attention from the authorities. In June 2008 a national report declared that the sports movement's vision of playful children's sports did not correspond to realities. On the contrary, a strikingly unanimous research community showed that 'competition fostering in early childhood forms the predominant logic', which runs the risk of creating a sports practice 'where selection and ranking are accepted early on as self-evident principles for promoting performance and results' (SOU 2008, 59: 236). The following year the government ordinance on state support to sport activities was supplemented by a *children's right perspective*, indicating that state support to sports is intended for activities compatible with the UN convention of children's rights (Proposition 2008/09: 126).

The RF vs the SOK in the power struggle for Swedish elite sports

A second controversy in Swedish sports policy has to do with the differences of opinion between the RF and SOK. Their cooperation difficulties may superficially seem as a traditional struggle for power over the control of talent development in Swedish sports and its funding. However, in reality the differences are much more multi-faceted due to the different structures and objectives of the organizations.

A first difference concerns *representativeness*. The RF represents nearly all association-organized sports in Sweden, whereas the SOK consists of the special sports federations whose sports are represented in the Olympic programme. From this follows that 36 out of the RF's 70 SFs are also part of the SOK – while the remaining ones are left outside without any access to SOK elite support.

A second difference involves the different *areas of responsibility*. The RF's mission is a broad one. According to its statutes, the confederation is 'the Swedish sports movement's coordinating organization' with the task to 'deal with concerns common to the sports movement nationally as well as internationally' (Riksidrottsförbundet 2009b). In practice it ranges from strategic decisions about the sports movement's future activities to funding allocation, opinion forming, sports development and contacts with the surrounding community. The SOK's tasks are much more limited, as they are about creating 'competitive Swedish Olympic teams in order to achieve good Swedish results in Olympic Games.' While the RF is responsible for both elite and breadth issues, the SOK's mission focuses explicitly on the top elite in a limited number of sports.

The organizations' *internal power structure* differs as well. The RF applies a system whereby most of the 200-odd votes of the assembly are distributed proportionally among the special sports federations on the basis of their number of clubs. The SOK instead applies the principle: one member association – one vote. This means that the influence of those SFs which are part of both organizations varies from one organization to the other. The Swedish Football Association, for example, had seven votes in the 2007 RF assembly, as against only one for the Swedish Fencing Federation. At the annual meeting of the SOK they had, however, one vote each.

Furthermore, different *allocation systems* apply to funding issues. In the RF most of the elite support forms part of the basic funding to the special sports federations. Since this support is chiefly allocated according to various quantitative measures, such as the number of clubs and active members, education programmes conducted, etc., the chances of receiving means for elite activities are largely tied to the relative size of the federations. In the SOK the talent support is allocated by assessing the potentials and needs of individual athletes (or teams). Nor is there any hesitation about giving greater financial support to athletes in financially weak sports. This is an attitude stirring mixed emotions. Most positive are of course small Olympic federations with scanty resources from the RF and few chances of receiving supplementary market revenues. For these the SOK's distribution principles may offer the only possibility to operate any talent development whatsoever. At the other end are those sports federations which would have received more funding through other distribution principles.

Finally, the organizations possess *different competencies* in elite sport issues. The SOK has worked operatively with talent development since the 1990s. The efforts made by the RF have, generally speaking, been more limited and supportive following the argument that the operative responsibility in elite sports issues lies with the individual special sports federations.

The relation between the RF and SOK has been subject to an almost continuous debate since the 1980s. On the initiative of the RF, a series of reports have analysed the internal structure, roles and working methods of the two parties. Proposals for a merger have been broached on several occasions, but are usually watered down to various forms of cooperation agreement.

The fact that the government in 1998 gave the SOK its own money for talent development has in no way reduced the differences. The RF has regarded it as in principle wrong that the government makes decisions about the sports movement's internal funding allocation. It has also been branded as unfair that the state has initiated a talent support which does not benefit all special sports federations.

The state's sports policy role and responsibility

There is no doubt that in recent years the state has increased its responsibility for elite sports. However, the role of the state in elite sports has also remained a much debated issue. This debate has been dominated by two major themes. The first, which is a matter of principle, concerns the RF's request for greater independence in allocating state support to sports. The second is a more traditional theme, in that the confederation in various ways has advocated greater public resources and new political reforms to further strengthen elite sports.

The discussion about the independence of the sports movement is linked to the strong increase of state support since the late 1990s – from ca. 50 million euros in 1998 to as much as 175 million euros in 2008. This development is a direct result of additional funding allocated to the sports movement via AB Svenska Spel, the national gambling company. The gambling money has been portioned out in different forms. Most of it has, however, been earmarked by the state for child and youth activities at the local level, either as local activity support or through a variety of time-limited projects (SOU 2008: 59).

For the RF the gambling money has created some ambivalence. A positive aspect was of course that sport was given more resources. More frustrating, however, was the fact that the money was earmarked for the local level and that the SF consequently could not share any part of the investment. For the RF, thus, the demand for more influence over issues of state allocation turned into a dual strategy, which involved demonstrating the principle of autonomy and simultaneously making room for using the gambling money from the local club level to the special sports federations in new ways (SOU 2008, 59: 349).

The RF's struggle was to some extent successful. By 2006 the government granted that at least part of the funding via the gambling market could also be allocated to the special sports federations. This was followed in 2009 by the special elite investment of a total of 20 million euros (this, too, financed out of a gambling market surplus). An even greater autonomy was achieved when it was decided that the SOK talent support should subsequently be allocated by the RF (instead of being earmarked by the government). This strengthened the confederation's influence over funding issues and simultaneously gave it a stronger power position in Swedish elite sports.

Parallel with demands for increased autonomy, the RF has – somewhat paradoxically – been striving for new earmarked grants to attract international events to Sweden. For this, the RF has emphasized the significant role played by international competitions in promoting tourism, creating employment, marketing cities, etc. as well as the view that it is unreasonable that the sports movement defray all the costs and take all the economic risks. Besides, both sport and the Swedish tourist industry will suffer every time a special sports federation, for economic reasons, declines hosting an international contest. These proposals, too, were positively received by the government, and in 2009 it promised to add new funding to the sports movement for creating a national competence centre with the mission to get more international sports events located to Sweden (Proposition 2009/10: 1).

Even tax relief has been requested. As an example, a state commission proposed in 2006 a number of measures for reducing the taxation of elite-related sports activities. This included abolishing the advertising tax for voluntary associations as well as introducing a 'sports practitioner account' to enable elite athletes to postpone the taxation of their sports incomes. The commission's proposals were very positively received by the sports movement but were never realized (SOU 2006: 23).

How successful has the Swedish elite sport system been?

It is always precarious to assess whether certain strategies or systems for sports talent development are better than others. The first problem is to determine what should be considered a reasonable level of performance for a specific country, given its unique sporting circumstances. Add to this the risk of contrafactual reasoning, i.e. the difficulty of determining in retrospect whether there would have been better results if the elite sport system had been structured differently. A discussion of the pros and cons of the Swedish elite sport system must therefore be limited to a few general observations.

With these reservations there are several reasons to consider the Swedish elite sport system relatively poorly developed. Sweden has never been anywhere near the form of state-organized talent development that characterized the Eastern bloc in the latter half of the twentieth century. Nor has there existed any equivalent to the American system with its extent of commercial sports and considerable talent development within the framework of college and university studies. By comparisons like these the Swedish popular movement model seems modest indeed. Attempts at coordinating elite sport strategies have been few, late in coming and, besides, overshadowed by a more generally structured state support to sports focusing on organizations and on activating children and young people.

Even in a Nordic perspective the Swedish elite sport system seems both decentralized and fragmentary. The economic terms for operating national team activities and talent development vary strongly from one sport to another. Besides, the conditions for inter-federation cooperation have been poor due to a democratic structure where the autonomy of the SFs has taken primacy. It must be admitted that these problems have been noted in recent years. Since 2009 the state has allocated further means to elite sports. In addition, attempts are currently under way to coordinate the disparate types of support lent by the RF and SOK. However, even if these elite efforts should be successful, there is still a giant leap to the coordinated systems for elite sports that characterize the Norwegian 'top sport miracle' and Team Denmark. In a wider perspective one might even question whether it is reasonable to talk about a Swedish elite sport system at all. Perhaps it is rather the *absence* of a specific elite sports strategy that is the chief Swedish characteristic?

However, one may also look at it the other way around. Without doubt, there are elements in the Swedish sports model that have benefited elite sports. Such elements are also found in the other Nordic countries. The first is the great openness within voluntary organizations. In Sweden it is more or less a tradition that children and young people should be given the chance to test a number of different sports to find an activity which suits them and which they are prepared to go in for. This is also done extensively. A major youth survey conducted in 2005 demonstrated that as many as 88 per cent of all young people between 13 and 20 had participated in more than one club sport and that close to half of them (45 per cent) claimed to have been active in four or more sports (Trondman 2005).

A second factor is the Swedish welfare model. The permanent funding to sport granted by the state in the early twentieth century has contributed greatly to enable the sports movement to grow to the current 20,000-odd clubs, distributed among 70 different special sports federations. Add to this the extensive historic support to facilities. The municipal expansion in the postwar years, not least, created an impressive sports infrastructure with publicly financed indoor and outdoor facilities: swimming halls, ski hills, football pitches, tennis courts, illuminated jogging-tracks and skateboard ramps. In addition, school gyms and playgrounds provided a variety of sports materials like tables for table tennis, baskets for basketball and goals for floorball. The very combination of Sweden as a welfare state and the approach to sports as a publicly prioritized leisure activity has created favourable terms for attracting children and youngsters to an active and varied sporting life by allowing them to try out different sports.

To summarize: A Swedish popular movement tradition in sports together with the comprehensive support from state and municipalities has created a relatively favourable opening for children to *discover* their talent – but after this it is largely left to the practitioners themselves to create the conditions for *developing* their capacity. To some extent, local clubs may contribute by offering qualified coaches and training facilities. Furthermore, the federations may with time supplement this by training camps and national team activities (for the very best). Still, it is up to the individuals to set aside time and acquire resources for their elite efforts, something that immediately creates great differences between different sports and their practitioners. In commercially strong sports like football, ice hockey and tennis there are good chances of obtaining sponsors, advertising contracts and salaries. For top athletes in the Olympic sports, scholarships are available via the SOK's talent support. For the others, however, nothing remains but to finance their elite efforts via part-time jobs, studies or financial support from families and other relatives (Lindfeldt 2007). For these athletes, sports are and will continue to be a voluntary leisure activity regardless of the level of their performance.

One important conclusion is thus that there is no uniform way of describing Swedish elite sports. Circumstances still differ too much between sports and federations. Nevertheless, it must be admitted that the terms of existence for elite sports have improved considerably since the late 1990s. Both the RF and SOK have developed strategies for paving the way for elite athletes from promising talents to potential medallists in international competition. At the same time, the state has given important recognition to elite sports by formulating explicit elite sport policies and by earmarking funding for elite sports purposes. Even though the RF keeps emphasizing the right of the special sports federations to decide about their own sports, the trend is towards increasing cooperation, joint federation efforts and centralism. The future will tell to what extent this process will result in a uniform Swedish elite sport system – and whether the effect of these changes will be to harvest more Swedish medals in international competitions.

5

Finnish elite sport – from class-based tensions to pluralist complexity

Jari Lämsä

It is not possible to understand the development of the Finnish sports movement and elite sports without a brief review of Finnish society in the early twentieth century. In Finland, sports and politics have been intertwined in an exceptional way. In Sweden and Norway, the tensions of social class-based sports completely disappeared by the 1950s. In Finland, both internal and external political conflicts maintained the class and language-based division of the sports movement well into the 1990s.

During the first half of the twentieth century, Finland was a superpower in terms of sporting success. It became a myth that Finland was placed on the world map at the Stockholm Olympic Games in 1912. At the Olympic Games between 1908 and 1936, Finland was the fourth most successful nation. Finland's athletes, however, succeeded in a limited number of events, mostly in track and field and in wrestling. The role of successful athletes and the status of sports played an important role in Finnish nation building. Sports and success in sports were taken seriously in spite of the general spirit of amateurism.

Success in sports did not, however, reduce political conflicts or the organizational fragmentation of the Finnish sports movement. During the first two decades of the twentieth century, Finland saw the emergence of a sports movement divided in terms of both language politics and social classes. The 1918 Civil War divided the nation, and this division also extended to sports. The non-socialist, Swedish and working class camps competed with each other, but they also efficiently recruited all the social classes and groups into the sports movement.

The political trends were also reflected in elite sports. The concept of elite sports was first used in Finland as early as the 1920s. The actual differentiation and institutionalization of elite sports did not start until after the Second World War, when the stiffening competition in international sports pushed Finland out of the limelight of success. Since the 1960s, the development of Finland into a welfare state was also reflected in the organization of sports. Class conflicts diminished and public sports political debate abated as a result of the corporate relationship between the sports organizations and the state. Also the increased resources curbed confrontations. Thanks to investments in full-time training and the role of the Finnish Olympic Committee as an elite sports organization, Finnish individual sports reached new successes in the 1970s. Even in the next decade Finland maintained its image as a sucessful elite sport nation.

In the 1990s, Finland tumbled into a deep economic recession. Finland also joined the European Union. The time was ripe for unifying the four central sports organizations. The process was initiated by the Finnish Central Sports Federation (SVUL), the largest non-socialist sports organization, which hoped to create one strong central sports organization for Finland. In this process to change the structure of Finnish sports, the SVUL itself went under. The other central sports organizations continued their activities on the basis of their new statuses. The new central Finnish Sports Federation (SLU) provides service and is the representative body for all the national sports organizations. The new organizational structure differs from that of the other Nordic countries.

This chapter discusses the main events in the structural change and its effects on Finnish sports culture and especially on elite sports. It starts with the early history of the Finnish sports movement and its division into language and class based organizations, followed by a summary of the main competitive sports organizations and the tensions in the period from the declaration of independence in 1917 to the 1980s. The institutionalization of Finnish elite sports took place in the late 1960s. The role of the *Finnish Olympic Committee* (FOC) as an elite sports organization was clarified. A major change in the system of Finnish sports organizations took place in the early 1990s, which was a period also characterized by economic depression and the rise of social neo-liberalism.

The chapter is mainly based on earlier research and on Finnish sport histories. Also original sources have been used in the chapters on elite sports and the structural change of Finnish sports. The currency conversion is based on the value of the euro in 2010 as per the Statistics Finland currency converter.

Birth and differentiation of the Finnish sports movement

The Finnish Gymnastics and Sports Federation, which later became the Finnish Central Sports Federation (SVUL) was established in 1906. The aim of the SVUL was to bring all the major national sport associations under its control. The main sports were 'everyman's sports', i.e. wrestling, skiing and athletics. The Finnish Football Federation (SPL) was established in 1907 to promote ball games. Women had established the Finnish Women's Gymnastics Federation ten years earlier in 1896. Its view of the competitive sports organized by men was highly critical (Laine 1984: 330–333).

The SVUL's early history was characterized by struggles between the Swedish and Finnish speakers about the control of the federation. In spite of occasional conflicts, the Swedish sports movement in Finland integrated itself with the non-socialist sports movement fairly smoothly. A considerably deeper gulf developed between the non-socialist and workers' sports movements. The confrontation between the working class and the non-socialists developed in the two decades between the last few years of the nineteenth century and the year 1917. During this period, the labour movement became an influential social force and its organizations covered politics, as well as trade unions and youth and sports movements.

The Civil War also influenced the Finnish sports movement. On 24 November 1918, the non-socialist SVUL decided to dismiss the sports clubs which had participated in the 'red rebellion' either as special military detachments or companies; as well as the individual members of the clubs who had lost their civil rights. The decision gave rise to the national organization of workers' sports movement in January 1919. A total of 56 workers' sports clubs established the Finnish Workers' Sports Federation (TUL), which became the central organization for all the workers' gymnastics and sports clubs (Hentilä 1982, 66–80). In practice, the establishment of the TUL meant the birth of two sports camps in Finland.

In the period of 1906–1993, Finland had a total of five sports organizations that could be classified as central sports organizations (figure 5.1). The main battles were fought between the SVUL and TUL. Competitive and elite sports formed the core in this fight between the various sports movements. The main issue was that of international representation in elite sports. In the beginning, the fight was about the separation of socialist and workers' worlds and separate camps in sports. Later, when the concept and sphere of sports expanded, the fight focused on removing overlapping structures.

Period of separate sports movements

Isolation of workers' sports movement

The 1918 civil war affected the Finnish sports scene for a long time. In the period of 1919–1939, there was no official cooperation between the TUL and SVUL. Both the sports movements created their own competition and training systems. As the right to represent Finland in international competitive sports were held by the SVUL's national sport federations, the TUL had to work hard to attract working-class athletes and keep them in the organization. The TUL built connections with international workers' sports movements in order to make it possible for Finnish working-class athletes to participate in international competitions. When the TUL, based on its policy decision, systematically refused to send its athletes to Olympic Games, a total of 77 athletes defected from the TUL and joined the non-socialist sports movement between 1919 and 1939 (Syrjäläinen 2008). They won a total of 31 Olympic medals – one quarter of the medals gained by Finns in the Olympic Games in 1920–1936.

The only cooperation organs that the TUL accepted in Finland were the state and municipal sports boards, through which also workers' sports received support. When the Finnish state first distributed government grants for sports in 1920, the SVUL's share was 42.5% and the TUL's share 30% of a total of FIM 200,000 (Vasara 2004: 31). Non-socialist Finland wanted to unify the fragmented system of central sports organizations. In the 1920s and 1930s, a total of three committees set up by the Finnish Council of State suggested the combination of the existing central organizations into one national central sports organization. The suggestions did not lead to any changes. During the period of right-wing radicalism in the early 1930s, the status of workers' sports weakened. During this period, several communist organizations were suppressed, including 160 workers' sports clubs (ibid. 2004: 108). In 1932–1934, the TUL also lost its government grants because the right-wing members of the State Sports Committee managed to set a condition that a central sports organization had to allow its members free participation in international competitions in order to be eligible for government subsidies. Based on its policy decisions in 1919 and 1921, the TUL did not, however, agree to this requirement.

Period of cooperation 1940–1959

Towards the end of the 1930's, the non-socialist hegemony got new features. In the name of national unity, the role of the Finnish state as a supervisory actor above the sports organizations entered the debate on sports. A more moderate group of sports leaders representing the political centre gained ground and advocated the unification of Finnish sports step by step through negotiations and agreements. In this development, a significant landmark was the speech made in the Finnish Parliament by Urho Kekkonen, the then minister of justice and an active sports leader, in 1936. Urho Kekkonen accepted the existence of the TUL and stated that the prerequisite for cooperation between sports organizations was a mutual acknowledgement of independence and equality. He regarded the establishment of the TUL in 1919 as justified (Hentilä 1982: 462; Halila & Sirmeikkö 1960: 495).

This change initiated a new period that aimed at cooperation between the central organizations. The first contacts between the SVUL and TUL took place at the beginning of 1938. The completion of the Helsinki Olympic Stadium and the right to organize the 1940 Olympic Games granted to Helsinki added momentum to the cooperation negotiations. Athletes from both the SVUL and TUL participated in the competition to celebrate the inauguration of the Olympic Stadium. The stadium became a kind of symbol of unity for Finnish sports. The first official cooperation agreement was concluded between the TUL and the Finnish Football Federation on 8 May 1939, followed by several cooperation agreements between the TUL and national sport federations. Plans for joint Olympic training between the SVUL and TUL were also made (Hentilä 1982: 478). The war that broke out between Finland and the Soviet Union on 30 November 1939 interrupted this development. When Finnish society started rebuilding the country after the armistice agreement at the end of 1944, the country was in turmoil.

The twenty years that followed the war marked a fragmented period in Finnish sports. In the beginning, workers' sports revived faster than non-socialist sports. In just a few years after the war, the TUL's membership tripled from 50,000 to more than 150,000 (Hentilä 1982: 103). The agreement signed between the SVUL and TUL in 1947 gave the TUL more authority concerning issues related to international sports activities (Hentilä, 1982: 60–70). In the early 1950s, the non-socialist and socialist sports movements almost reached an agreement. The core issue was about joining workers' sports clubs in (non-socialist) national sport federations. There were strong tensions within the two camps. As a result, both the social democratic party and the workers' sports movement divided into two wings. In the TUL, the group that supported joining in the non-socialist sports movement was left in the minority. It established the Central League of Workers' Sport Clubs (TUK) in 1959. Finland now had five central sports organizations.

Political complications influenced cooperation between the central sports organizations. The 1952 Olympic Games brought them together to join forces to ensure the success of this important international sports event. The Olympic Games are remembered as 'the Olympic Games of all times' in Finland – not because of the success of Finnish athletes but because of the successful organization of the games. The Olympic harmony was, however, short-lived. A few years after the Olympic Games, cooperation between the SVUL and TUL was practically non-existent in all sports. An understanding was eventually reached, where the TUL's athletics division became a member of the Finnish Athletics Federation (SUL) and the TUL provided a list of the clubs that belonged to its athletics division. At the same time, all competition activities were declared open to all. The SUL would be responsible for coaching, which meant that the TUL was expected to subordinate its athletics training to the SUL (Halila & Sirmeikkö 1960: 589). This practice, which created dissatisfaction especially at the TUL's grass-roots level, was later included in the agreements between several other national sport federations and the TUL (Hentilä 1982: 399–401). It did not take long before peace was broken again.

From Olympics crisis to unity

The disagreements in Finnish sports culminated at the end of the 1950s when the workers' sports movement was divided into two. Those positive to cooperation with the non-socialists established the Central League of Workers' Sport Clubs (TUK), whereas the communists, who had taken control of the TUL, and part of the social democrats insisted on an absolute independence of the organization. In June 1959, the TUL cancelled all the cooperation agreements with the SVUL and national sport federations, which meant that it was left out of all international competitions. For the 1960 Winter Olympics, however, the central organizations were able to agree on a team which also included participants from the TUL. An agreement was reached at the last moment by establishing an 'Olympics 60' Sports Club, which the TUL's Olympic candidates were able to join. However, Finland participated in the Rome Olympic Games without athletes from the TUL. Finland's results were disappointing, only five medals.

The relationship between the SVUL and TUL governed the Finnish sports policy up till the 1960s. When the central organizations expanded their cooperation by an agreement concluded in 1966 to include national competition activities in it, the essential disagreement between the organizations was solved (Hentilä 1982: 99). Finnish athletes were free to participate in competitions organized by the different sports movements. The issue of international representation was agreed on in separate cooperative committees. The agreement served as a basis for cooperation until 1990, but attempts to unite organizations which were fuelled by different ideologies still failed.

In the 1960s, Finnish society underwent a radical and fast change from rural to industrial and service society. The rise of a welfare state and expansion of the public sector also affected sports. The role of the public sector in sports culture had expanded since the 1960s, and the disagreements between the central sports organizations were transferred to the sports political organs of the state. Public quarrels between the non-socialist and workers' sports organizations faded away (Juppi 1995; Kempas 1986: 278), and the state sports administration strengthened. The Ministry of Education established an office for sports and youth affairs, and the State Sports Committee was transferred under the control of the Ministry of Education. The new State Sports Committee consisted of ten representatives from the political parties and five representatives for the sports organizations (Juppi 1995: 198; Vasara 2004: 165–166).

The social changes that affected sports meant that the concept of sports expanded. Sports were seen as physical activity that concerned all population groups (Vasara 2004: 198–202). The Sports Act in 1979 was a landmark which defined sports as an essential part of a welfare state and therefore entitled to government subsidies. The Act also defined the division of duties between the public sector and sports organizations, leaving the responsibility for the actual organization of sports and physical activities to sports organizations. The public sector was defined as responsible for setting general sport political goals and maintaining the financing system. The Act made it possible for sports clubs to receive government subsidies through municipalities. The 1980s were a decade of high activity in sports facility construction. A total of 9,400 new sports facilities were built in Finland (Vasara 1992: 387).

Unifying the field of sports in Finland was a project that took 70 years to complete. Between 1919 and 1989, the TUL, SVUL and other central organizations conducted negotiations on more than thirty different models for a national central sports organization. For the non-socialist sports leaders, a one-national-organization model almost became an obsession, and for quite a long time it was justified in view of competitive and elite sports only. Towards the end of the 1970s, the SVUL made a sports political decision according to which there was no reason to maintain a fragmented system of sports organizations in Finland. However, the establishment of a single central sports organization by forceful means did not seem a realistic alternative any more. On the other hand, the TUL's view of cooperation was based on the idea of cooperative committees and developing their activities (see the figure below). Cooperative committees had helped the TUL reach half of its goals: The TUL's athletes were able to participate in international competitions and the TUL was able to organize competitions of its own. Even if the TUL was represented in the cooperative committees, its leaders felt that the real power was still in the hands of the SVUL's national sport federations. The TUL was just a 'silent partner'. The cooperative committees needed to make a lot of improvements concerning equality and fairness in decision making (Kempas 1986: 278–280).

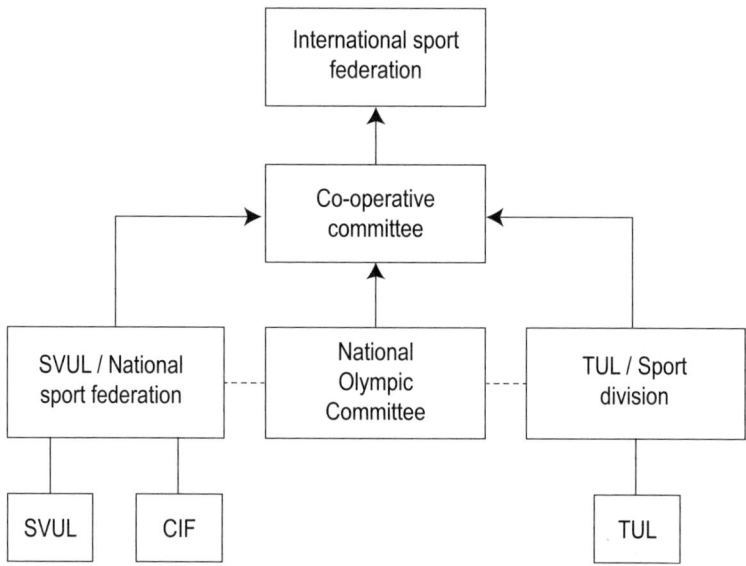

Figure 5.1: The TUL's view of the representation of Finnish competitive sports in international sport organizations. Source: Kempas 1986: 323.

Differentiation and development of elite sports in 1960–1990

Until the early 1960s, both competitive and elite sports in Finland were closely connected to the models and coaching culture created in the early twentieth century. In the years that followed, elite sports were differentiated from the rest of sports and it developed into a special domain with its own structures. The roles of the national sport federations and the Finnish Olympic Committee as elite sports organizations expanded. Competitive sports became an accelerated profession, and demands for special treatment of elite athletes at school and in military training increased. Elite sports also received a lot of criticism. Such criticism touched upon the nature of elite sports, the increasing utilization of social resources for elite sports, and relevance of the old structures of sports (Heinilä 1982).

Up to the mid 1960s, the coaching of Finnish Olympic athletes was mainly taken care of by national sport federations and clubs, and by the TUL's sport divisions and their clubs. The main task of the Finnish Olympic Committee was to elect Finland's Olympic teams and the practical organization of Finland's participation in the Olympic Games. The Committee also provided financial support to potential Olympic athletes for a year or two before the Games. A general principle was that Finland should participate in Olympic Games with as large a team as possible (Laine 2007: 217). Coaching was mainly based on the experience and traditions of each sport. For instance in skiing, Veli Saarinen acted as the chief coach for 31 years, and in athletics Armas Valste's coaching career lasted for 25 years. At the international level, competition became harder. This was reflected in the declining success of Finnish athletes at the Olympic Games. However, it was not until the bottom was hit in 1960 that changes in coaching were really initiated.

Since the 1960s, Finnish elite sports was developed systematically. This was made possible by the strong growth in state subsidies. The grants increased five-fold during the 1970s (Hentilä 1982). The development of elite sports was also supported by the new sports organizations and new roles between the various actors. The central sports organizations developed and maintained the basic functions that were important for competitive and elite sports, e.g. recruitment and training systems. Especially in coach training, huge leaps were made in the 1970s and 1980s, when the central organizations adopted responsibility for coach training for all sports. The main responsibility for athlete coaching was still with the SVUL's national sport federations and the TUL's sport divisions and their clubs. Training camps were organized by national sport federations in sports institutes and abroad. Since the 1940s and 1950s, a comprehensive network of sports institutes was in place. All-year training was made possible by the 1963 Act on Sports Institutes which strengthened the role of sports institutes as elite training centres. In the 1970s, the Finnish Olympic Committee declared itself as Finland's elite sports organization.

The Finnish Athletes' Federation reforms: its organization and coaching system

The changes in elite sports support started practically at the same time within the Olympic Committee and in the Finnish Athletes' Federation, the SVUL's largest national sport federation.

In the Finnish Athletes' Federation, the change process was launched after the fiasco of the European Championships in Budapest in 1966. The new management of the Finnish Athletics Federation also found new ideas and development models from the world of business. The result was a comprehensive development process in which the activities of the Federation were systematized on the basis of the principles of management by objectives, the objectives being the procurement and training of top-class athletes who would succeed in international competitions. Teams were established for coaching, training and financial management. These teams worked alongside the traditional trustee representatives and they were supported by expert organs called triangles, whose members were recruited from various fields of society. The triangles that worked under the expert management team were medical, mental, research and career triangles. In this way the Finnish Athletes' Federation effectively utilized a wide range of Finnish expertise to support its coaching system (Finnish Athletes' Federation, 1979).

To begin with, the change in the SUL focused on the head office, its coaching system, elite athletes and their coaches, but since 1973, development processes were also launched at the club level. Internal management teams were established in sports clubs for coaching, training, junior sports and financial management. Competition activities were developed especially for children and adolescents by creating a junior sports system for 10–14 year olds. The competition format was launched as a club-specific point collection competition in 1968, and the SUL, TUL and *Apu* magazine organized the first national junior sports event in 1970. These competitions received a lot of publicity and attracted large numbers of people to sports activities. At the beginning of the 1970s the *Finnish Ski Federation*, sponsored by the largest newspaper in Finland, launched a similar junior sports event called Hopeasompa (Silver Ring). Hopeasompa is an important talent hunting event in Finland still today.

Finland's good connections to both Western and Eastern Europe proved an advantage. Especially in the 1970s, Finns actively participated in seminars in different European countries to acquire new information on sports research and coaching. The Finnish government concluded international bilateral sports cooperation agreements on expert exchanges and visits. Also sports organizations established new international connections. Based on its background, the TUL had extremely good relations with Eastern European countries. For instance in 1975–1979, the TUL had nine visiting coaches from the Soviet Union, eight from the German Democratic Republic, and six from Czechoslovakia. They trained Finnish coaches at the TUL's Sports Institute (Kempas 1987). As the first western party, the SUL also concluded a four-year coaching and athlete-exchange agreement with the Soviet sports authorities (Salo 2007: 239).

The SUL's change process also produced results. In 1971, Helsinki organized the European Championships, which were a success both economically and sports-wise. At the Munich Olympic Games, Finland won three gold medals in long distance running, and in the 1974 European Championships, Finland won ten medals and was the fifth best nation. The status of athletics as the main form of sports became stronger in Finland.

The Finnish Olympic Committee becomes an elite sports organization
Actual measures to reform the Finnish Olympic Committee were launched in 1965. The Board of the Olympic Committee established a special coaching committee whose duties included making proposals to the board on the distribution of coaching funds, as well as guidance and monitoring of coaching provided by the federations. Apart from the members of the Olympic Committee Board and coaches, the members of the coaching committee included experts who mostly represented the field of medicine. During its first term, the committee launched the Olympic Committee's own coach training by organizing coaching seminars in 1966–67 and by intensifying the utilization of sports medicine centres in testing athletes. After the 1968 Olympic Games in Mexico, the change and activities were estimated as positive but insufficient in view of future success (Laine 2007: 224).

Since 1969, the Olympic Committee has hired a full-time chief coach. The model for this post was found in East Germany and West Germany. The chief coach's field of duties expanded and his role in reforming the Olympic Committee was significant. In practice he planned, organized and supervised the operative activities of the Olympic Committee connected with coaching. He asked the national sport federations for their Olympic coaching plans, checked them and presented them to the Board of the Olympic Committee. He monitored the implementation of the coaching plans, organized meetings and training courses for the Olympic coaches, followed international developments in coaching, and informed the Olympic Committee and the national sport federations of all important issues (Finnish Olympic Committee, 1969).

There was a fear the Olympic Committee would become a new central organization. The representatives of the national sport federations also wanted to protect their turfs in the area of coaching. They did not want the Olympic Committee to have any duties that would directly concern the coaching of athletes. The Committee should be 'the coach of the coaches'. This title was also unofficially used of the Chief Coach of the Olympic Committee. In spite of the criticism, the Olympic Committee implemented reforms that allowed it to raise its status above that of the national sport federations concerning the development of Finnish elite sports. The demands that the Olympic Committee presented to the national sport federations concerning systematic and goal-oriented activities in, e.g. coaching did lead to the modernisation of the concept of elite sports among the national sport federations and to a more realistic evaluation of their own states (Seminar of the Finnish Olympic Committee, 1976 (7605): 11).

The development that started in the late 1960s brought the Olympic Committee close to an umbrella organization model in the area of Olympic sports. Apart from the National Sports Council, the Olympic Committee was the only national organization in which all the central sports organizations and national sport federations had been full members since the 1950s. In practice, the Olympic Committee earned its status and role in elite sports through several different processes. It adopted several coordination tasks, e.g. (1) athletes' coaching grant system, (2) training and seminar activities for coaches and other central sports officials, (3) hiring of professional coaches, (4) financing of research and development activities connected with elite sports, (5) financing of coaches' field trips abroad, and (6) development and strengthening of the Olympic Committee's own organization.

In the 1970s, the economic situation of the Olympic Committee improved. In 1969, the Olympic Committee and the Ministry of Education agreed on financing plans for the Olympiad – the period between two Olympic Games – to secure resources for the expanding development work. Coaching grants of various types and levels formed the framework for the support system of the Committee. From 1968 onwards, coaching grants were distributed for the whole Olympiad, not just for two years before the games. The athletes were classified into A, B and C classes. Class A coaching support was meant for potential Olympic medallists, Class B for athletes who aimed at being among the top eight athletes; and Class C for those who aimed at being among the top 16 athletes. This classification remained in place to the end of the 1990s. In the 1970s and 1980s, the Olympic Committee supported 120–200 individual athletes annually. The men's ice hockey team also received support from the Committee. Athletes also received grants from the central sports organizations, and the major national sport federations distributed coaching grants. The support of the Olympic Committee was always distributed through national sport federations. The strongest federations were able to combine their own grants with those received from the Olympic Committee and distribute larger amounts to their athletes.

Other significant forms of support included coaching, intensification and research grants. Starting from 1974, the Finnish government started to distribute a special grant to the central sports organizations and the Olympic Committee for the purpose of hiring professional coaches. In 1976, the grant was FIM 1.7 million. This grant made it possible to double the number of full-time coaches in Finland. The Olympic Committee and the central organizations cooperated in the distribution of the grants to avoid overlapping. At the end of the 1970s, the SVUL estimated that the coaching grant was a significant step in the development of Finnish elite sports (SVUL 1977). In the 1980s, the government support to hire coaches expanded, and during the following decade the Olympic Committee made considerable investments of its own in hiring professional coaches.

The increased resources made it possible for the Olympic Committee to support the participation of athletes in training camps abroad, especially in sports in which training was difficult in winter. The share of this special grant rose up to 30 percent of the total grants distributed to the member organizations of the Olympic Committee. The coaching grant was discontinued in 1992, when it was combined with different kinds of equipment grants and special grants into an intensification grant, which aimed at directing elite athletes to domestic and international training centres through their national sport federations.

In addition to the various forms of support, the Olympic Committee built a new kind of elite sports culture that was based on research and expert knowledge. Sports research had been supported by the Finnish government since the beginning of the 1950s, but it was not until 1966 that systematic sport research was launched by the newly established State Sports Committee together with the State Committee for Sport Research. The importance of research knowledge was also understood in the sports organizations. The SVUL was the first to establish a scientific committee of its own in 1964. The committee organized both national and international seminars, carried out or commissioned different kinds of research and development projects, and analysed problems in the system of sports organizations (SVUL 1981: 232). When the work of the coaching committee of the Olympic Committee got under way, part of the duties of the SVUL's scientific committee were transferred to the coaching committee, and the know-how of the various experts was made available to both the organizations. Finnish sport research reached a high international level as early as the 1970s.

Conflicts between research, development and sports rules emerged in Finland at an early stage, when sport research was raised as one of the means to secure success in sports. At the end of 1973, the Olympic Committee gave a research grant for a project to study the advantages and disadvantages of anabolic steroids. On the international sports scene, too, the use of hormones was a topic of interest. The distinction between allowed and forbidden hormones was redefined – for instance anabolic steroids were forbidden from the beginning of 1975. The financing of the Finnish research project was discontinued, when it became public knowledge in 1977 (Kanerva 2007: 254–258).

Speculations on the use of doping among Finnish athletes were part of the reverse side of the coin of success in the 1970s and 1980s. Since then, a few athletes have admitted the use of forbidden substances and methods, but most have strongly denied having been involved in any forbidden activities. Doping news has, however, regularly filled the headlines in Finland since the 1970s. Martti Vainio was the first athlete in the Finnish sports history to lose an Olympic medal because of his doping offence in the Los Angeles Olympics in 1984. The Finnish sports organizations and the Finnish government had established an anti-doping committee two years earlier in 1982. The committee became an independent organization and withdrew from direct contacts with sports after the doping scandal at the World Ski Championships in Lahti in 2002, in which six top Finnish skiers were caught using forbidden substances.

The strengthening role of the Finnish Olympic Committee in elite sports and the period of planning culminated in the first national elite sports strategy in 1987. In the strategy, the Olympic Committee was profiled as the representative body of elite sports, i.e. Olympic sports. According to this definition, the Olympic Committee was a channel through which the public relations of elite sports were managed and through which international development trends in elite sports were communicated to the central sports organizations and national sport federations. The goals of the strategy included a significant increase in the state sports subsidies, development of training facilities for the youth, professionalisation of training, and the establishment of training centres and a research centre for Olympic sports (Finnish Olympic Committee 1987).

The 1980s has been described as a period of strong growth and institutionalization in the system of Finnish sports organizations (Heikkala 1998: 96). Especially the economic resources and personnel numbers of the national sport federations grew significantly. The system of sports organizations also remained fragmented. New sports were introduced in Finland and some of them, such as aerobics and floorball, did not adopt the traditional organizational model. They organized partly on a commercial basis or allied themselves with non-sport organizations. In elite sports, too, new sports and new kinds of heroes emerged. Keijo Rosberg, who won the Formula 1 Championship in 1982, brought a new kind of professional image to the Finnish sport scene. However, it was not until ice hockey broke through in Finland that the Finnish sports scene changed forever. In the 1980s and 1990s, ice hockey became the first professional sport and at the same time the number one spectator sport in Finland.

Neo-liberalistic thinking already arrived in Finland in the 1980s, but it was the economic recession in Finland and the social upheavals in Eastern Europe in the 1990s that properly led to a new era. Finnish society turned its face to the west. Finland joined the European Union in 1995 and adopted the euro as one of the first EU countries in 1999. Finnish sports hit the realities of the 1990s harder than many other sectors of society. The plans and future images that were presented in the elite sports strategy in 1987 were buried in the structural change that took place in Finnish sports.

Structural change in Finnish sports 1989–1993

The 1980s were a decade of consensus in Finnish sports. The relationships between the central sports organizations were smooth, and sports policies were outlined mainly in the spirit of cooperation. New strategies were, however, developed in the background, and the future of Finnish sports was outlined in a way that differed from the traditional way of thinking. One move was made in the SVUL's strategy for 1990–1993 titled 'Sports Offers New Things'. The sports strategy project challenged the old structures that were based on the competitive and elite sports traditions dating back to the early twentieth century. According to the sports strategy:

> Finland has been run onto the world map often enough through international success stories for which we owe thanks to especially skiing and athletics. The new sports vision is based on an innovation arrived at through extensive cooperation of the participants in the development of a new sport strategy. The key result is the acceptance of the 'sport for all' principle (Sports strategy project).

According to the sports strategy project, sports should be organized into sectors: elite sports, youth sports, health-enhancing physical activity, and adapted physical activity. It was admitted that this choice was challenging in view of the old settings of competition and distrust prevailing in the field of sports. Another idea that was raised in the strategy project was the replacement of the government grant system, which was affected by old political fights, by a new system based on management by results, i.e. the organizations would receive government grants on the basis of their real results.

The most important result of the sports strategy project was a new ideology for the reforms of the 1990s. In hindsight, there were defects in the strategy, e.g. the exclusion of trustee leaders and club level representatives from the group. Besides, the strategy project was dominated by large national sport federations, leaving smaller federations the role of outside observers only (Heikkala 1998). Towards the end of the project, there were also disagreements among the participants. The organization of sports at the regional level was an issue in which the opinions of the SVUL, the TUL and the Ministry of Education differed so much that a shared position could not be reached.

As a result of the 1990s' economic recession, the struggle between the central sports federations for resources turned against the organizations themselves. Support for overlapping organizations did not fit the new public management ideology. It was based on ideas implemented in the public sector, moving from management by norms to management by results. The Ministry of Education appointed a working group to make proposals on sports organizations' profit areas that would be the most important in view of the development of the sports culture and on the evaluation criteria of the results. This working group published its report on 31 January 1992, and summed up the idea of performance-based management as follows:

> The Ministry of Education will adopt the new public management system from the beginning of 1993. This means that the Ministry of Education itself becomes a profit centre. Among other things, performance based management means that the Ministry of Education manages its own units and supports various activities through financial frameworks and by agreeing with the units concerned on the objectives to be set for their activities. The units will be independent both functionally and economically, free of detail-level interference in terms of financial management and management by norms (Ministry of Education 1992: 1).

The basic idea was that breaking down the overlapping administrative structure of sports organizations – especially the central sports organizations – would release resources that could be focused on supporting actual sports activities. The overlapping structures were seen to concern especially the SVUL and TUL (Ministry of Education 1992: 38). The working group also discussed possible ways of cutting down administrative costs, e.g. excluding the administrative costs of sports organizations fully or partly from state subsidies in order to direct the grants to grass-root level activities more efficiently (Ministry of Education 1992: 39). The transfer to the new public management system in 1995 meant giving up the old government grant system dating back to the 1920s, in which the grants were distributed through the central sports organizations to the national sport federations and district organizations. Finland was the first Nordic country to adopt the public management system in sports.

The structural change had, however, started before the adoption of the public management system. It started when the SVUL's Chairman, who at the SVUL's General Assembly in 1989 made a proposal for one national central sports organization. A single central organization was justified by efficiency considerations. According to simple mathematics, the SVUL and TUL employed a total of 520 clerical staff and maintained 54 regional organizations, which all had training and coaching systems of their own. The integration of resources would allow dozens of millions of euros to be used for the support of club activities (SVUL 1989). The overall responsibility of the national sport federations for the development of their own sports and for their results was also emphasised in the chairman's address.

The integration process turned into a fight between the two largest central organizations, the SVUL and TUL. In this fight, the Finnish Football Federation, the Swedish Sports Confederation (RF) and other sports organizations were left out as bystanders. The Ministry of Education officials and politicians actively participated in the process, especially towards the end. There were no significant breakthroughs during the first two years. The SVUL was active. It made plans for the new structure and pressured the opposite party to participate in the negotiations. The TUL did not agree to participate in negotiations that aimed at its abolition and the integration of its operations in a new national central sports organization. The TUL wanted to develop its cooperation with the national sport federations to promote Finnish sports and was also prepared to strengthen the position of the Olympic Committee in elite sports. At the end of 1991, the SVUL drew up a new strategy and started looking for solutions that did not include the integration of existing central organizations.

The non-socialist sports leaders turned to the state. Ex-Prime Minister Harri Holkeri was appointed Chairman of the National Sports Council. One of his tasks was to lead the integration process. In early 1992, the process was accelerated, and at the same time the Finnish government assumed a stronger role. The working group on performance-based management appointed by the Ministry of Education completed its work. It considered that government subsidies maintained overlapping structures in sports (Ministry of Education 1992). Sometime later, the National Sports Council convened the sports organizations for negotiations on structural changes to be made in Finnish sports.

There was no love lost between the SVUL and TUL. The SVUL stuck to its demand for a model dominated by a national sport federation, with a national service and representative body established to support the federations. All government grants should be given to the new central organization, and the districts should manage without direct state subsidies. The TUL demanded that the national sport federations be given an independent status first – free from the SVUL. The TUL warned that the new organization should not even resemble the SVUL. The TUL's Chairman even suspected that the reason for the SVUL to rush the structural change was due to the SVUL's economic difficulties.

In spite of the widespread suspicions and accusations, 85 sports organizations, the Ministry of Education and the National Sports Council convened to round-table negotiations on 2 June 1992 and agreed on the organization of the change process. After this meeting, the project proceeded fast. The first measure was to appoint an advisory committee of 16 members who represented the central organizations, national sport federations, other sports organizations, Ministry of Education and the State Sports Committee. The most important result was produced in five working groups which outlined the different sports sectors and the regional operations of the new sports organization. As each central organization considered its own regional model the best, conflicts could not, however, be avoided. In spite of the tensions, the second phase started on 28 August 1992. A new working group should prepare the core issues for the new organization and draw up a Letter of Intent for the purpose of its formation. The working group preferred a lean organization which would concentrate on providing services, contrary to the SVUL's idea of a strong central organization. The TUL, on the other hand, wanted to concentrate elite sports to the Olympic Committee and keep its own operations as unchanged as possible.

A turning point was when the SVUL's severe economic problems became public towards the end of 1992. In order to improve its self-sufficiency, the SVUL had during the 1970s launched intobusiness activities with the funds it had obtained through the sale of its gaming company Veikkaus Oy to the Finnish state. Some funds were invested in real property and in ski resorts. The SVUL's investments in the Sport Institute of Finland in Vierumäki and the Vuokatti Sports Institute were considerable. The share of loans in the financing of the activities was 90 per cent.

The revenues were significant until the early 1990s, when the economic depression quickly drove the SVUL into a liquidity and security crisis. Towards the end of 1992, the SVUL tried to cope with the situation by selling everything except the Vierumäki and Vuokatti Sports Institutes. According to the SVUL's chairman, the organization had 'neither debts nor assets' (SVUL 1992), but this was not true. The SVUL's debts eventually amounted to FIM 400 million, and the organization had to turn to the government for help. As a result of the financial crisis, the SVUL lost some of its grip on the ongoing reform process, in which it had called the shots until the end of 1992. The SVUL's difficult rescue operation took several months and gave the other organizations a chance to increase their influence. The SVUL's problems also shifted the power towards the Ministry of Education and political actors. As the SVUL's financial difficulties also threatened two sports institutes and several national sport federations, which were governed by the SVUL, the criticism towards the old, notorious central organization structure gained momentum.

Despite the problems, the reform of the sports structure advanced. The main organizations accepted the Letter of Intent concerning the new organization in the round-table negotiations of 27 January 1993. In the background, however, the wheeling and dealing on the final structure and top posts went on. The Ministry of Education outlined a new performance-based sports appropriation model. The Minister of Culture, who was responsible for sports, issued statements in which he threatened to distribute all the government grants directly to sports clubs. An official of the Ministry of Education stated that the government would only subsidise independent regional organizations, and according to the Budget Director of the Ministry of Finance, sports could be left totally without government subsidies. The fight over the new organization continued. When the SVUL's financial problems continued, the Prime Minister intervened. He assigned the Chairman of the Ski Federation to prepare a report on the SVUL's economic situation and on the integration process in Finnish sports. The report proposed that both the Sport Institute of Finland and the national sport federations be granted additional financial support.. The Finnish government approved the proposal on 23 June 1993. The solution saved the SVUL from bankruptcy, but it also sealed its destiny.

In spite of the SVUL's problems, the reform process was approaching a conclusion. The final battle on the new organization took place in a small group of 12, which decided on the number of the votes of the members, seats on the board, and regional issues. The SVUL, and especially the national sport federations, demanded that the new organization should have a wide and representative trustee-based administration consisting of a general assembly, council and board. Such an arrangement had, however, proved inefficient and resource-consuming. Both the SVUL and TUL convened once more to thrash out the results and consequences of the negotiations.

The new central organization, Finnish Sports Federation (SLU), was established on 16 November 1993. A total of 93 organizations signed the Memorandum of Association. The role of the Finnish Sports Federation was defined as that of a service and representative body. It was joined by all the national sports organizations and eight independent regional organizations. Later, the number of regional organizations grew to 15. Completely new actors on the sports scene were the sector-based organizations focusing on children's and youth sports, health-enhancing physical activity for adults and elite sport. The status and role of the Olympic Committee as a sector organization was left open. Of the previous central organizations, the SVUL discontinued its operations, and the Finnish Football Federation became a national sport federation. The TUL and CIF lost their central organization status, but continued as ideological sports organizations and continued to receive government grants. In the new situation, the TUL became the SLU's largest member organization.

According to Juha Heikkala (1998), who studied the system of Finnish sports organizations in the 1990s, there were three elements behind the structural change: growth, differentiation and professionalisation, all of which gained ground in the 1980s and the 1990s. These factors speeded up the structural change, which led to the opening of the structures of sports organizations, pluralism and complexity. Transfer from the old corporative system took place through formal unification, i.e. all the organizations joined the SLU, but in practice the transfer created a more fragmented, multi-centre structure (Heikkala 1998: 139). The individual organizations gained freedom and independence, but on the other hand, lost the security provided by the old and familiar structures.

One of the most significant consequences of the structural change was that the government subsidies to the sports organizations were transferred to a new performance-based system, in which the results depended on the weightings of the sectors, i.e. children's and youth sports, adults' health-enhancing physical activity and elite sports. The weighting of children's and youth sports was defined as 50 percent, adults' health-enhancing physical activity 25 percent, and elite sports 25 percent of the imputed total subsidies (Ministry of Education 1995). A significant change was the transfer of decisions concerning state support to the Council of State (Ministry of Education 1996: 14). In the old corporative system, the central organizations first distributed the appropriations between themselves and then inside the sports movements. In the new system, the power of the sports organizations as redistributors was reduced to near nothing. This led to a new lobbying culture. Every national sports organization was responsible for its own activities and its relationship with the state.

Status and organization of elite sports after the structural change

The key issue in the reform of the Finnish sports system was the removal of the overlapping structures of competitive and elite sports activities. During the whole process, practically no attention was paid to the overlapping structures of the other sectors. The TUL gave up its own elite sports activities, which were transferred to the national sport federations. The centralised structural (area/regional organizations) and functional support systems (training and recruitment) were discontinued, and the national sport federations were left to rely on their own activity and resources. A significant feature was the abandonment of the trustee-based decision-making system.

The original objective of the change, which was cost efficiency, turned out to be more or less rhetoric. Converting the talks and plans into practice and laying off people proved a difficult task (Heikkala 1998: 100). In 1995, after the structural change, the number of sports organizations in Finland was 114 (Ministry of Education 1995). Since then the number has grown to 130.

The process was criticised for being elite sports oriented (e.g. Hentilä 1994). After its completion the elite sports sector launched strategic plans based on cooperation between the Ministry of Education, the Olympic Committee, national sport federations, and the SLU (Strategy 1994). In addition, significant elite sports projects were implemented, e.g. the establishment of the Research Institute for Olympic Sports in 1990, athletes' grant system in 1995, and the youth programme launched by the Olympic Committee in 1996. In the new structure, the development of elite sports at a national level has however, proved challenging, and no major improvements have been achieved.

One important challenge has been the management and coordination of elite sports. The Chairman of the Olympic Committee wanted the organization as an independent actor in the area of Olympic sports. Many of the national sport federations which were not in the Olympics programme supported the transfer of all elite sports under the control of the Olympic Committee. This was justified by equality considerations: Olympic sports enjoyed extra support that came through the Olympic Committee (*Helsingin Sanomat* newspaper 1994). There was a hot debate on the issue both inside the Olympic Committee and in the whole sports community. In 1996 the Olympic Committee promised to expand its activities as a representative body to all sports. Still, it wanted the SLU to adopt part of the responsibility for supporting non-Olympic sports. This would be in line with the Swedish model, where the central organization is in charge of the general and non-Olympic elite sports matters and the Olympic Committee concentrates on the Olympic sports. However, in the new Finnish system, the SLU's role as a supporter of elite and Olympic sports remains insignificant.

Another challenge has been the weakness of the vertical connections from the club and regional level to the national elite sports organization. The connections have depended on the activity of the area and regional organizations. In sports with a limited number of participants and representatives, the connections have been practically non-existent. In the new system, elite sport was defined as activities at least at the level of national team youth and adult sports. Defining elite sport as mainly adult sport represents big challenges for sports clubs. They are expected to produce potential elite athletes and bring them to the gates of adult level sports, from where the national sport federations and the Olympic Committee would pick them for Olympic coaching. Also, in the new pluralistic sports culture, traditional elite sports seem to have lost influence. This is partly due to the increase in health-enhancing physical activities among children and adolescents. Elite sports have had to compete with several other often lighter forms of sports that have emerged on the sports scene. In the 1990s, Young Finland Association 'Nuori Suomi' actively expanded its activities in sports past traditional sports clubs.

Finnish elite sports did not foresee the rise of professionalism as the leading ideology in sports. In the 1990s, the fights about the integration of class-based sports federations still continued in Finland. It was not until after the Olympic Games in Lillehammer and Atlanta that the first signs of the crisis in the Finnish sports system were recognised. In these games, Finland's goal was 20 medals but the result was only 11. In Lillehammer, it was the second time in the history of the Winter Olympics that Finland did not get a gold medal. The failures were explained to be due to faults in the state sports appropriation system and in the youth programme of the Olympic Committee. Single efforts to develop elite sports did not, however, bring results.

Apart from the problems caused by conflicts within the sport movement, the doping scandal involving Finnish skiers at the World Ski Championships in Lahti in 2001 added to the depression. The scandal changed the sports debate in Finland. People's faith in old ideals was shattered.

The structural change was labelled as elite sports-oriented, but in hindsight, elite sports lost the most in the reform. The old structures that had supported competitive and elite sports fell apart and the sports movements disintegrated into a complex mesh of organizations. In the 2000s, several studies have emphasised the significance of the coordination of the national sports system as an important success factor. In Finland, the debate on coordination has continued, and several plans have been made, but the results have been weak.

PART III

Success stories

Introduction

This purpose of this section is to describe and discuss successful periods in specific Nordic sports during the last decades. Chapter 6 focuses on Swedish tennis and golf, chapter 7 on Norwegian women's handball, chapter 8 on men's ice hockey in Finland and chapter 9 on Danish track cycling. Each of these cases provides an example of a Nordic sport that has achieved sustained extraordinary international results. The cases are consciously picked to reflect variety in sports: male and female, individual and team sports, summer and winter sports, and 'major' as well as 'minor' sports regarding national and international prevalence and degree of professionalization. Rather than presenting some kind of 'typical' Nordic success formula, thus, the section aims to provide different examples of Nordic sports' sustained success within a diversity of sporting contexts. However, by placing emphasis on the processes leading up to the breakthrough, and key incidents and strategies in maintaining international success, it might still be possible to trace similarities in the different roads to excellence.

The chapters follow a similar structure, consisting of three main parts. First, the sustained success of the sport in question is documented. This includes a brief description of the sport's history and position in a national context, and an overview of the international results achieved over a specific successful period of time. Second, the development and conditions related to the breakthrough on the international scene is discussed. Organizational and cultural conditions as well as individual initiatives and competencies are taken into account. Third, the chapters illuminate the ups and downs and future prospects for the actual sport. Issues touched upon are the degree of institutionalization related to the challenge of maintaining good results, processes of knowledge production as premises to reproduce success over time, and coaching cultures marking the sport in question. By following similar structure and themes when digging into the particularities of the specific sports, we hope that some common key elements and processes will emerge despite differences in the sports' resources and size. This will be further elaborated in the concluding comparative chapter.

6

The Swedish 'golf and tennis miracle' – two parallell stories

Johnny Wijk

Swedish tennis and golf sports have had an unequalled success during the last few decades. In both sports, groups of players have reached an international top position, and some even advanced to number one in the world ranking. Both sports are well established worldwide. Sweden for a long time played a humble role. Suddenly, however, the picture changed and Swedish players became extremely successful. How could this happen? The development of Swedish tennis and golf represents a piece of interesting and remarkable sport history, as examples of unique success stories.

This chapter focuses on various perspectives and explanations behind these success stories. It is essential that this has not been a question of just a few successful top individuals. It concerns the development of a structure from which new world elite players emerged one year after another for several decades. What is interesting is the collective success and its structure rather than individual examples. One important point is the clear parallel development which Swedish tennis and golf have undergone with a time lag of about 10–15 years. Is there some common pattern?

All sports development takes part within a societal context. This is captured in a theoretical model which points out different levels of explanatory factors:

The top level is called *General social conditions* involving basic factors like climate, national economy, subsistence level and social space for leisure activities.

The next level, *General sport conditions*, concerns what sport investments are made by society, how many sports facilities are built, the general interest in sports from government and private sponsors, and how big a proportion of the population takes part in sports activities.

The third level, *The conditions of a specific sport*, comprises factors like the national tradition within the sport in question, its support from society in the form of facilities, the availability of the sport, the number of local clubs, the number of athletes, the strength of the sport federation, television and press interest in the sport, and its idols and fixed stars as well as the level of international competitiveness.

The fourth and last level is termed *The performance of a specific sport*, which in this context is represented, for instance, by factors like the quality of coaching education, training methods, competition strategies and talent development, technical and tactical knowledge, the development of new techniques and new tools. (For a more thorough description of my model, see *www.Idrottsforum.org* 2010–12–15)

The aim of this model is to elucidate the discussion about a *'success spiral'* with a view to explaining sustained success periods of a sport within a country. Before entering this discussion, we will briefly describe the overall development of Swedish elite tennis and golf.

Description of the elite successes within Swedish tennis and golf

The 'Swedish tennis miracle' concept became well known and established in the 1980s. It described the broad wave of success of Swedish men's tennis, with young Swedish players pouring forth year by year on the international tennis competition arena. Swedes advanced quickly on international rankings and soon a whole group of them were to be found in the absolute world elite. At one time six Swedish men were among the 20 best players in the world, and the Swedish team reached the world finals in the Davis Cup national tournament contest seven times in a row. The rest of the tennis world asked: What actually happened in the strange country up north with long winters when it was not even possible to play tennis outdoors?

The 'Swedish golf miracle' concept is not as well-known and established. It was launched internally within golf with an evident association to the tennis miracle, in order to mark that a similar positive development had taken place in Swedish golf. In the *Svensk Golf* journal, for instance, the editor-in-chief, Anders Janson, began in the late 1980s to use this expression. It referred to the rapid expansion in the number of new players and courses then going on in Sweden, but also to the initial Swedish successes in international amateur golf. He claimed that, in the long run, this would also lead to great successes at the professional level: 'one day it will happen, perhaps not before 1990 or the year 2000, but *one* day it will happen; that a Swedish golfer will win one of the really big golf tournaments, like the British Open or the US Masters!'

At the time this prophesy was probably mainly looked upon as an unrealistic dream, but it came true much quicker than the writer himself imagined. A year later the vision was a fact, and it was a young Swedish woman, Liselotte Neumann, who achieved the sensational performance of quite unexpectedly winning the US Open. A little more than ten years later Swedish golf victories in professional tournaments all over the world had become an everyday event. A success wave kept rolling, which was of at least the same quality as Swedish tennis had already experienced.

Statistics of Swedish victories and international level players

The elite development in Swedish tennis and golf can be described in various ways. A starting point is the total number of Swedish victories in professional world tours in the two sports, structured by decade, from the 1960s to today. Such a compilation clearly demonstrates both the explosive development and the parallel inter-sport development with a time lag of about 10 years.

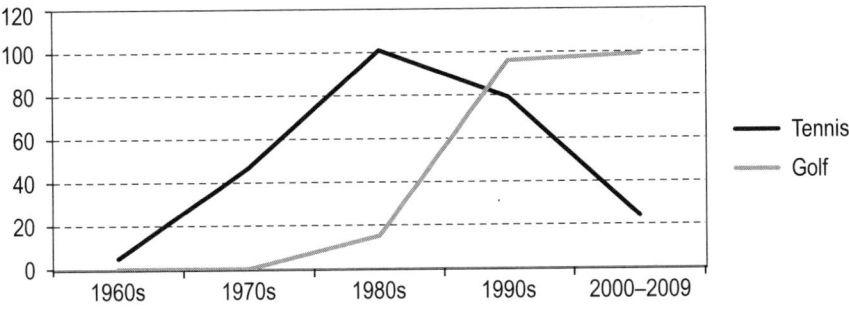

Figure 6.1: Individual Swedish tournament victories in international professional tours.

Figure 6.1 indicates the total number of victories in professional tours for the two sports. From looking upon a Swedish victory as a unique and sensational event, Swedish victories could be counted by the dozen. The curves also point to a division into phases, which in turn suggests rise, peak and fall, as will be analysed below. The parallel development of tennis and golf as regards victories at the international level is an interesting fact in itself. There is, however, one significant difference between the two sports: in tennis 95 per cent of those who have been part of the success wave are men, whereas in golf success is equally distributed between women and men.

It is certainly true that tennis with Björn Borg and golf with Annika Sörenstam have had one superstar each. However, a great many other players have pulled off victories. In tennis there are about 30 different players – 27 men and four women – who have won international tournaments. In golf there are 15–20 different players of either sex behind the victory statistics. The collective success is also illustrated by the fact that the men's tennis team in the Davis Cup national team tournament advanced to as many as 11 world finals in the 1980s and 1990s. Similarly, Swedish women golfers in the late 1990s dominated the European women's team challenging the USA in the Solheim Cup. Six out of twelve players came from Sweden. The rest of Europe – including the British Isles which always used to prevail in the history of golf – shared the other six places. Only a couple of years earlier this situation would probably have been considered entirely unrealistic.

The broad collective wave of success can also illustrated by the number of *different* Swedish players who have qualified as tournament pros in each sport. Figure 6.2 below shows the number of tennis players ranking among the 100 best in the world. For golf it shows the number of Swedish players who have qualified to play in the two superior professional tours in the world, the European and the US tours. The statistics are divided into five-year periods with an annual average of the number of Swedes to be found in the world elite in tennis or golf.

The figure shows that Swedish women's tennis had, on average, one player among the 100 in the world top throughout the period, with two players in the odd year, and none at all another year. This roughly corresponds to what could be 'normally' expected from a country with the population size of Sweden. For a long time this was also the situation for Swedish men's tennis. Björn Borg's breakthrough in the 1970s had a deep impact in the supreme world elite. However, the big collective rise to success took place in the 1980s, with about 10 players firmly on the 100 list. Many of them were even among the top 10. The peak lasted till the late 1990s, when the number of highly ranked players plummeted. In the 2005–2009 period tennis was down annually to an average of 2–3 male players among the top 100. At the beginning of 2010 it has decreased further to 1–2 players.

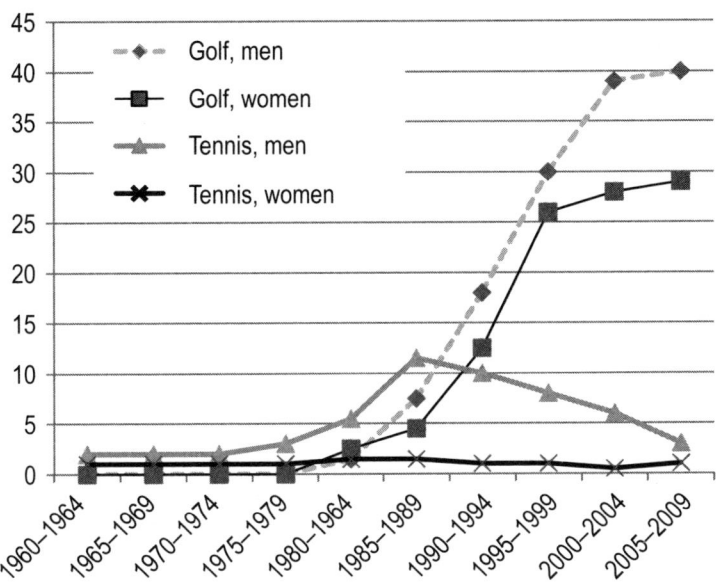

Figure 6.2: Number of Swedes in the world elite. For tennis; the number among the top 100 in the world, for golf; the number of those qualified for the pro tours.

Swedish golf only had the odd player qualifying for the world elite before the mid-1980s. Towards the end of the decade things happened quickly. Soon there were about 10 men and five women per year who qualified for the salons of the pro world. The situation then began to improve by leaps and bounds, and throughout the 1990s the number of professional Swedish players kept growing. Just after 2000, nearly 40 men and 30 women qualified annually for the pro tours, among 250–300 top of the world. Each year some players have disappeared from the list, not doing well enough or qualifying for the next season. However, they have been continuously replaced by new Swedes. Now, in the early 2010s there is some indication that the wave of success has abated. The number of Swedish players among the very best in the world may have gone down slightly and there is some anxiety about failing recruitment. Still, the total number of professional players is almost the same, and in 2009–2010 a couple of new Swedish players have started to advance to the international level.

The 'success spiral' of tennis and golf

As demonstrated above, Swedish tennis and golf have both had a successful development at the international elite level. How did this come about? This is of course a difficult question to answer as there are plenty of possible explanatory factors. However, the model presented in the introduction, covering different levels of society and sports, offers a way to understand this mystery. The challenge is not only to explain success for a few individuals at a certain time, but also the continued success of new talents, one generation after another. What is it that starts a *success spiral*? What is it that sustains it for decades with new successful athletes year by year? And why does the success wave go down sooner or later?

Success factors at the structural level: The development into a broad 'popular sport'

It seems that a basic factor behind the elite successes of Swedish tennis and golf is the quick transformation from restricted narrow upper-class sports to relatively broad popular ones. Both sports were for a long time activities primarily reserved for the upper levels with few established clubs and a limited number of members. However, this pattern was broken thanks to several factors.

Quantitative development within tennis – breakthrough in television, attracting the young

Tennis in Sweden experienced a clear public and mass media breakthrough in the early 1960s. A few successful players like Kalle Schröder in the 1940s followed by Lennart Bergelin and Sven Davidson in the 1950s drew attention among people interested in sport, but it was during the 1960s that tennis reached the entire population in a new way. This happened due to a combination of a couple of sensationally successful Davis Cup tournaments. It attracted attention to the players Jan-Erik Lundqvist and Ulf Schmidt. The fact that the Swedish Television chose to broadcast these matches live from the town of Båstad played an important role.

The first really hot event took place in the summer of 1962 at the European finals against Italy. Thrilling matches were broadcasted live on television for three days in a row and were reported to have been followed by a million viewers from their homes. The daily papers caught on. There were huge headlines and pictures even on their front pages – which was completely new to tennis – followed by a several-page detailed coverage on the sports pages. King Gustavus VI, who took a great interest in tennis, was at Båstad and the royal homage on the court itself provided a natural angle for the press. In tennis Sweden had never been anywhere near such public scenes. The crowds reacted as if it had concerned football. Båstad was described as 'unbuttoned for the first time, "the upper classes" stood up in their seats roaring like football fans round the tennis arena'.

In the summer of 1964, the Davis Cup successes were repeated. A series of live broadcasts on television attracted some million viewers every time. Television coverage culminated with the world semi-finals against Australia with the world's best players at Båstad. They included the number one player Roy Emerson, supported by Fred Stolle, and the new young star John Newcombe. The Australia match created a tennis fever in Sweden that started several weeks before, and the daily papers were crammed with articles about tennis. *Tennistidningen* ('the *Tennis Journal*') published a leading article which claimed that tennis was now on its way to becoming a sport for all just like football and ice hockey. Elderly ladies were heard discussing over a cup of coffee the chances of 'Janne and Uffe' in the Davis Cup. Makeshift tennis courts were arranged all over the place. Youngsters played tennis with park benches turned upside down as nets and pieces of string as lines, and every single sports shop was reported to have sold out its tennis rackets and balls.

The early 1960s successes and subsequent exposure in the mass media triggered an internal discussion in tennis about how best to follow up and broaden the sport. An illustrative article was published in 1962, written by the leader of the tennis district of Gothenburg. He pointed out the dilemma that club recruitment to tennis schools mainly consisted of the club members' children. This was not so strange in itself, since they had been trained by their parents at an early age and demonstrated great talents while still young. But tennis missed lots of talents because of the narrow selection. It would be much better if schoolmasters and physical education teachers helped to find the real talents, rather than the tennis clubs making their selection among club members' children. For them tennis was looked upon as a hobby on the side of studies and a professional career. It was among the boys and girls who did not intend to go on to higher academic studies that the chances of finding those who really wanted to sacrifice their best years for tennis were the greatest, according to the author of the article.

The discussion made an impact on the Swedish Tennis Federation. It declared that it was now high priority to find new talents who had the right physique, ball sense and attitude to tennis. Another issue was that it was high time to build new courts, and quickly. There were even rumours about setting up tents that could be inflated by warm air to make it possible also to play in the winter. Great expectations were associated with these so-called 'Barracuda tents', named after the producing company. Another article from 1965 emphasized the need for setting up ball boards or ball walls on all sport grounds and schoolyards and in residential areas where young people could start playing tennis. It was among the crowd of ball-kickers that the chances were best of finding tomorrow's great tennis players.

The 1960s tennis expansion may also be described in figures. This was the decade when the broad foundation for tennis was created in Sweden. In the first half of the twentieth century the number of tennis clubs in the country experienced slow growth. Towards the end of the 1950s there were just above 400 clubs. During the 1960s there was an explosion resulting in duplicating the number of clubs. In less than 10 years 450 new clubs were formed, reaching a total of nearly 900 in the early 1970s. Thereafter, not so many clubs were added; in 1985, the peak year, they amounted to 939, and then the number gradually dropped. Membership figures also exploded in the 1960s, from ca. 25,000 to 55,000 tennis members – an increase by 120 per cent in 10 years.

The strong new interest in the tennis sport also entailed an increase in support from society. Municipalities offered sites, grants or municipal loans to support the building of new tennis courts and, later on, special indoor halls as well. Soon every Swedish municipality had both outdoor courts and, eventually, facilities for playing tennis indoors, which were made available the year round by cooperation with the local club. This is one important factor behind the success of Swedish tennis.

Quantitative development in golf – the sport working to become a 'folk sport'

Swedish golf can display the same type of quantitative expansion and endeavour to broaden its social recruitment with the aim of becoming a 'folk sport' like tennis. However, in golf one cannot point to a definite mass media breakthrough like that of tennis. One person who contributed early on to making golf known, and also advocated the potential of golf as a folk sport, was the well-known ice hockey player and sport idol Sven Tumba. He was caught by the game. In parallel with his ice hockey career he started travelling round the country to take part in various stunts with the purpose of making golf more popular among the general public. According to Tumba, golf was an excellent game for everyone interested in sports, and too much fun to let managing directors keep it among themselves. Tumba trained assiduously and become one of the very best in the country, even joining the national team in golf, his third sport after ice hockey and football. Being a celebrity with great public relations skills, Sven Tumba managed in the late 1960s to get some of the biggest international golf stars – including Arnold Palmer and Jack Nicklaus – to come to Sweden and take part in exhibition contests.

However, golf had problems acquiring space on television. The very first golf game broadcast on Swedish television was in 1966. A few short films showed summaries of the US Golf Championship. A minor breakthrough for golf on television took place in 1973 when Göran Zahrisson, a famous television sports reporter, commented on an English film from the Ryder Cup, the big team competition between the USA and Europe. This film with the international stars of the time was split up into five one-hour programmes and was a success among the viewers. Only in August 1977 – 15 years after tennis – was golf shown live on television for the first time.

Gösta Netzén, a county governor, wrote a critical contribution to the debate in 1972. He claimed that the Swedish Golf Union had missed the potential for becoming a national folk sport. He maintained that the union devoted itself chiefly to competition golf and the established clubs. Instead it should forcefully advocate golf as a sport offering excellent recreation, outdoor life and physical exercise for the general public regardless of age, sex and social position. The general development in Sweden had led to the closing down of thousands of farms. This created an excellent opportunity to plead for golf courses and an open landscape instead of shrubbification, according to Netzén.

The Swedish Golf Union did listen to the criticism and in 1973 formed a special information committee with the task of trying to find the best ways of broadening the sport. The committee stated that everyone seemed to agree that golf ought to become a folk sport. The question was how to achieve this. Should one start from the top or from the bottom – via municipalities, schools or television? In the mid-1970s the Golf Union presented a long-term plan called 'Image', which stressed the importance of broadening the sport to reach new population groups. Among other things, it had started 'Riksgolfen' – a national golf campaign for attracting non-golfers to try out the game more easily. This initiative turned into a huge success with upwards of 100,000 starters.

In a number of articles and chronicles in the *Svensk golf* journal one can follow how the advocates of golf argued for broadening the sport in the mid-1970s. One editorial from 1975, for example, pleaded the importance of erasing the notion of an 'upper-class sport'. He suggested a major propaganda drive for a description of golf as not a particularly expensive sport. The average golfer lay only insignificantly above the average income in Sweden at the time. In this context it was also observed that Swedish golf lacked strong representatives in the public sphere, who could prompt the development, as had been done, for instance, in both tennis and ice hockey. The Ice Hockey Federation under its strong leader Helge Berglund – also city commissioner in Stockholm – had managed exceedingly well in the 1960s and 1970s to promote ice hockey as a municipal concern. Artificially frozen ice rinks had mushroomed everywhere, whereas in golf there were only a few locally supported courses in the whole of the country.

The sport started growing strongly in the 1970s to nearly explode in the 1980s and 1990s, with regard to both new clubs and members. The just over 100 golf clubs and the 40,000 members in the early 1970s grew to 275 clubs and 300,000 members in the early 1990s. The Swedish golf boom accelerated in the 1990s until it reached its peak a few years into the twenty-first century. At that time as many as 600,000 Swedes were enrolled in 450 golf clubs, which made golf the third biggest sport in Sweden by the number of members. Around 2005 the membership curves turned down for the first time and a number of clubs experienced financial problems, as newly established golf facilities kept being inaugurated in spite of falling demand.

Availability and social broadening as key factors for success

The story of the building-up phase in Swedish tennis and golf is about broadening the social appeal. The new youngsters came from broader segments of the population – not least from the rapidly growing Swedish middle class – and no longer solely from families where the parents themselves practised the sport. Both sports can be said to have climbed down the social ladder in Sweden. It became available to nearly all young Swedes to try out and even go on practising them, depending on their interest and talents – an almost unique situation for these two sports in an international perspective.

Growth and social broadening became possible in practice thanks to 'the Swedish sports model'. Its core is local clubs with a social movement background, with municipal funding and a basic ideology stating that all citizens are welcome. Very few sports clubs in Sweden have been private and thus excluding new members and athletes. This also became the main model for tennis and golf – with the exception of a few exclusive clubs in the big cities. This availability for practising sport – often locally, and also often with the possibility of having a coach lead the training at a fairly low cost – created a very broad recruitment base.

The availability of a sport is an important factor in the success spiral sketched above. However, it leaves out a central question: What makes some sports more attractive than others? This is a question with many layers, but there is one aspect which has probably favoured both tennis and golf in Sweden. The Swedish welfare development has entailed the growth of a broad middle class. With increasing financial resources and the ambition to climb the social ladder, the growing middle class was looking for new cultural and social ways of expressing itself, including the choice of sport. In sociological and pedagogical research there are many studies indicating that the choice of a sport is often closely tied to a social perspective. The important thing is not only where you stand on the social ladder, but also how you prefer to be viewed and how you wish to change your social identity.

Such a view is expressed by, for instance, Pierre Bourdieu in 'Sport and Social Class' (1978), an article where he describes how the world of sport offers a broad social choice and that choosing a sport is associated with where you are – or wish to be – on the social ladder. Hans Bonde (1988) follows a similar argument in his essay 'Den hurtige mand' ['The fast man'], setting up a model of ideal types based on sex, social group, occupation and social identity to explain how sport is layered. There is also Bo Schelin's sociology dissertation *Den ojämlika idrotten – om idrottsstratifiering, idrottspreferens och val av idrott* (1985) [*Unequal Sport – on Sport Stratification, Sport Preference and the Choice of Sport*], containing studies of a large number of athletes which show that every individual has a social framework within which a number of sports are socially acceptable. Lars-Magnus Engström's study *Idrott som social markör* (2006) [*Sport as a Social Marker*] not only confirms the thesis that the choice of sport is connected with social group, but demonstrates that the entire physical pattern of exercise, health and leisure habits is linked to social class and social identity. Sports like boxing, rugby and others that require hard physical contact and strong physical strain are primarily positioned on the lower rungs of the ladder. Football (soccer), athletics, gymnastics and motor sports flourish on the middle rungs, whereas sailing, equestrian sports, downhill skiing, golf and tennis are typical sports at the upper end of the social ladder of sport.

A central hypothesis here is that two structural movements going in different directions joined together in a final goal. The growing middle class wished to 'climb up' in its social identity. To improve its social capital it was willing to allow the children to play tennis and golf – sports that are traditionally associated with the upper layers of society. Meanwhile, both tennis and golf in Sweden worked very deliberately on 'climbing down' the social ladder, to get rid of the upper class stamp and expand its recruitment in broader population layers. When these two structural movements converged, a very favourable situation was created in Sweden for the two sports, a situation that was unusual – probably unique – in an international perspective. For about a decade this was to turn into a strong competitive edge for each of the sports in the international competition arena.

Success factors at the sport level: National youth contests, coach education programmes and team building

The strong influx of new youngsters, the intensive building of new tennis courts and golf courses backed up by both public and private resources thus provided excellent basic structural conditions. This will, however, still not be sufficient for international success. The central national federations for tennis and golf were both quite small and had few employees. This meant that they could not affect the development very much on their own. The Swedish sports model was built, as mentioned, primarily on the idea of local clubs running basic sport activities and training. The national federations and the regional district organizations were, however, allotted some special tasks.

Talent selection and national youth contests

When young people increasingly turned to tennis in the mid-1960s, the question was how to take care of the best talents. Since the 1950s, school championships in tennis had been arranged, and now the Swedish Tennis Federation launched the idea of a new national junior cup. To begin with, every club in the country was to arrange a local competition to select the best boy and girl of each age between 11 and 18. The winners would then go on to the district level, from where the best would advance to regional finals and eventually to national finals.

Kalle Anka, a magazine for young people, entered as the main sponsor and the annual basic inventory of tennis talents in Sweden was soon a well-known success. It became the model for several other sports as well. For decades all the tennis clubs in the country were involved in carrying forward their best boys and girls. When expanded, the system could be compared to a fine-meshed net, to catch every young Swedish person who had shown a talent for tennis. In the year 1970, by the way, the names of two of the final champions in the *Kalle Anka Cup* were Helena Anliot and Björn Borg, both world players to be. Going over the names of the youngsters reaching the national finals in Båstad year by year, a striking number of them were found, when grown up, among the world elite.

Swedish golf was one of the sports that observed the success of tennis with its *Kalle Anka Cup*. In the mid-1970s it started a golf equivalent called the

Colgate Cup. Just as in tennis it was a matter of finding talented youths via competitions at club and district levels and eventually in national finals. After changing its sponsor the championship became known as the *Föreningssparbanken Cup.* The golf sport continued to develop the idea of national youth contests. In the 1990s it created a Swedish tour system for young people, where boys and girls in different age groups first took part in district competitions, for advancing to regional or national contests.

National team activities, coaching education, team culture and strong leader profiles

One important task for a central sport organization is to build up a national system for coach education. In 1952 the Swedish Tennis Federation hired Bill Lufler, an American, as national tennis instructor. The task was to develop and train national team players as well as educating new instructors and coaches for the local clubs. Lufler worked in Sweden for nearly 10 years. He developed a great number of basic coach education programmes, and also wrote a couple of coaching manuals which included the most important special tennis techniques. Like a number of other sports, tennis later developed a coach education system involving several steps. The first two were adapted for the district coach level and the two upper ones for central courses at the national level. In 1971 the 'Swedish School of Sport and Health Sciences' (GIH) started a special tennis coach programme for elite coaches. In the early 1970s, the Swedish Golf Federation started its own coach education directed towards proficient Swedish golf players with different courses running for a two-year period. In 1972 GIH started special education for future elite coaches in golf.

Both tennis and golf are individual sports and in the international arena team games definitely take second place. In Sweden, however, both tennis and golf have emphasized extensive national team activities. Golf achieved many fine amateur successes in team playing in the 1970s to 1980s for junior girls and boys. This signalled that a breakthrough was imminent even at the professional level. By far, most Swedish tennis and golf players who later reached the world elite have been members of Swedish teams. This has stimulated a team culture in these otherwise manifestly individualistic sports. Also, in 1978 Sweden was first in the golf world to introduce a national league team, still a most unusual phenomenon in international golf. There is in all likelihood a strong link between the Swedish successes in tennis and golf of representing one's club in league games as well as doing training and competing collectively. In tennis a couple of coaches became famous for developing the collective team spirit successfully; Lennart Bergelin, Hasse Olsson, Jonte Sjögren and Calle

Hageskog – all leading the men's team to Davis Cup victories. The golf coach Pia Nilsson – with a background as a professional player in the USA – has made a name for herself both in Sweden and internationally for her good leadership and her way of developing individuals while still being part of a team.

In tennis, Sweden was first in the world to create special teams on professional tours. A group of three to four players shared a coach and were sponsored by a company. They travelled together to professional competitions, competed, trained and boarded together. The idea was to create a strong team spirit, as in club or national teams, to achieve better individual successes. First out was Team Siab in 1981 including the young talents Mats Wilander, Anders Järryd, Joakim Nyström and Hans Simonsson with Jonte Sjögren as their coach. This team building drew attention internationally and the successes of those involved were substantial. Two of them even became number one in the world; Mats Wilander in singles and Anders Järryd in doubles. During the 1980s and 1990s other teams were formed in Swedish tennis, but the phenomenon did not have much impact in other countries. However, this organizational model petered out in Sweden, too, in the late 1990s. Presently it is apparently on its way to disappearing. The new Swedish world players seem to prefer having their own coaches and travelling more by themselves, in accordance with the traditional international pattern.

Successful team building is also a major factor in the story of Swedish golf. In the early 1980s a couple of Swedes – on both the men's and the women's side – started approaching professional games on the world tours. A number of talented young men under the leadership of Jan Blomqvist had for three years formed part of a development group aiming at the great amateur contests. In the 1982 Amateur World Championship, the players Ove Sellberg, Magnus Persson, Krister Kinell and Per Andersson succeeded beyond expectations. The team came second after the USA. This triggered investments in professional careers and in 1983 – two years after tennis – the first golf team, Team Saab, started, including the first three above-mentioned players. Three years later, in 1986, a second team was formed by the name Team Volvo with Jesper Parnevik, Johan Ryström and Carl-Magnus Strömberg as players. Just as in tennis these three travelled together sharing a coach and sharing accommodation during the European pro tour.

Team thinking among Swedish golfers has lingered on into the twenty-first century. Caroline Hedwall is a new 20-year old rising star. She was interviewed after the Swedish women's team – including Anna Nordqvist and Pernilla Lindberg – had won gold in the 2008 Amateur World Championship. The recurring question asked by foreign journalists was how little Sweden could keep producing new world golfers all the time. She always answered that there were two things which distinguished Sweden most from other golf nations. The first was the system of open clubs where in principle any young person was welcome to play. The other was the distinct team spirit and solidarity created inside the club teams, the national junior tournaments and the national youth teams. The players then took the team spirit with them into the pro world, where there were many other Swedish women who took care of each other and made it easy even for the newcomers to feel secure on the tour. There was nothing like it in the other nations, she said.

Sport practice: Technique, systematic training, physical development and US college games

Have Swedish tennis and golf invented some new technique or training tricks which brought about the success at the international level? When Björn Borg in the early 1970s had his breakthrough in the world elite, there was immediate talk about the new style of playing that Borg demonstrated. The double-handed backhand was not in itself a new shot. Several players before Borg had used two hands – some of them at both forehand and backhand. However, the combination of high top-spin shots, very quick footwork and a strong basic fitness kept him running on the court hour after hour. At the beginning of his career it was mainly on slow clay courts that his style of playing did him justice. Soon, however, Borg developed his game to become as successful on faster courts, but his safe play from the back court remained his hallmark.

It is, however, not obvious that Swedish players who came into the world elite during the 1980s had a distinct style. A great many of these certainly used two-handed backhand and stable backline playing, but far from all of them. Mats Wilander's game was to some extent a reminder of Borg's, whereas Stefan Edberg's serve, volley and attack tennis, for example, was the absolute opposite. The Swedish tennis successes in the 1980s and 1990s may have partly been due to the introduction of new tennis techniques with a novel type of shot, but just for a short time, since this could be quickly copied by the rest of the world. Within Swedish golf there is nothing to suggest that any new Swedish playing technique can form part of the explanation of the successes. Most coaches working in Sweden came from England, and a number of the training camps for the best young players were located abroad with foreign coaches engaged.

Rational training and physical development

There is a great deal of evidence that both Swedish tennis and Swedish golf actually contributed something that was new about training methods, training quantity and physical development. The Swedish quantitative breakthrough in tennis drew attention to the fact that many of them had earlier engagement in several different sports. Basic training had given them a strong physique and fitness that was unusual in the tennis elite, whose foremost players relied more on fine technique than strong physique. Several Swedish stars had even been successful in various sports when they were younger; for instance bandy, football and ice hockey. They were used to hard physical training and devoted much more time to physical training and fitness than other players in the world of tennis. Recruitment to tennis in the rest of the world was still much more restricted socially to children and young people from the upper layers of society – members of private clubs with high fees – where hard physical training was not a natural part of growing up. The Swedish breakthrough in tennis happened at a time when the sport may be considered as still underdeveloped as far as rational training, both physical and mental, was concerned. This was an advantage that lasted for just over a decade. In the 1990s, however, a new generation of tennis players emerged elsewhere for whom hard physical training was a natural prerequisite.

Interestingly, the same development is found for Swedish golf. Along with the broadening of the recruitment, youngsters with a broad sports background got into contact with the sport. The new generation of young Swedish golfers started to train harder, in a more rational manner, and with more recurrent exercises. This was already being noticed by the golf leaders of the period. In an article from 1977 it was stated that Swedish golf owed most to the British when it came to the introduction of golf sport, courses, equipment and instructors. However, when it came to rational training and training persistence, Sweden had a great deal to teach the British. The Swedish men's team had spent some time at a training camp in Northampton. English newspapers and even the BBC noted the systematic Swedish training methods and the fact that the players had made almost a thousand training shots a day each in the middle of the winter when British golf players scarcely trained at all. John Cockin, a British coach who arrived in Sweden early on to help build up golf, declared in 1995 that the Swedish development had surpassed all his dreams. In articles which drew a great deal of attention, Cockin had initially criticized young Swedish golfers for being too lazy, spoiled and upper class, and unwilling to spend the time necessary for being successful in competitions. However, later on, in the 1980s, a new type of juniors turned up; the upper class stamp disappeared.

Suddenly there were ordinary young people with an interest in sports who realized that hard training and a great deal of time were required to learn the game properly.

Similarly, Lars-Erik Sandler, a golf leader, declared in 1986 that foreign journalists were now talking about 'the Swedish golf miracle' – thanks to the much noticed Swedish successes in international amateur golf championships. They were now anxious to learn about the secret behind it. According to Sandler, the chief explanation was that Sweden was the first country that started with systematic training, physical development of the whole body, agility training, nutrition analyses and mental coaching in golf. One of Sweden's most successful players on the men's side was Jesper Parnevik. He made an interview in 2008, looking back at 20 successful years in the world elite. During his first year in the European tour he started training even harder than before. He got up at five in the morning for a running exercise and then often spent up to 12 hours a day on training fields and courses. According to Parnevik, there were at the time extremely few world golfers that trained really seriously at all, while the Swedes really made a mark both by fitness training and by their patient slogging round the training tracks for hours on end.

US colleges

Being a talented young player and considered as one of the best in the country is one thing, another is to manage to get established in the professional world arena. This is a needle's eye that only a few talents have the strength to get through. However, surprisingly many of the established Swedish professionals both in tennis and in golf have in their upper teens spent a period at an American college or university. Alongside studies they have been drilled hard in their sport by training daily under professional coaches. In the college teams they have then participated frenetically in matches within the American tournament system. During some period school teams travel and compete intensely against other schools and universities and occasionally live almost like professional players. Of course, not all Swedish college-team juniors took the final step into the professional world level; some went home instead – sometimes with a university degree in their luggage – to become good national players and coaches.

The Swedish world elite women golfers are very strongly linked to previous college games. For nearly all this has been part of their career. The touring season in the USA finishes with an individual college championship, where every state introduces the very best, who meet later in a national final. Winning this final is usually a guarantee of a subsequent world career. As many as four Swedish golf girls have managed this. Annika Sörenstam became college champion in 1991 and her sister Charlotta sensationally repeated the performance in 1993. Mikaela Parmlid won in 2003 and Caroline Hedwall in 2009. In tennis, Mikael Pernfors achieved the very unusual feat of winning the US college title two years in a row, 1984–1985. He was virtually unknown back in Sweden when he left for the USA. However, in 1986 he went straight from college to Paris, and there from a first-year pro advanced to the French Open finals, going quickly from 'nowhere' to establishing himself among the top world elite. There is hardly any doubt that college sports in the USA has been important for toughening, developing and selecting the very best suited tennis and golf players. Perhaps other successful Swedish sports – for instance swimming and athletics – also have received similar advantages from the American college system.

A cautious hypothesis is that the Swedish sport model for tennis and golf has been successful in sifting out youth talents with a thorough basic training. Many have later had the chance of being matched in the severe competitiveness of American colleges. It is in the USA that the final screening has taken place. Those who have best managed the tough training, the travelling, and the competitions, have become ready to enter the hard professional life.

In Sweden there are sports upper secondary schools that offer talented young people advanced training in parallel with their studies. Many sports have a national sports upper secondary school of their own, like tennis in Båstad or golf in Klippan. This is certainly a good thing, but it is doubtful to what extent this has helped in developing talents to world stars at the top elite level. The marked difference from US college sport is that in the latter, hard training in sharp competition is paramount.

Summarizing analysis: The different phases of the success spiral, the rise and decline of Swedish tennis and golf

There is no easy answer or no single factor that explains the extraordinary success of Swedish tennis and golf. It is not enough to seek the answers just inside the sports; the explanation must also be sought in the development in society. A number of different factors behind the successful development are included in a *success spiral*. Societal structure, the sport structure, and the actors' practising of the sport converge to create a favourable situation with good chances of achieving successful athletes.

Tennis and golf in Sweden have experienced an almost parallel success spiral, with a time lag of about 10 years. A chief success factor is the strong quantitative increase in both sports. This happened partly because a quickly growing middle class identified with new social habits in its endeavour to achieve a higher social status, where tennis and golf fitted in well. Partly it is due to the deliberate strategies of the sports themselves to become more of folk sports with a broader recruitment. 'The Swedish sport model' with its open clubs welcomed everybody to participate, even in tennis and golf. In an international perspective, this was unique. The intense development began with building courts and courses, educating coaches and beginners' schools. It is neither strong national federations, large national sport schools, nor spectacular individual trainers which lie behind the successes of Swedish tennis and golf.

With international successes, mass media idols were created, who further heightened the interest. This was especially important in tennis with its big television exposure – in golf it took longer for the idols to emerge. A common factor is that more systematic and physical training methods became a natural element, as well as the willingness to organize in teams, and cooperating in training and preparing for competitions even at individual contests. Both tennis and golf have built national systems where young players have concurred to select the most talented players. A surprisingly high number of Swedish world stars in both tennis and golf, have taken part in the US college sports system with tough practice and competition just before their international breakthrough.

The success spiral may be divided into five different phases reflecting rise, peak, slow decline and, perhaps, real fall.

Phase 1: Few practitioners, limited popular support, the odd international success
The first phase is characterized by few practitioners, a highly specialized sport that interests and engages only a small part of society. As for tennis and golf, both were established as sports in the upper social layers. In tennis there were in the first half of the twentieth century a few odd Swedish players with successes just below the world elite, whereas in golf this was rare.

Phase 2: Evolving into a folk sport, increased social interest, a few world stars on their way
For both tennis and golf the Swedish welfare development was favourable. A broad middle class with money to spend emerged with increased leisure, better economy and an interest in marking higher social belongingness, where sports like tennis and golf were attractive. Tennis experienced in the late 1960s a period of strong quantitative growth in both the number of new clubs and

the number of players. For golf the same development started a little more than ten years later. International successes and mass media focus on new idols spurred the interest; sponsors appeared; municipalities supported; clubs employed coaches; new training methods were developed and central coaching courses and national youth competitions got under way.

Phase 3: Established folk sport with strongly built up structure, groups of new world players
In the third phase the sport takes its place as a broadly established folk sport with a large supply of local clubs with good resources and coaching capacity available to large parts of the population. Central federations are responsible for national youth investments, coaching education and a national competition system screening for new talents. A broad social interest from the media and sponsors makes a good influx of resources possible. Great competition successes at the world elite level, with in principle every age group repeatedly producing new athletes with the capacity to reach the world elite. Team building and team play in colleges in the USA facilitate the step into the international elite. New idols keep creating new models. Swedish tennis entered this phase in the 1980s and remained there until the late 1990s. Swedish golf reached there in the mid-1990s and has so far, by 2010, not yet left it. It still produces several new players annually who establish themselves on the professional tours, but at the same time there are distinct reports about a noticeably declining inflow of young people into golf. The golf success spiral seems to have started moving less smoothly.

Phase 4: Past the peak but still a solidly broad sport, good elite successes at a lower level
In the fourth phase the decline has started. Fewer young people join in, as other sports become more alluring. Elite successes at the world level have declined. International competition is growing in line with welfare development and broadened recruitment in the rest of the world. Training and technique development happens in other parts of the world. For Swedish tennis, this phase occurred in the second half of the 1990s. No new talents kept streaming in as they used to, while the tennis world changed. In several countries tennis exploded in about the same way as it had done in Sweden, a clear example being Spain, where the sport was broadened socially and a remarkable number of new Spanish world players emerged in the 1990s. After the fall of the wall and the split-up of Yugoslavia, tennis players began pouring forth from Russia, Serbia and Croatia – not least on the women's side.

The game of tennis also developed with harder, faster and flatter shots, where the earlier Swedish style of playing no longer held sway. Massive training and physical build-up became something self-evident throughout the tennis world. All told, nearly all the previous advantages Sweden had had within world tennis at the beginning of the twenty-first century had disappeared, and there was even talk about Swedish players now training too little and, above all, leaving their serious commitment to tennis until too late an age in comparison with the rest of the world. The question for Swedish tennis at the beginning of the 2010s is whether it will manage to stay on in phase 4, or lose its edge and lapse into phase 5.

For Swedish golf there is still no obvious decline at the world level to be seen, but it might hover on the borderline of phase 4, according to the above discussion. World competition in golf has clearly sharpened with many new countries where golf has undergone social broadening and is quickly beginning to produce a great number of world stars – not least with reference to the Asian golf miracle in the first years of the twenty-first century. A clear example is women's golf in South Korea, which has experienced a very quick and sensationally broad success wave that widely surpasses the Swedish one, with some 25 South Korean women players established in the world elite on the US tour today.

Phase 5: Back as a small limited sport, only the odd success at the world elite level
The fifth phase means that the circle is closed, that the spiral of success has made its round and the sport in question is back at phase 1. This is no unique development, as there as many examples in Swedish history of sports that have experienced the full trip from a strong rising period, a success peak with many stars in the world arena, the beginning of decline and then being relegated again to an obscure place in international competition. There may be many reasons: shifting social interests, young generation changes, the popularity of other sports, and the development of sport techniques and training methods.

The next decade will show whether Swedish tennis on the men's side – the women's side not having experienced any notably rising success – will finally go all the way back to phase 5 after its fantastic period of success that lasted for a couple of decades. The chances of staying on in phase 4 – with about one new world player roughly every second or third year – are relatively good, thanks to a solidly built-up structure, and a stable position in phase 4 must be looked upon as very good for a small country. Swedish golf is, however, still surfing high on its success wave and seems to be able to remain in phase 3 with one or two new world players almost every year on both the women's and the men's sides, an incredible success story, which has so far lasted for about 15 years. Due to the decreasing interest in golf among Swedish youngsters and the sharpened international competition it is, however, reasonable to soon expect a small decline at the elite level and consequently a descent into phase 4, where Swedish golf will, however, probably stay for a decade or two.

Concluding remarks

The success histories of Swedish tennis and Swedish golf have been analysed as a *success spiral*. For other sports the success story may look somewhat different; a success spiral may, for instance, start in different ways – quite often via a few successful individuals creating starlike positions and attracting a great deal of attention. However, for a period of success to last beyond these single individuals, a solid underlying structure is required, which manages to keep producing and further developing new age groups of athletes all the way to the international elite. Few sports manage this for any length of time. Alongside tennis and golf, swimming for both men and women, men's table tennis and men's handball are additional examples. Of these, swimming is the only sport that still manages to keep the success wave at its peak in phase three, according to the above model. Men's table tennis and men's handball have after decades of international success now in the early twenty-first century experienced that the success spiral has lost momentum; and suddenly there are fewer players in the new generation who can take over at the international level.

Swedish athletics illustrates the challenges of sustained success. Around the turn of the millennium a whole group of athletes born about the same time won World Championship and Olympic medals. They became popular national heroes and fine representatives of the sport. In spite of this, it is highly uncertain whether there will be any follow-up with new generations of stars in athletics after this particularly successful generation. It is doubtful whether athletics in Swedish has the solid structure required and also whether big crowds of young Swedes will choose athletics of all sports in the future. The next few years will supposedly provide the answers, but there is an obvious risk that Swedish athletics will soon relapse to a rather obscure position in the world arenas. The big successes may only be temporary, and linked to a limited group of special individuals. Sports like tennis, golf, swimming, equestrian sports, ice hockey and all forms of skiing probably have a much greater chance in the future of fairly frequently watching one or another new Swedish athlete take up a position among the very foremost at the world elite level.

7

Norwegian women's handball
– organizing for sustainable success

Lars Tore Ronglan

Until the mid-1980s, women's Norwegian handball had not won any medals in any international tournament, neither European club tournaments nor championships for national teams. In fact, Norway had never placed better than number seven in the World Championships before 1986, and it had not qualified for any Olympic tournament. Although the most widespread and popular female sport in Norway in the 1960s, 1970s and 1980s, the federation's effort to increase the competitiveness of the national team did not yield significant international results. Then, in 1986, the national team quite surprisingly managed to reach the bronze final in the World Championships. They beat the German Democratic Republic (DDR) and won Norway's first medal ever. During the next two and a half decades Norway dominated women's handball internationally. No other national team won as many medals in international championships from 1986 to 2010 as Norway.

This chapter takes a closer look at this 25-year period of sustained success. First, the international competitiveness of Norwegian handball will be documented, including a description and brief discussion of the differences between club results and national team results over the last decades. This is followed by an analysis of the breakthrough for the national team in the mid-'80s, and the maintenance of good results in the coming decades. Four phases are discussed; (1) The *breakthrough* in 1986, (2) how the success was *repeated* (1987–93), (3) how key elements of the success formula were *institutionalized* (1994–2000), and (4) how they had to be *renewed* due to changed environmental conditions (2001–10). The conclusion discusses the challenges Norwegian handball faces today in the efforts to continue to succeed internationally.

Women's handball in Norway: Brief history 1937–1986

Handball became organized as a national sport in Norway in 1937, when the Norwegian Handball Federation was established. Contrary to Sweden and Germany, where the sport developed as a 'men's game', handball developed into a 'women's sport' in Norway, as it did in Denmark (Skjerk 1999). It was introduced as the 'first team sport' for women in Norway. Lippe (1994) considers this crucial for the development of handball as a 'women's sport' in this country. Female players dominated the handball federation; already in 1940 girls and women constituted 69 per cent of the total number of players (Lippe 1994). Moreover, the first Norwegian Championship and the first national team consisted of females. When the first international match was played between Norway and Sweden in Oslo in 1939, 10,000 spectators watched Sweden win 3–1 (Nordberg 1997). The fast growing popularity of the new game was reflected in a newspaper title in 1939, stating that 'handball has become the women's football' (Lippe 1994).

During the 1950s, 1960s and 1970s handball fortified its position as the most popular female team sport in Norway. The number of players grew steadily, and two thirds of the players were girls and women. However, Norwegian elite handball did not achieve same level as the best European nations. Statistics from the Norwegian Handball Federation reveals that the Norwegian team lost more matches than they won during these three decades. Additionally, they lost almost every match played against the Eastern European countries dominating the sport in this period, like Yugoslavia, Romania, the Soviet Union and Czechoslovakia.

In the 1960s, the Norwegian team did not qualify for the World Championships (WCs). In the 1970s they qualified for three WCs, placing as number seven as the best result. The team did not qualify for the Olympic tournaments in 1976, 1980, or in 1984. During the first years of the 1980s, however, Norway achieved improved results within youth handball. The junior national teams were more often competitive in international tournaments. Although they did not win any medals in the Junior World Championships, the junior teams were quite close in 1981 and 1985.

7 NORWEGIAN WOMEN'S HANDBALL – ORGANIZING FOR SUSTAINABLE SUCCESS

At the start of the 1980s the situation for Norwegian handball can be summed up as follows: The sport was the most widespread organized sport among girls and women. Systematic talent development work in the elite clubs and the federation had produced a generation of well skilled young players. This was facilitated by a better infrastructure. The state policy had emphasized the building of sport halls during the 1960s and 1970s. This gradually improved the training facilities for players and clubs around the country (Goksøyr, Andersen, & Asdal 1996). In this way, state policy compensated for a traditional disadvantage in Norwegian handball when compared to its international competitors, namely the lack of training and match arenas.

International dominance the last 25 years

Handball is dominated by European teams. Internationally, teams compete in club tournaments like the European Cups and in national team tournaments like World Championships and the Olympics. Thus, assessing a nation's position in international handball can be done by looking at the international results either of the national teams or of the elite clubs located in the country. In the following, we will present both the results of the national team and the elite clubs from Norway over the last 25 years. The numbers illustrate that Norway's international dominance in this period primarily is based on the national team's extraordinary success. In the end of the section the differences in national and club team results are briefly discussed.

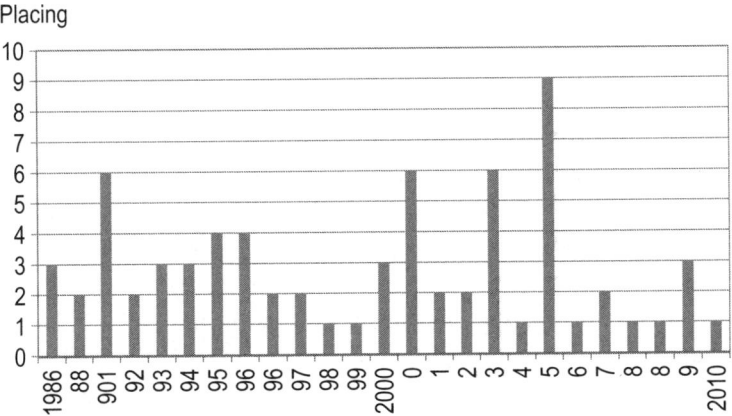

Table 7.1: National team results in European Championships, World Championships and Olympics 1986–2010 (25 play-off tournaments in total)

In the last 25 years (1986–2010), a total of 26 international play-off tournaments has been organized; 11 World Championships (WCs), 9 European Championships (ECs) and 6 Olympic Games. Out of these 26 international championships Norway qualified for 25 (missed the Olympics in 2004), and reached the bronze final or final 21 times. The team has won 19 medals – 7 gold, 7 silver and 5 bronze medals – during these last 26 championships (see table 7.1).

Winning 19 medals out of 26 possible make Norway the definitively most successful nation within women's handball during this period. Other major medalists are the Soviet Union / Russia (13), Denmark (11), Korea (10) and Hungary (8) (see table 7.2).

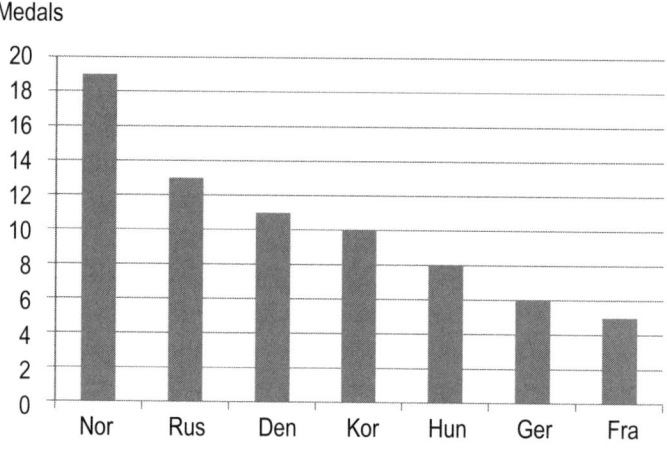

Table 7.2: Number of medals won in European Championships, World Championships and Olympics 1986–2010

Moreover, if we compare the three most-winning nations (Norway, Russia and Denmark) we see that Norway, in addition to having won most medals, has less up and downs than their competitors. During this period Russia did not qualify to three play-off tournaments and Denmark four, compared to Norway's one. While Norway has only one placing below number 6 (no 9 in 2005), Russia has placed below number 6 four times and Denmark five times. Thus, Norway's 'average placing' during 26 tournaments is 2.7, while Russia's average is 3.9 and Denmark's is 4.5.

If we move from national team results to results in the European Cups for clubs (E-Cups), a quite different picture appears. The E-Cups are organized by the European Handball Federation (EHF) and recognized as the most important club tournaments in Europe. The best clubs from most European countries participate. Since the start of the 1990s, the EHF has organized four E-Cups annually for women's club teams. The best clubs in each nation qualify based on their performances in the national leagues the previous season. For a club team to win the most prestigious E-Cup, the Champions League, can be compared to a national team winning the European Championship.

From 1994 to 2009 the EHF has organized four European Cups each year, meaning that totally 60 E-Cup finals have been played in this period. Grouping the finalist clubs according to nationality gives a picture of the dominating nations in European club handball during this period (see table 7.3).

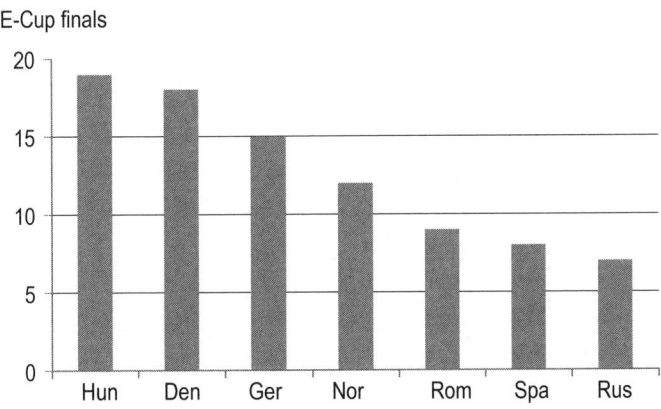

Table 7.3: Finalists from different nations in the European Cups 1994–2009

In contrast to the national team results, clubs from Hungary, Denmark and Germany have been more successful than Norwegian clubs in the European club tournaments (table 7.3). The trend becomes even clearer if we look at semifinalists in the Champions League (CL), the most prestigious club tournament (table 7.4). While Danish and Hungarian clubs have reached the semifinal 10 and 12 times respectively, Norwegian clubs have reached the CL semifinal two times during these 15 years. Eight European nations have performed better than Norway in the Champions League, in terms of reaching the semifinal (table 7.4).

The differences between the Norwegian national team results (tables 7.1, 7.2) and elite club results (tables 7.3, 7.4) the last two decades are significant. Norway has had the most successful national team internationally, winning

19 medals over the last 26 championships. In contrast, Norwegian club teams have rarely managed to reach the finals in the European Cups. It can be argued that national team results are a more valid indicator of a nation's competitiveness, due to increasing migration of players in professional club handball. For example, a recent study showed that the amount of foreign players in the Danish women handball league increased from 13 per cent in 2000 to 33 per cent in 2007 (Agergaard 2008). In recent years successful Danish clubs in the European Cups have signed a significant number of Norwegian players. Another example is the well-performing Austrian club (Hypo Niederösterreich) in the Champions League (table 7.4). To a large extent it has been composed by players from Eastern European countries.

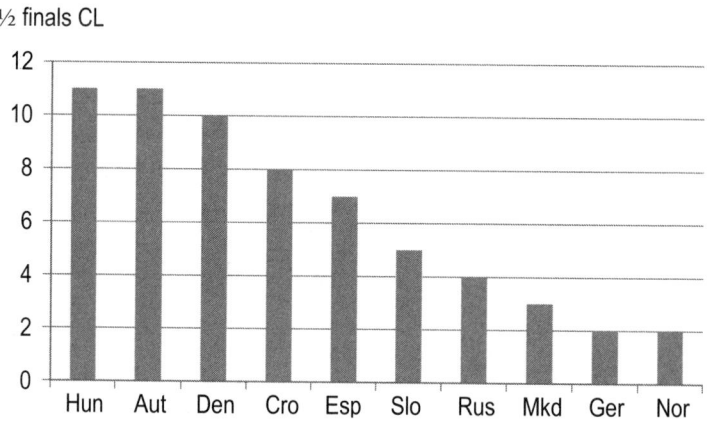

Table 7.4: Number of semifinalists / finalists in Champion League 1994–2009

However, the fact that several clubs from at least three nations have performed significantly better than Norwegian clubs in the European Cups (table 7.3), indicates that the national club leagues in Hungary, Denmark and Germany over the last 15 years have kept a higher standard than in Norway. Despite increasing migration, most of the elite players – and almost all of the young talents – are after all playing in the domestic league. Given that the Norwegian league provided a weaker competitive context, this situation should not benefit the national team in Norway. This suggests that the quality of the national team the last decades has not been a pure reflection of the work being done in Norwegian club teams. On the contrary, the performance level of the national team has definitively been higher than in the national elite clubs. This makes the sustained success of the Norwegian national team over this period even more interesting to study.

Framing of the story

The discussion of the development in Norwegian women's handball the last 25 years is divided into four periods. This division reflects major processes that dominated the different periods. Specific incidents introduce or frame each phase. The first incident was the *breakthrough* itself; winning the bronze medal in the 1986 World Championship. To understand the breakthrough, environmental conditions and internal processes leading up to the championship are discussed. The breakthrough introduced phase two; lasting from 1987 until 1993, it was characterized by *repetition* of the success and stabilization of the 'new' performance level within the team. A change of head coach after the World Championship in 1993 introduced phase three. It lasted from 1994 until 2000. In this period, *institutionalization* of the success formula was emphasized; including talent development systems, knowledge production and coaching strategies. Phase four was introduced by increased player turnover and varying results by the turn of the century. This last period (2001–09) was characterized by *renewal* of the success formula reflecting changing economic and environmental conditions.

The four phases cannot be completely separated from each other. Rather, the movement from 'breakthrough', to 'repeated success', to 'institutionalizing' and 'renewing' the success should be seen as a gradual transition. Both the division into phases and the emphasis on processes that define the different periods are based on documents, field observations, and interviews with key informants within the team, handball federation and elite sports organization in Norway. To a certain extent the phases coincide in time with changes in team leadership. There was a total change of the coach team in 1994 (head coach plus assistant coaches) and a partial change in 2001 (replacement of the assistant coach). The assistant coach recruited in 2001 replaced Marit Breivik as head coach in 2009, an incident that may also signify a new phase. This potential 'fifth phase' will be touched upon in the final section which outlines future challenges for Norwegian women's handball.

The breakthrough in 1986
During the first half of the 1980s, Norwegian women's handball did not make any significant progress pointing towards the bronze medal that was won in

1986 World Championship. The talent development in Norwegian handball had improved, but the new generations coming up had still not been capable of beating the best international teams in their age group. The medal in the Senior WC 1986 was totally unexpected. The huge national media coverage from the championship was unanimous in describing the achievement as a 'sports adventure' coming totally 'out of the blue' (Andersen 2005). Journalists labeled the team as the 'bronze team' and their coach as a 'magician'.

The achievement in the WC 1986 was surprising for several reasons. Three will be discussed here. First; international women's handball was at the time completely dominated by the Eastern bloc countries, which were still strong regimes with few signs of the crisis that was to come. Second, the economic situation in the Norwegian Handball Federation was critical. In fact the federation was nearly bankrupt a few months ahead of the championship. Third; the team experienced a chaotic leadership situation less than two years prior to the championship. The new head coach suddenly quit in 1984 and the inexperienced assistant coach had to take charge of the team on short notice.

Until 1986, the Eastern bloc dominance in international women's handball was virtually total. 23 of the 24 medals in the eight indoor WCs organized since 1957 had been won by Eastern European countries; particularly the Soviet Union, GDR, Hungary and Yugoslavia. The only medal won by a Western European country was Denmark's silver medal back in 1962. A similar situation characterized the Junior World Championships. No nation managed to interfere in the total Eastern European dominance until Korea entered the podium in 1985. Hence, the Norwegian senior medal in 1986 might be understood as a 'breakthrough' in more than one sense. It not only lifted Norwegian handball onto the international scene, it also represented the first step in breaking the Eastern European hegemony over the sport.

Within men's handball the Eastern European domination was equally strong; and here a similar 'Western breakthrough' did not happen until 1990 (Sweden). The male Swedish victory in the WC 1990 coincided in time with an unstable and chaotic political, social and economic situation in several Eastern European nations. This may (temporarily) have weakened their competitiveness in international elite sport (Merkel 1999). In 1986, however, the sport systems in Eastern European regimes like the Soviet Union and GDR were well organized and their 'state amateurism' still worked (Green & Oakley 2001). This comparative observation makes the Norwegian breakthrough even more remarkable.

A second factor making the 1986 success a surprise was the economic situation in the Norwegian Handball Federation (NHF). Hosting the men's World

Championship in 1985 turned out to be far more expensive than expected. The NHF faced an economic crisis in the first half of 1986. The situation was so critical that some persons, among them the president and the general secretary of the federation, decided to risk private funds to save the federation from bankruptcy (Andersen 2005). As a curiosity, it can be mentioned that Marit Breivik, later the successful head coach of the national team for 15 years, was part of the private rescue operation as a member of the board in 1985. This 'private' rescue operation was in fact what made it possible to send the national team to participate in the World Championships in 1986. Of course the economic downturn restricted the NHF's activities, including the national team preparation for the championship. On the other hand, the restricted economic freedom also forced the federation to prioritize strictly. The result was a clearer focus on the women's team (as opposed to the men's) within a long-term strategy. Hence, one could argue that although economic problems limited team development in the short term, it laid the foundation for a long-term commitment that really paid off.

Indirectly, the economic situation was part of the reason why Sven-Tore Jacobsen, a young and rather inexperienced coach, became the head coach of the national team two years ahead of the WC 1986. After a disappointing World Championships in 1982, the NHF had decided to hire an internationally recognized coach. A contract had been signed with an experienced Yugoslavian coach with good merits. However, soon afterward he withdrew from the contract for personal reasons. As a kind of emergency solution, the intended assistant coach (Jacobsen) was supposed to be in charge of the team for a limited period of time. However, promising results and the economic situation contributed to make the temporary coach permanent prior to the WC 1986.

In sum, one could conclude that two apparently unwanted incidents – economic problems and an unforeseen change of coach – turned out to be a lucky strike for the NHF. Jacobsen was a kind of coach that suited the national team perfectly in the 'breakthrough-phase'. He was creative, charismatic and enthusiastic, truly following the motto 'the sky is the limit' (Bernhus, 1988). Although he obviously was a demanding coach due to his immense energy (ibid.), he had a significant impact on his players, especially the new generation of talents that he gradually integrated in the team.

Several biographies from these players emphasize how important Jacobsen's knowledge and attitude was in the 'breakthrough-phase' in the mid-1980s (Bjerkrheim & Nordberg 1999; Gynnhild 1993). The stories and personal anecdotes of Jacobsen's behavior indicates that he displayed social skills and an 'impression management' (Goffman 1959) important to really make a difference as a coach (Jones, Armour & Potrac 2004). Coaches' energy and personal charisma may be even more important to stimulate a 'breakthrough' than it is to stimulate a continuation of a success (Ronglan 2011).

Finally, it is worth mentioning that there may be a thin line between placing number six and winning a bronze medal in a handball championship. When trying to understand the national team's breakthrough in 1986, coincidences and luck should be taken into consideration. For example, because the Romanian team lost by one goal in the last second against Czechoslovakia, Norway's draw result in the last game turned out to be enough to pass Romania due to a better goal difference. This was enough to qualify for the bronze final. However, it does not mean that luck 'caused' the Norwegian medal. Rather, it is just a recognition of the 'circumstantial luck' (Bailey 2007) that may be needed to succeed in a tournament competition.

Circumstantial luck: the circumstances in which one acts introduce luck (ibid. 371), may in the handball context mean that results in matches involving other teams turn out in your own favor. To be 'lucky' with incidents on which the team itself has no influence (e.g. other matches) may partially explain the outcome of one championship, but hardly the outcome of 25 championships in a row. Thus, while luck may possibly play a role in creating a single success (a 'breakthrough'), the luck factor is over time equalized between competitors in sport. When we now turn to the repetition of the handball team's good results, we therefore have to look at more systematic relations and processes to make sense of the story.

Phase 2 (1987–93): Repetition of the success

A breakthrough in international sport is always about surpassing previous achievements. Consequently, if the success is going to be more than just a single event, the performer has to stabilize his or her performance on a higher level than it used to be. The necessity to 'transcend your current performance' is 'the core of the logic of competing' (Heikkala 1993: 397) marking elite sport in general. The bronze medal won in the WC 1986 meant that the national team was for the first time qualified to an Olympic tournament (Seoul 1988). The basic short-term challenge was how to repeat the success one and a half years later. Having taken a step upwards and become the 'silver team' in 1988, the next challenges were to repeat the top-three placing in the WC-90 and again in the Olympics-92 and the WC-93. In this way, the first 6–7 years after the breakthrough was characterized by a quite narrow focus aimed at revisiting the podium, and thereby confirming that the team belonged to the definitive international elite.

The major strategy applied by the Norwegian Handball Federation in these 'pioneer years' was to *maximize the team's* preparations for each upcoming championship. The national coach's requests for more training camps, more tournaments abroad, an expanded staff, and better economy were fulfilled, despite resistance from the other part of the organization. For example, because of the rapidly increasing activities of the national team, there was a growing dissatisfaction among the elite clubs which frequently 'lost' their best players to national team activities. In the late 1980s and early 1990s, the conflict between the national coach and some elite club coaches became so intense that the federation continuously had to mediate and solve problems between the parties (national team / elite clubs). The NHF strongly supported the national coach, and continued to prioritize national team development.

In the early 1990s, the Norwegian woman's national team spent more than twice as many days per year at training camps than the equally successful Swedish men's national team. This illustrates an overall difference between Norway and Sweden regarding the distribution of power between sport federations and clubs. At the same time it underlines the NHF's strong willingness to spend money and resources to maintain the national team's success – 'at the expense' of club development, some representatives from the clubs would argue. Undoubtedly there was much noise and disagreement marking Norwegian elite handball in this phase. This was a consequence of clear priorities and leadership. However, the national team / club team conflict was also exhausting for the parties, including the involved players. Thus, it can be argued that even though conflicts were natural and maybe necessary when establishing the new performance level, they had to be reduced to be able to maintain good results over time. This gradually happened during the institutionalization phase in the mid-1990s.

To understand the NHF's strategy in phase two it is important to recognize how the first medals won in 1986 and 1988 also represented a *commercial breakthrough*. The commercial breakthrough was expressed in two ways; (1) a huge media attention, which led to (2) a rapidly increasing sponsor interest. The sudden and intense media interest surrounding the 'bronze team' from 1986 and the 'silver team' from 1988 was exploited by the NHF to sign long-term and lucrative sponsorship deals. Thus, the NHF's difficult economic situation in 1986 was turned into a solid economic recovery. In fact, the economic turnover in the NHF increased by 30 per cent in two years, more than in any other national federation in the country (Ronglan 1992). Additionally, a large number of young girls (and boys) started playing handball in the latter half of the '80s. The growth of active members was, at least within the federation itself, viewed as a consequence of the increased public interest created by the national team success. No wonder – given these positive consequences – that many recourses in the 'pioneer years' were used to optimize the team's conditions to prepare properly for each upcoming championship.

During phase two (1986–93), the national team players went from being 'pure amateurs' to become 'semiprofessional' athletes, receiving part-time salaries from the NHF. This *professionalization process* was, among other things, aimed at extending the careers of the key players. The principle adopted by the NHF was that each player got her salary increased in line with increased experience as a national player (number of championships played) (Ronglan 2000). In this way the NHF's strengthened economy was strategically used to keep the experienced players in the national team for a longer period of time, thereby counteracting the traditional turnover problem caused by players quitting 'too early'. To a new elite nation with a limited pool of top players, this strategy was probably productive in reproducing good performances the first years.

The strategy made it easier to increase the 'working load' on national players (training camps, etc.) and at the same time extend their careers. The NHF's wage policy was particularly effective because the elite clubs still were 'amateur teams' in the 1980s. Consequently, most of the players got paid as national players, but not as club players. Distributing salaries based on 'seniority' rather than pure 'performance' may seem unusual viewed from today's professionalized team sport, but it was essential to secure necessary continuity in the late 1980s and early 1990s. For example, five to six players held central positions in the national team during the whole period 1986–93, and reached on average about 200 played national games before they retired.

In addition to improved economy and strategic use of money, the national team's *improved ranking* and reputation internationally was utilized to further strengthen team preparations in the late 1980s. After the breakthrough it was easier to get invitations to quality tournaments abroad, which provided the team with additional international experience at the highest level. The team became a more interesting training partner ('sparring partner') to other elite milieus, and the head coach and federation managed to establish relationships with handball teams and experts in various European countries. These experiences fostered valuable knowledge exchange and production for the benefit of the Norwegian team.

The NHF's decision to apply for, and being chosen to host, the World Championships in 1993 contributed to further increase public interest in women's handball in Norway. It also had a positive effect on key players' motivation to work hard and extend their careers during the early 1990s. The championship in Norway in 1993 represented the end of what I have labeled phase two, resulting in another bronze medal. Contrary to the WC 1986, the medal this time was a bit disappointing given the thorough preparations, the home advantage, and the fact that the team after several repeated successes now was an established candidate for the podium.

To sum up; phase two (1986–93) was characterized by a narrow focus aimed at stabilizing the team's performance on a higher level than it used to be and thereby confirming that it belonged to the definitive international elite. The major strategy adopted by the NHF was to maximize the team's preparations before each upcoming championship. The number of training camps increased, participation in international tournaments was intensified, the support staff grew, and players moved from amateurism to semi-professionalism. This comprehensive professionalization process was facilitated by a growing public and commercial interest in the team. The development was guided by clear priorities and strategies by the decision makers in the federation and the head coach of the team. As a consequence, there was increased conflict between 'club interests' and 'national team interests'. Establishing the national team as part of the international elite was a time-consuming and resource demanding process, accompanied by disagreements and resistance within the federation.

Phase 3 (1994–2000): Institutionalization of the success

Phase 3 represents a period where a more profound institutionalization process took place. The 'success formula' was more clearly anchored within the handball organization. After the turbulent and rather conflict-ridden 'pioneer years', this gradual institutionalization process accelerated throughout the 1990s. Like the previous period, this period also culminated with a World Championships organized in Norway (1999), now with the Norwegian team on top of the podium. Three dimensions of the institutionalization process are central: (1) a more consistent and structured talent work, (2) an increased cooperation with Olympiatoppen, and (3) the implementation of a long-term and uniform coaching strategy.

Phase 3 was introduced by the change of the head coach after the WC 2003, a change that in itself contributed to the institutionalization process. The outgoing coach (Jacobsen) was a barrier-breaking, charismatic, but also controversial type of leader. The incoming head coach (Breivik) had a solid organizational and club-based background. She was considered competent and was welcomed when she entered the job. She had acquired coaching experience through six years as coach in the best national elite clubs. She had also been elite sport director in the federation during Jacobsen's period as national coach. This background, combined with a more team-based approach to problem solving, reduced the level of conflict.

However, a new leadership style alone could not remove tensions and conflicts embedded in different interests and competition for limited resources. Club interests versus national team interests was still a topic for debate. Still, the intensity of the debates decreased, and cooperation between club coaches and national coaches gradually replaced competition between the parties.

With the new head coach, and the history of the team, the focus expanded. The key question throughout the 1990s was how the success could be facilitated in a long-term perspective, not only reproduced from one championship to the next. Consequently, establishing a solid *talent development system* became important. The federation used considerable energy and recourses to hire competent youth national coaches, some of them full-time. The head coach was involved in the hiring process and responsible for coordinating and following up the recruits.

The talent development system involved a network of regional talent groups and coaches supported by the central coaches hired by the NHF. On the one hand this nationwide network represented a form of decentralization, in the sense that talent development got a more clear focus in the regional departments of the federation. On the other hand the talent development system was centralized, since the NFF-hired coaches coordinated the activity, designed the content of the programs, and contributed to educating the talent coaches. Consequently, also the role of the national team's head coach changed. In addition to being responsible for the daily performance development within the senior national team, she coordinated and monitored the junior national teams and the broader talent development work.

The talent work led to visible performance improvements from the mid-1990s. In 1995, a Norwegian team for the first time won a medal in the Junior World Championships. The following two years Norway continued to reach the bronze final in the junior championships. Several players from these generations contributed some years later to the two first gold medals won by the senior national team (EC 1998 and WC 1999). However, an interesting observation is that the Norwegian senior team in relative terms performed significantly better than the junior teams from the mid-1990s until today. During 16 junior championships (WC and EC) from 1995 until 2009, Norway won 6 medals, while for example Denmark won 8 and Russia 10. These results differed significantly from the distribution on the senior level (see table 7.2: Norway 17, Russia 12, Denmark 11).

Although talent development in Norway improved through the '90s and onwards, other nations did better. It seems that Norwegian players to a greater extent managed to further increase their performance after becoming senior players by the age of 20. Alternatively, the talent development systems in other countries may have been so 'successful' that more of their players' performance potential was reached at an earlier age. Although this is speculation, it illustrates the complexity embedded in the concept of 'talent development' and the difficulties in finding valid measurements of it (Trancle & Cushion 2006). Nevertheless, the Norwegian international senior results consistently exceeded the junior results. This suggests that more than an improved talent development is behind the sustained senior success.

During the '90s, female handball in Norway gradually became more *integrated as part of Norwegian elite sport*. The interaction between the handball federation and Olympiatoppen was intensified, as was the cooperation between the handball team and other successful team sport milieus in Norway, particularly women's football (World Champions 1995 and Olympic Champions 2000). When Olympiatoppen started its involvement in handball in the early 1990s, the support was primarily economic. With increased competence within Olympiatoppen, the interaction involved several aspects such as coaching support, nutrition, and physical training programs.

From the mid-1990s the national handball teams regularly used Olympiatoppen's training center in Oslo for training camps and testing. Here, networks with athletes and coaches from other sports were developed and formal as well as informal knowledge exchange took place. Thus, the facilities and competence provided by Olympiatoppen contributed to integrate the handball team as a significant part of the Norwegian elite sport milieu. In addition, given that the successful period of Norwegian handball already had started when Olympiatoppen was established in the late 1980s, the relationship between handball and Olympiatoppen was of mutual benefit.

Norwegian handball may be viewed as a precursor of the overall Norwegian 'elite sport adventure' emerging in the 1990s (Hanstad 2002). The institutionalization process within Norwegian elite handball ran parallel to the development of Olympiatoppen as the central node within the overall elite sport network. The reciprocity between the handball team and Olympiatoppen was strengthened by strong personal bonds between the head of Olympiatoppen (Stensbøl), the coach of the handball team (Breivik), and the director of the handball federation (Hertzberg). Rather than culminate at the end of the 1990s, the close link between elite handball and Olympiatoppen continued after the turn of the century. When Breivik ended her 15 year-long career as head coach of the handball team in 2009, she was immediately recruited by Olympiatoppen as a full-time senior coach responsible for team sports.

The last aspect of the institutionalization process to be discussed here is related to Breivik's extensive leadership period. It was marked by a *'holistic coaching philosophy'*, which may illustrate the long-term perspective adopted by the NHF. This long-term strategy was facilitated by an extraordinary stability in the NHF's leader group during the 1990s. Both the director and the vice-director of the federation occupied their positions from the mid 1980s until 2002. Further, only two persons held the position as president of the federation during the same 15 year period. Last but not least, only two head coaches were in charge of the team from 1984 to 2009; Jacobsen for 9 years and Breivik for 15 years. This rather unusual stability in leadership positions compared to sport organizations in general contributed to predictability and probably made it easier to stick to the long-term strategies chosen in the early 1990s.

An important aspect of the long-term thinking was the head coach's implementation of a 'holistic' coaching philosophy. Central elements were to stimulate players' autonomy and empowerment, and to work towards a 'balanced' performance enhancement that also involved other arenas in the players' life (Ronglan 2000). Such a holistic approach to coaching was in line with Olympiatoppen's basic philosophy and thinking (Hanstad 2002). However, it differed from the traditional authoritarian coaching practices still dominating national (Ronglan 2000) as well as international elite team sport (Potrac, Jones & Armour 2002). The new holistic approach introduced unfamiliar methods. Consequently, extensive time was needed to implement this model and to provide full benefit of the working methods. Moreover, it was necessary to adopt a similar philosophy within the junior national teams, to ensure a smoother transition from the junior to the senior level.

The implementation of a unified coaching philosophy across the NHFs national teams could benefit from the senior coach's role as 'team leader' of the junior national coaches. Her involvement in the hiring processes and education of these coaches made it easier to coordinate philosophy as well as coaching practice. The career of the present senior head coach Thorir Hergeirsson as illustrates the point. He was hired as a full-time coach in the federation in 1994, and worked as junior national coach in close contact with the senior coaches during the 1990s. Each player entering the senior team in the latter 1990s had experience from training camps and championships led by Hergeirsson. In 2001, he became Breivik's assistant coach; a position he held until he was hired as head coach when Breivik quit in 2009. The example demonstrates how continuity was emphasized and how consistency in leadership and coaching was obtained.

To sum up; the institutionalization process characterizing phase 3 (1994–2000) was facilitated by stability in leadership positions and clear, long-term strategies. A broader perspective on sustainable success led to a solid talent development system and the unified implementation of a holistic coaching practice. During this decade, the relationships to Olympiatoppen and other elite sport milieus were intensified and the knowledge exchange expanded. Team results gradually improved throughout the 1990s and culminated with two gold medals won at the European Championships in 1998 and World Championships in Norway in 1999. The NHF had a stable and solid economy, leading to good conditions for the senor team and to an expansion of NHF-hired coaches and staff working with elite handball.

Phase 4 (2001–10): Adversity and renewal

After the Olympics in Sydney (2000), some experienced players ended their national team careers. In 2001 Breivik replaced several people in her staff, among them the assistant coach. These changes introduced a new phase marked by a stagnation of the federation's finances and a gradual shift in the power relation between the federation and more professionalized clubs. During this period the team experienced more ups and downs in results. Contrary to the high and steady performance level during the 1990s, the team placed as low as number six in the 2000 European Championship, six in the 2003 World Championship, and nine in the 2005 World Championship (table 7.1). Adversity and change created, from time to time, turbulence around the team. Still, the team won the same number of medals during this period (eight) as in the preceding one, including twice as many gold medals (four vs. two). This development raises questions about how renewal was achieved. An important part of this is how the professionalized European club handball influenced national team conditions.

The squad of 16 players winning the bronze medal in the Olympics 2000 consisted mainly of players from domestic clubs, with the exception of three individuals playing abroad. The growing professionalization of some foreign leagues made an increasing number of Norwegian players move abroad over the next years. Thus, in the middle of the decade about half of the national team performed as professional players outside Norway, particularly in Danish clubs. The rapid professionalization of the Danish League during the first years of the decade (Storm and Almlund 2006) included growing salaries as well as an increased performance level. This combination attracted elite players across Europe (Agergaard 2008). In 2006 a total of 14 Norwegians played in the Danish League (ibid.).

This emigration of Norwegian players had two important consequences. First, it contributed to a shift in the power balance between the Norwegian federation and the clubs supplying players to the national team. Second, the 'emptying' of the best players from the Norwegian League created opportunities for other players to take over important roles in Norwegian clubs. This may have been beneficial for the talent development situation in Norway. Let us take a closer look at these developments.

With the professionalization of the Danish Handball League, Danish club budgets increased on average by 150 per cent from 2000 to 2005 (Storm & Almlund 2006). From being semiprofessional in the 1990s, the biggest clubs developed into enterprises paying their key personnel – foreign stars like some of the Norwegians – salaries almost in line with the Prime Minister's (ibid.). The biggest clubs could spend more money to develop and run their teams than the Norwegian Handball Federation could spend on the national team. This tendency was reinforced by a slight decrease in the federation's finances during the same years. Consequently; the national players abroad, or in the one dominant Norwegian club, developed greater commitments to the club as their main employer.

This shift in the distribution of power and recourses between the Norwegian federation and professional clubs 'forced' the federation to take club interests more seriously. Due to club interests, as well as financial stagnation, the number of national team training camps was reduced compared to the 1990s. The national team more frequently 'released' players for club preparation. Also, players sometimes canceled national team activities because of club obligations or the need for recovery. In this way the national team became more dependent on the performance work in the clubs to uphold and increase its own level. The criteria for player selection to the national team gradually changed. The vast majority of national players were consistently selected from three to four of the dominant Scandinavian clubs, reflecting the clear hierarchy of the clubs. This made it easier to apply specific club-based player constellations and to integrate club-based playing styles into the national team.

However, the new situation did not lead to any changes in the coaching philosophy implemented during the 1990s. The national team was still marked by a holistic coaching philosophy aimed to stimulate players' empowerment and long-term development. An aspect of this philosophy was to view talent development as an integrated part of national team development. Paradoxically, the emigration of elite players to foreign clubs may have contributed to make talent development work easier in Norway than in countries like Denmark and Germany. The lower quality of the Norwegian league lowered the threshold for young talents to gain playing time and experience on the highest national club level.

In Denmark it was debated whether the massive immigration of foreign elite players might have blocked domestic talents' natural career paths by reducing their possibilities to gain match experience at the highest level (Hjort, Agergaard & Ronglan 2010). This discussion was intensified when Denmark experienced a significant reduction in national team performances in the 2005–09 period, while their elite clubs continued to qualify to finals in the European Cups. A similar situation existed in German handball, where the Bundesliga-clubs bought lots of Eastern European players.

In 2006 the senior national team coaches Breivik and Hergeirsson decided to form a 'recruitment team' consisting of players between 20 and 25 years old. There was a significant performance gap between the junior (under 20 years) and senior national teams. The intention was to create an additional qualitative training and competition arena for the 'second best' players in Norway. This increased the pool of hard working elite players 'knocking on the door' to the senior team. Such a coach initiative and follow-up of a broader group of players illustrates how the new situation also influenced the role of the national team coach. In addition to performing 'hands-on-coaching' on the court, the coaches operated to a greater degree as 'orchestrators' (Jones & Wallace 2006). This involved instigating, organizing and maintaining oversight of an array of tasks and individuals. With more players abroad they developed more long-distance coaching with extensive use of video clips, e-mail and internet.

To sum up, phase 4 was marked by weaker conditions for the national team. This was due to a stagnation in resources, a reduction of team-based preparation periods, and less 'control' over the players. Although the team experienced more ups and downs in results, it still won medals with the same frequency as in the previous decade. It avoided the significant performance decline that the Danish national team experienced.

The weaker conditions for the Norwegian national team were to a certain degree counteracted by improved conditions for the best players in their professional clubs (quality of training and match) and for the talents in the domestic league (playing time). The intensified work to follow up talents and create suitable training and competition contexts for a larger group of elite players contributed to the continuation of the success.

Last, but not least, we should not underestimate the importance of the accumulated experience gained through the history of the team. 'The best preparation for playing an Olympic final is to have played an Olympic final before'. The team's sustained success provided the participants with unique experiences during international tournaments. The merits of the team in general and the head coach in particular may have been decisive in making the right priorities during team preparations and championships.

What now?

Time will show whether the Norwegian women's national team is able to continue its success during the coming decade. Thorir Hergeirsson replaced Marit Breivik as head coach in 2009. This represented a clear continuation of the basic philosophy adopted during the last 15 years. The economic recession hitting the Danish League at the start of the new coach's period, indicated again changing conditions relevant to the team. Norwegian national players may move home to domestic clubs (as seems to be the current trend), or other European leagues may take over the hegemony and attract the best players. Further, the financial situation in the NHF, and the competing priorities between 'elite and mass sport' and between 'male and female' handball in Norway, will affect the national team.

Contrary to the 1980s and 1990s when the NHF prioritized the women's team due to its exceptional results, the improvement of men's handball in Norway over the last years has been accompanied by increasing support from the federation. If the men's national team makes an international breakthrough in the near future, similar to the women's team in the '80s, it may have positive as well as negative consequences for the women's team. Such a situation might broaden the Norwegian elite handball milieu and stimulate experience-based knowledge exchange across gender borders. In addition, it would probably increase the public and commercial interest in the sport as such. However, it may be difficult for a small country to keep both a men's and a women's team within the ultimate international elite, as exemplified by the situation in Denmark over the last two decades. Here, the national teams for men and women have alternated in being a leading team on the international scene.

The level of international competition is another important aspect. Maybe 'new nations' will appear on the international scene, or old powerful nations will experience a renaissance and regain their competitiveness. Already former Soviet republics (e.g. Ukraine), Balkan countries (like Croatia and Slovenia), and an old handball 'superpower' like Romania are again climbing on the result lists. The efforts to introduce handball on other continents have also brought some results lately. China (Asia), Angola (Africa) and Brazil (Latin America) have regularly reached placements from sixth to eighth in World Championships and Olympic Games in the period 2004–2009. Brazil is hosting the women's World Championships in 2011, as part of the international federation's strategy to further globalize the sport. If this succeeds, the international competition might be tougher, making it harder for the Norwegian team to maintain its hegemony.

Finally, it is necessary to return to the Norwegian team's own performance work; which, at the end of the day, remains the crucial aspect. Independent of a tough competition context or changed environmental conditions, the team must manage to constantly reproduce its high quality work to uphold good results. An important part of the 'success formula' is the balance between continuity and renewal. The NHF and the women's team have during the last decades managed to combine continuity of key personnel and key processes with necessary creativity and innovation. Time will show if they manage the balance as well in the future years.

8

Lions on the ice: the success story of Finnish ice hockey

Jari Lämsä

Introduction

In the Calgary Olympics in 1988, the Finnish national ice hockey team – 'the Lions' – beat the then Soviet Union in their last battle by 2–1. The victory gave Finland the Olympic silver medal and its first World Championship or Olympic medal in a sport in which success had been eagerly anticipated. From 1954, the Finnish national team had regularly fought in the World Championships and Olympic Games against the big teams: the Soviet Union, Canada, Czechoslovakia and Sweden. In the 22 organized Olympics or WC tournaments, the country came fourth or fifth a total of 17 times. The first Olympic medal was a surprise, but it reflected the determined efforts since the 1950s. The increase in the number of players and active parties, together with improved facilities and training skills had formed a sustainable basis for international success of ice hockey. As with other Finnish sports, ice hockey is based on the voluntary training done in hundreds of sports clubs. However, unlike other sports, ice hockey developed towards professionalism already in the 1970s.

The chapter analyses the rise of Finnish ice hockey since the beginning of the 1960s. The focus is the process of professionalization. In a sports organization, the process of professionalization can be linked to either the sport itself and to the training, or to the administration of the organization and procurement of resources (Seippel 2010). Essential factors are the development of facilities, commercialization of the sport and the rise of its popularity, as well as the development of training and skills towards the Finnish way of playing. The development of Finnish ice hockey can be divided into three phases characterized by amateurism, half-professionalism and full professionalism (Mesikämmen 2002). The transfer from amateurism to half-professionalism occurred at the end of the 1960s in connection with the loosening of the international amateur regulations (cf. Billing, Franzén & Peterson 2004). The development towards full professionalism was gradual. Only in the 2000's, did all the main series of ice hockey begin to function as companies.

The choice of ice hockey as a success story of Finnish sport is based not only on its international success, but also on its position in the development of domestic sport. Traditionally the international success of Finnish top sport had come in individual sports, but since the 1990s success had dwindled. Ice hockey had been able to achieve continuous international success ever since the beginning of the 1990s. The growth of ice hockey in the 1960s and '70s coincided with major changes in the Finnish society. People moved to towns and learned to enjoy the rhythm of the industrial working and leisure hours. It is with this development that the growth in the popularity and professionalization of ice hockey can be connected. Increases in personal wealth and leisure made possible new habits of consumption. Ice hockey, as a hard and fast game of the towns fitted this image well (Mesikämmen 2002). In the 1990's, ice hockey grew to be the leading Finnish sport.

The chapter in organized as follows: The first part briefly describes the history of Finnish ice hockey and the success of the men's national team. The second part examines the development of Finnish ice hockey and the prerequisites of success before the actual breakthrough (years 1975 to 1988). The third part analyses the breakthrough of Finnish ice hockey and its golden era (1988 to 2001). The final part discusses the ups and downs as well as the challenges of Finnish professional ice hockey from 2001 and onwards. The chapter is mainly based on interviews of ice hockey experts and on existing studies.

A brief history of Finnish Ice Hockey

Ice hockey was developed in Canada in the 1870s, and the International Ice Hockey Federation(IIFH) was founded in 1908. The international competitions formed and spread fast, as the first European Championships were organized as early as in 1910; it became an Olympic sport in 1920, and the first World

Championships was held in 1930. In Europe, ice hockey was an amateur sport for a long time, whereas in the North America, professional series have a long tradition. This difference became important after the Second World War, when the Soviet Union and Czechoslovakia became the most successful ice hockey countries. Ice hockey became a sport of the 'cold war' – a symbol of the battle between the capitalistic and socialistic models of societies (Soares 2007). The supremacy of the socialist countries in ice hockey lasted till the beginning of the 1990s.

The disintegration of the Soviet Union and the transfer to professional sports confused the ice hockey world and new nations rose among the successful countries. Among these was Finland. Finland was not one of the pioneering countries of the sport. The game started in the city of Tampere in 1928, initiated by a Finnish engineer who had studied in Canada and later brought home some ice hockey sticks (Kaukalon Leijonat 1989: 9). At the beginning, ice hockey only took hold in a few larger cities of southern Finland. Tampere, Helsinki and Turku became the ice hockey centres where the development of the game took place more rapidly.

Ice hockey was first incorporated into the Finnish Skating Federation; speed-skating and figure skating were the sports of this Federation. The Football Federation also competed for ice hockey and organized the first Finnish Championship tournament in 1928. The same year, the first test match against Sweden was played. The competition between the federations was soon finished, as in 1929, the Finnish Ice Hockey Federation was founded. This stimulated the development of the sport. During the next decade, a Finnish Championship League (FCL) was started (1934). Another national level was formed beneath the FC-series, giving the winner a possibility to rise to the championship league. In addition to this, the federation organized camps for the national team at the Sports Institute of Finland. At the end of the decade, Finland also participated in its first World Championship, where it lost all five games. Only from the year 1957 did Finland participate regularly in the Olympic and WC-tournaments.

Ice hockey had to compete for a position in the Finnish sports culture. During the first half of the twentieth century, Finnish sport was concentrated in small communities in the countryside and it was dominated by individual sports. In winter sports, mainly cross-country skiing, ski jump and skating, the importance of the clubs in the countryside was greater than in summer sports. (Häyrinen & Laine 1989).The fact that the development of ice hockey developed in the cities turned out to be a winning tactic, as it happened at a time when the Finnish society became more urban. A first sign of this was when ice hockey passed bandy in popularity in the 1960s. The construction of artificial ice rinks and, a little later, ice hockey halls, contributed to this.

Football is the most popular game and biggest spectator sport of many nations. In Finland football is the biggest sport in terms of the number of amateur players, but its popularity as a spectator sport doesn't even come close to that of ice hockey. In 2010, ice hockey was clearly the most popular sport in Finland. Fourteen teams play in the professional league of Finnish ice hockey, the FC-league. During the 2009/2010 season the turnover of the owners of the FC-league was 80.9 million euros. The players' fees were about 30 million euros. The median pay of the players was 63,500 euros. The difference between the top-most series of ice hockey and the same level of football is big. The national football league, the Veikkausliiga, also has 14 teams. In the season of 2010 the turnover was less than 20 million euros. The median pay of the players was 21,000 euros.

After football and gymnastics, ice hockey is the third most popular sport of youngsters in Finland. 101,000 children and youngsters below the age of 18 play ice hockey; 93 per cent of them are boys. 51,000 children and youngsters play ice hockey in an organized way in clubs. This popularity is an important foundation for the competitiveness of ice hockey. So is the amount of training among the youngsters. As many as 71 per cent of children's or youngsters' club players train at least three times a week. In football, the corresponding figure is 47 per cent, and in athletics 20 per cent (Liikuntagallup, 2010).

Although Finland is not the most successful nation in ice hockey, the country has been one of the major powers of the game since the 1990's. In the seven Winter Olympic Games from 1988 to 2010, Finland has won five medals: two silver and three bronze. Finland has won two world championships, in the years 1995 and 2011, in addition six silver and three bronze medals. Finland's position in international ice hockey is reflected in the medal statistics of the World Championships. In the period of 1976 to 2011, 33 World Championships have been organised in total and 99 medals have been won. The most successful nation has been Sweden, with 23 medals. However, the disintegration of the East European countries at the beginning of the 1990's makes comparison difficult. Taken together, the number of medals by Czechoslovakia (13), the Czech Republic (10) and Slovakia (3) adds up to 25, a total which exceeds Sweden's. The total number of medals by the Soviet Union and Russia was 20. Canada won 14 medals, Finland 11, and the USA two medals. Finland won its first WC medal as late as in 1992. After that, Finland is the second with its 11 medals after Sweden (15 medals).

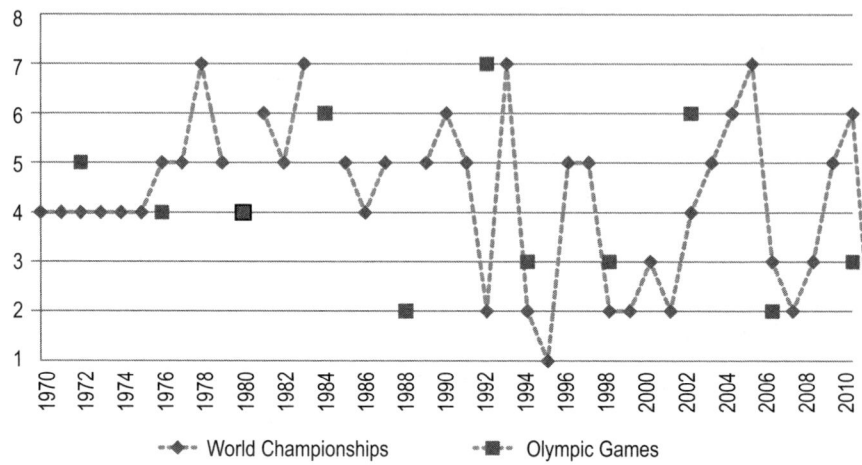

Figure 8.1: The ranking of the Finnish national team at the Winter Olympics and World Championships, 1970–2010

Ice hockey is a modern game where facilities and equipment are important. In North America, ice hockey has been an indoor game from the beginning. Also in Europe, the first indoor arenas were built at the beginning of the twentieth century. In Finland, the development of ice hockey started slowly and only speeded up at the end of 1950s with the building of artificial ice rinks. Such rinks improved the operating conditions of the Championship series. No longer did weather conditions cause cancellations of games as much as before and the number of games could be doubled.

The target of the next decade was to get an ice hockey stadium for Finland. The International Ice Hockey Federation granted the WC tournament to Finland for the year 1965, but on the condition of building a stadium. At the beginning, the idea was to organize the WC tournament in Helsinki, but the plans of the city and the timing of the WC tournament did not converge. Instead it was Tampere, the centre of Finnish ice hockey, that became the host of the WC tournament (Kaukalon Leijonat 1989: 40; Mennander & Mennander 2003). Although Finland was not successful in the tournament, the events attracted more than 200,000 spectators.

In Finland the municipalities have the main responsibility for building and maintaining sports facilities. The initiative for building sports facilities also always comes from the local level. Ice hockey halls were large investments and often the multipurpose use of them had to be negotiated, so that the demands of different sports could be accommodated under one roof (Nygren 1980; Mennander 1997). On the other hand, the strong development of the Finnish welfare state in the 1970s and 1980s made more extensive building of sports facilities possible. The investments by the state and the municipalities in sports facilities were multiplied during this period (Juppi 1995).

From 1975 the Ice Hockey Federation played an active role in the building of ice hockey stadiums. At the beginning of the 1970s, the building of ice hockey stadiums was argued from the point of view of competitive sports and their needs, but from the early 1980s the federation emphasized that halls should be built to support the activities of children and youngsters. The new strategy worked. In a welfare state perspective, this justification was considered more legitimate. Beside the competitive ice hockey stadiums of big cities, lighter practice ice hockey halls started to emerge. Halls were built in ever smaller communities.

The construction of ice hockey halls was decisive for the professionalization process of Finnish ice hockey (Mesikämmen 2002). The numbers of players increased. The license system describing the number of players was implemented by mid-1970s. At that time, there were about 20,000 ice hockey players, reaching 30,000 in 1982. Ice hockey became an indoor sport at the national level during the 1970s. The number of spectators increased and the indoor facilities offered better possibilities for commercialization of the supplementary activities. The players' shirts had got the first advertisements as early as during

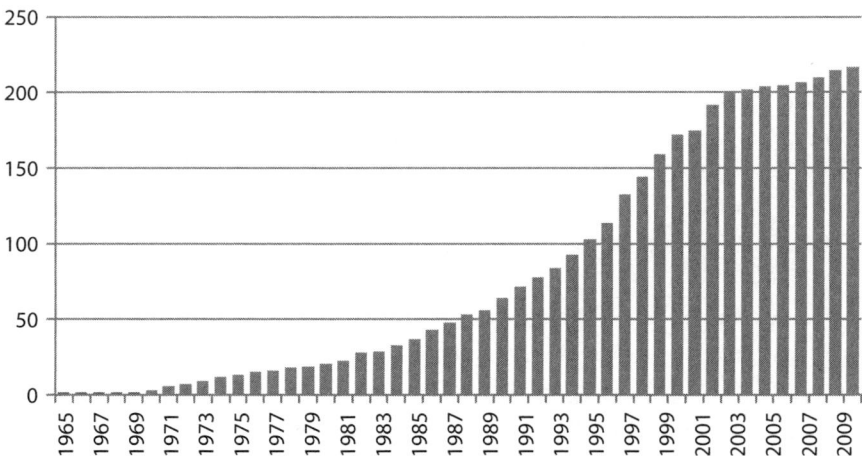

Figure 8.2: Building of ice hockey stadiums in Finland 1965–2010. (Source: The Finnish Ice Hockey Federation 2010)

the season of 1959 to 1960. Next advertisements spread to other equipment and to the sides of the rink, to the ice and to the stands. Parallel to this commercialization, the player fee system also developed. However, until the 1990s, these trends were based on bypassing the amateur regulations.

FC League and professionalization

Finnish ice hockey started to move from a leisure activity to a new phase in 1970's as the topmost series level became more professional. With the strict amateur regulations, the operations often occurred under double standards. The recruiting of players occurred under cover of studying or some other reason. The players were not officially paid. It was done 'under the table', or some teams played in the name of a certain company, and the players had a nominal work relationship to the factory (Kaukalon Leijonat 1989: 56).There were no models of professional ice hockey in Europe, since professionalism had only existed in Great Britain previously (Mesikämmen 2002: 110). When the Finnish Ice Hockey Federation started to support the professionalization of the sport by founding the FC League in the mid-1970s; the model was taken from the NHL.

The transfer to semi-professionalism in Finnish ice hockey started in 1970. The Montreal Urheilu Oy, which manufactured ice hockey sticks and equipment, rented the Tappara team of Tampere for three years. According to the contract, the company was responsible for the expenditure of the team, but it also got all the income. The project was met with widespread skepticism. Attempts to make money by the Tappara ice hockey team were generally condemned. The public image of Finnish sport was very heavily based on amateurism. However, these strict regulations were also bypassed in the case of Tappara. Montreal Urheilu paid the 25 players an annual fee of 5,000 to 7,000 euros (in 2010 value), ostensibly for advertising the Montreal ice hockey sticks. The tax authority also examined the operations, but could not find any wrong doing. So, it was a question of interpreting the rules of the sport itself (Wacklin 2005: 89–107).

The example from Tappara was not unique. Also in other cities, businessmen had invested money in the clubs. Still, in Tappara, the change was more comprehensive. It also covered training and marketing. A former top player was put in charge of the training. He systematized Finnish ice hockey training and made it more comprehensive. A model was sought particularly from athletics which had created a new success culture since the end of 1960s. The target was to win the Finnish Championship with their own players. This was done after a couple of seasons. Thanks to the new marketing ideas and the increase in popularity, the financial result of the team was also positive (Wacklin 2005: 108–113). Although the players became semi-professional in the 1970s, they officially maintained their amateur status. At the same time, more and more players got a side job in ice hockey.

The players that founded the Ice Hockey Players Association had the NHL player association as its model. The national team players and the Ice Hockey Federation had argued about the player fees for the games played at the national team. The best players in the country earned as much as 46,000 euros (in 2010 value) tax-free a year, in addition to the bonuses and subsistence allowances. As for instance the total duration of the WC tournament with camps was almost two months, the difference between the series team fees and national team fees was big. In 1973, attempts were made to correct this difference. The players were able to negotiate better fees for themselves, but at the same time, the federation made the rules of behaviour for the players during the tournaments stricter. The Players' association was the first European ice hockey organization for representation of players' interests which noted in its aims, for instance, representing the professional, social and sporting interests of its members. The association took quite a direct stand in favour of developing ice hockey as a professional sport (Kauhala et al. 2003, 16-18).

The Finnish Ice Hockey Federation had created the FCL already in 1975. The operation and administration of the League was planned on the basis of experiences gained from the earlier Serial Clubs and on the professional series in North America, mainly the National Hockey League. In Europe, there were no similar ice hockey series. The administrative model for the FC League was taken from the earlier federation. The play-offs system was copied from the NHL. The NHL transfer system was adapted to the Finnish context. The distance between the FC League and the Ice Hockey Federation was underlined by selecting Tampere for the domicile of the League administration instead of Helsinki (Kaukalon Leijonat 1989: 57).

Within a relatively short period of time ice hockey became the number one spectator sport in Finland. In the mid-1980s, the FC League had one million seasonal spectators. The game got more visibility in the media than before. The founding of local radio stations increased the local and regional fame, as in every league city, the games could be heard live on the radio (Mesikämmen 2002: 113). However, only in the 1990s could ice hockey make the first significant television contracts.

Training

From the 1960s onwards, the Finnish national team regularly participated in the Olympics and WC ice hockey tournaments. During almost the whole of the 1960s, the position as main coach for the national team was held by foreigners. The Canadians Joe Wirkkunen and Derek Holmes were followed by the Czechoslovakian Gustav Bubnik. From the Canadian coaches, the effective and simple ice practice and culture of making an effort were learned.

The NHL champion, Carl Brewer, brought a practical example of the Canadian way of playing; he was central in the club team Helsinki IFK as a player and trainer during the 1968-69 season. Just before Brewer arrived, Finnish ice hockey had allowed checking everywhere on the field. With the leadership of Brewer, HIFK learned to carry out the hard Canadian style of playing. Thanks to Brewer, Finnish ice hockey players obtained skills from and got contacts with the NHL (Kauhala et al. 2003: 15).

The Czechoslovakian Bubnik did important work in developing Finnish ice hockey. He combined so-called skilled ice hockey and systematic playing. In his coaching, the starting point was to develop individuals, but overall effort aimed improving the capacity of working together as a disciplined team. The reforms worked, and Finland beat Czechoslovakia in 1967 and Canada in 1968 for the first time on the WC level.

At the beginning of the next decade, Finland arrived at a crossroads. Contacts with Canada were good. The Soviet Union also gave know-how and skills. From Czechoslovakia came skillful coaches. Every year the national team went to Sweden for practice tournaments. Despite the development and new ideas, Finnish ice hockey was still far from a goal-oriented and systematic elite sport. The players were mainly amateurs. Their number of annual training hours were a third of those of the corresponding numbers in the major powers of the game. Information and international contacts, however, increased faith in the Finnish training model. This led to a number of initiatives.

Systematic research and analysis of ice hockey was initiated. By means of the analyses, information was obtained on the effects of training and playing. The exploitation of sport science research had already become more intense in the individual sports. At the beginning, the ice hockey coaches who had studied in Jyväskylä exploited the doctrines from individual sports. Many training methods were copied directly from, for instance, athletics, and at the same time physical training was stressed. Also systematic programming of training became a part of ice hockey training. Even individual training programs were made for the players. An ice hockey hall had been built in Vierumäki, at the Finnish Sports Institute in 1973. At the end of the decade, the Institute started systematic physical testing of players, videoing and game analyses.

Methods, know-how and analyses were developed mainly in Jyväskylä whereas Vierumäki formed a centre where things were tested, developed and applied to practice. For the Olympics of 1980, the Ice Hockey Federation had 25 players tested. 15 of them were seen to have complete physical prerequisites to play top ice hockey during a whole game. After the Games, it was seen that these players were successful in the tournament, whereas the players who were at a lower physical level failed. As late as in the 1980s, the tests were criticized, but as they developed clubs, coaches and players learned to exploit the tests in appropriate ways (Mennander & Mennander 2004: 177).

The Sports Institute had even earlier had an important role in the training of juniors. The Ice Hockey Federation had started the super camp activities in Vierumäki as early as in the 1950s. In the beginning, each of the 17 districts sent their own team to the camp. The Federation gathered the national junior teams for different age groups from the players of these teams (Mennander & Mennander 2003: 322). These camps gradually developed into the core of the junior training system of the Finnish top ice hockey. They were based on the joint camp of the best players of the age group, testing and national team operations of different age groups, as well as the development of coaches. The systematic testing operation started in the 1970s and made it possible to monitor and compare the characteristics of players.

The growth of information and know-how created a need for improved coach education, particularly after the founding of the FC League. The educational programmes developed as a cooperation between the different central confederations of sport and federations of separate sports in the 1960s mainly served the needs of lower series and juniors. Ice hockey participated actively in the development of these education systems. In the 1980s the professionalization of ice hockey coaches went further. By the mid-1980s, the top coach school became a requirement for coaching teams in FC League ans the 1st division. The school lasted for a year during which the coaches had five teaching periods. With this school, the know-how of coaches was improved, which had a significant impact on the culture of Finnish ice hockey training. The top coaches of Finland could be gathered around one table to discuss and develop the sport. Cooperation and a similar understanding of ice hockey were created among the coaches. The school formed a basis for the future development of Finnish ice hockey.

The international breakthrough of Finnish ice-hockey came at the end of the 1980s when the national team won the Olympic silver medal at the Calgary Winter Games. The success was mainly viewed as a result of improved physical training. In the preceding years the training hours had increased and the training had become more versatile. Improved skating skills were also a major focus and ice camps were held in the summer, too. The national team was regularly tested. The test results and the analyses based on them helped to screen and develop new top players, based on corresponding test results of other top players. Increased know-how was combined with professionalization of players, and many clubs hired professional physical trainers from the beginning of the 1990s. Also, the professionals abroad learned to train more effectively during the summer season.

The improved capacity of the Finnish players made it possible to challenge the other major ice hockey nations. An elite coach from the Soviet Union, Vladimir Jursinov, arrived in Finland at the beginning of the 1990s to coach a Finnish FC League team. His contribution was the personal skill development of players and he elevated the training culture to a new level. From the so-called Jursinov's school, many players were taken to the Finnish national team and to the NHL in the 1990s.

The most important success factor for the national team was, however, the development of the Finnish style of playing. From the 1960s, Finnish ice hockey had been subject to many foreign influences. The core of the Finnish style of playing started to crystallize in the 1980s. The analysis of ice hockey as a tactical game was developed at the University of Jyväskylä. Initially, football analysis was exploited, but fairly soon it was noticed that the games are quite different. In ice hockey, there is a small field which is clearly divided into areas. Also, changes of direction happens fast whereas in football there are more space and times to react.

Game analysis in Finland started according to the Canadian model, from the analysis of individuals. A comprehensive statistical model had been created around the work of the NHL players supporting the star cult of the professional sport. In Finland the team soon became the basis of the game analysis. One game was deconstructed into as many as 60,000 observations, and that game was analysed for as long as several months. It was noticed that 80 per cent of the attacks ended in failure. There were many attacks and they only last for a couple of seconds. As a result of the analysis, the conclusion was that the best and fastest attack was created by stealing the puck from the opponent by defending and directly turn towards an attack. This strategy became the brand of Finnish ice hockey in the 1990s. Analysts also studies how and where scoring situations originated both in the Finnish team and in the opponent teams. The coach had the analysis of the previous period available in the brake, and could exploit it to make tactical changes during the match.

The Finnish game analysis formed a strong competitive advantage during the 1990s. The game analysis helped break the myth that a Finnish team could never succeed because Finns are individualists. In the 1980s, the development of ice hockey had been based on improved individual training, but during the following decade, the Finnish ice hockey team was better organized than their opponents. The pieces of the puzzle fell into place in the WC tournament of Stockholm in 1995. Before that, Finland had won an Olympic silver medal in 1988 and Olympic bronze medal in 1994 as well as World Championship silvers in the years 1992 and 1994.

The Swede Curt Lindström was hired as head coach of the Finnish national team in 1993 and he led the team to an Olympic bronze medal and a WC silver medal in his very first year. Lindström succeeded in creating a unified team. He was able to eliminate all clans and cliques and generated a new kind of self-reliance in the players. In the 1995 WC tournament, Finland took its first victory by beating the host nation, Sweden, in the final. The significance of this victory in Finland was huge.

The final breakthrough of Finnish ice hockey coincided with many turning points in the wider society. When the East European socialist countries disintegrated and at the same time, their supremacy in international ice hockey was broken. There was room for new high-fliers in the field of international ice hockey. Finland took advantage of this. However, the success was also connected to national issues. As a result of the Eastern European collapse, Finland approached Western Europe and joined the European Union at the beginning of 1995. An economic depression and widespread social change had caused insecurity in the whole society. The World Championship in ice hockey was symbolically important. It attracted hundreds of thousands of Finns to celebrate spontaneously on the streets. A strong ice hockey ecstasy was felt in Finland, as the NHL lock-out brought many Finnish NHL stars to the FC League during the season of 1994 to 1995.

The World Championship crowned the determined work done for several decades. The central process was professionalization in various aspects of the term. Important steps were taken in the 1990s towards full-time players and commercialization. Helsingin Jokerit was the first Finnish ice hockey club to organize as a company. A few years later the club was bought by Hjallis Harkimo, who had become famous as an around-the-world sailor. As the owner of the club, Harkimo took his models from the NHL. He understood that to be successful as a business, ice hockey not only needs a good team, but also a stadium of its own by means of which it can create revenue to the owners. Jokerit was made into a brand with determination. This was done mainly with the lead of a young and talented player, Teemu Selänne. Media and charity campaigns brought results. Selänne became an incredibly popular player and Jokerit a brand name. The transfer of Selänne to the NHL in 1992 enforced the contacts of the owner of Jokerit to North America and made the selected direction of development stronger.

Finnish ice hockey stadium construction was elevated to a new level in the 1990s. A new multi-purpose stadium was built in Turku. It could be used for many different entertainment and sports purposes in addition to ice hockey. The hall in Turku cost 33 million euros of which the government paid 3.4 million euros. A bank from Turku bought the rights for the name of the hall. The Hartwall Arena completed in 1997 in Helsinki became a milestone of the new kind of hall concept. The Finnish Ice Hockey Federation wanted a new hall for the WC tournament of 1997. The cost was unprecedentedly high. The tournament brought a profit of 8.7 million euros (Mennander & Mennander 2003: 138-141). The concept of the Arena was inspired from North America, but developed further. After Helsinki, a similar hall has been built in several European cities, among others, Hamburg, Prague, Tallin, and Malmö. In the following years, the arenas became a Finnish export product.

In addition to the building of arenas, the professional operation of the ice hockey teams developed quickly. Almost all FC League teams had a full-time coach at the beginning of the 1980s. At the end of the decade, most of the players were also full-time professionals. As players saw ice hockey as a potential paid career, their attitude to playing and training became more serious. The Ice Hockey Federation profited from the WC tournaments organized in Finland. The first big success was the tournament of 1982 which brought in a profit of 3.7 million euros (in 2010 value). In 1991, the profit was 4.8 million euros, and in 1997 as much as 8.7 million euros. After this, the Ice Hockey Federation decided that tournament profits should be distributed directly to the clubs. In addition the national team has become a strong brand name and sponsorship object, and contributed to strengthen the Federation's financial situation.

The FC League of ice hockey turned itself first into a co-operative, and in the 2000-2001 season, into a limited company owned by the 13 league teams. At the same time, the League became a 'closed' series, from which no team dropped out for the three following seasons. This decision was, however, not an easy one. At least some strong actors would have wanted to invest in a European professional league in which the biggest Finnish clubs would have joined. Already in the 1990s ice hockey had been exposed to international competition, when the first players transferred to North America to play as professionals. In the 1980s, the transfer of players to North America was felt mainly as negative for the success of the Finnish national team. In the 1990s and especially after the so-called Bossman decision, the flow of players from Finland to abroad escalated (see figure 8.3). At the end of the 1990s, a transfer of more than 200 players abroad from Finland was registered. Traffic of players to Finland also increased, but not significantly. The lock-out of the NHL in the season 1994 to 1995 caused a clear peak in the player transfers.

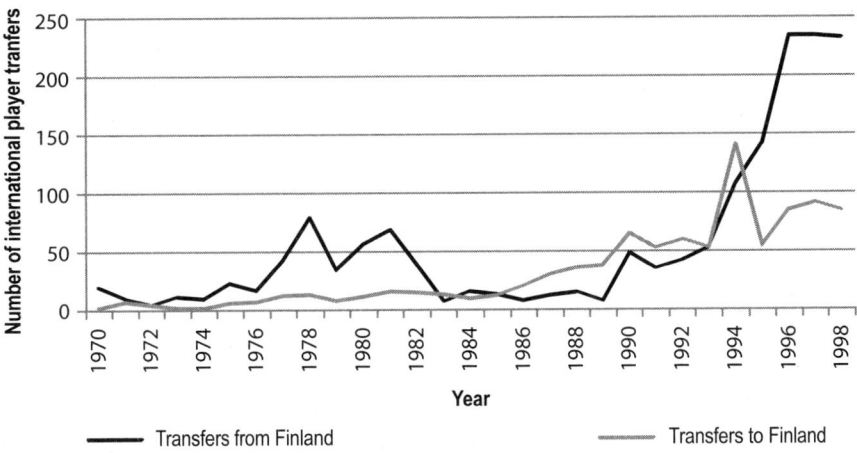

Figure 8.3: The number of international player transfers from and to Finland 1970–1998. (Source: Lämsä, J. 1998)

Future challenges of Finnish ice hockey

The success of Finnish ice hockey peaked in the years 1992 to 2001, when Finland won nine medals in the 13 highly valued tournaments. There has been success in the following decade, too. In the Olympics, Finland won medals in 2006 and 2010. Still, Finland was less successful than in the preceding decade, but in 2011 the Lions again won WC.

There are many reasons to ponder the future of the Finnish ice hockey. First of all, changed regulations of the sport have affected the Finnish style of playing, which has been based on strong defense and good goalkeeping. Many new, rising countries have also based their game on similar principles. The International Ice Hockey Federation has reacted to this development. They have made alterations in the rules enforcing the position of the attacker. For instance, disturbing with a stick is more easily punished, and the midfield offside has been eliminated. As a result of these alterations, Finland along with others, has to learn new style of playing which is no longer based on just fast change of direction and counter-attacks. Finnish ice hockey has been developed towards controlled attack.

Second, there has been an extensive public discussion on training and particularly on the relationship of the junior activities to the adults' top ice hockey. In 1987, a project specializing in the spontaneous sports activities of children and youngsters – Young Finland Association – was founded. All Finnish children and youngsters should have the right to do the sport that they like at the intensity that they like. According to the 'Everybody plays' ideology, early specialization and competition will lead more players to quit early. Those considering the matter from the point of view of top ice hockey claim that the Finnish junior activities have degenerated compared to the development of other countries just because of this excessively levelling training culture. Finnish ice hockey juniors are behind especially in playing skills.

The talent identification and development system of Finnish ice hockey is based on the planned camping and national team activities of the different age groups. The basic development of these talented ice hockey players is done in the clubs. The federation scouts for talented players. Through regional and national events the best players are selected for the national teams of different age groups. The best known event is the so-called Pohjola Camp. The annual event at the Finnish Sport Institute gathers the best 14 to 15 year-old players from different regions. The Pohjola Camp has a history of more than 50 years and all the time it has been a scouting camp. If a young player goes through all the phases of the system, he will have an experience of about 100 international games when he is 20 years old. From time to time, also in Finnish ice hockey, there has been discussion of founding so-called talent-hatcheries in the sport institutes. So far, these models have not been carried out.

Finally, it can be said that the rise of Finnish ice hockey has been a process in which the 'regularities of the big wheel' have led to international success. The factors influencing the rise have been the steady increase in the players and actors, increase of resources, and development of know-how. Professionalization, on the other hand, has been a process through which ice hockey has become separated from other Finnish sports. The decisions made by the sport in the 1970s anticipated the future correctly. Finnish ice hockey actors believed in success, although they had to wait several decades for it. In the end, the disintegration of the East European socialist countries gave the necessary space for the rise of Finnish ice hockey. In the 2000s, Finnish ice hockey has met new challenges, but so far, Finland has taken the role of fostering and developing a country of ice hockey. Finland can still produce good professional players and also refine their skills to team success.

9

The revival of Danish track cycling

Klaus Nielsen and Aage Hoffmann

Track cycling is an old sport in Denmark, with sustained sporting success for more than a century. In terms of active participants it has always been a minor sport, but Denmark has still maintained a position among the best track cycling nations in the world. The sport has had a prominent place in the public attention. However, from the 1980s and onwards the Danish international position was challenged. One important reason was the increased number of track cycling events in the Olympic Games. This significantly sharpened the international competition in the field. Another reason was the problems with basic facilities in Denmark. The Danish cycling tracks were of substandard quality, and Denmark also fell behind in relation to facilities, technology and funding. Danish results deteriorated significantly in the 1990s. From 2000 Denmark was without a single cycle track for a period lasting more than four years, and things went from bad to worse. Danish track cycling was declared dead and buried as an elite sport.

However, after a period of almost complete absence at the top international level, Danish track cycling has rapidly regained its position as one of the Danish sports that consistently wins medals in the Olympic Games and World Championships. This revival is the result of a strong emphasis on coaching, technology and optimization of support from the Danish elite sports institution, Team Denmark. It also reflects a successful niche strategy, with clear priority of some of the Endurance events in track cycling. This is indeed a success story. It is even seen as a case of best practice according to Team Denmark. Important lessons can be learned from this case in relation to the role of strategy, prioritization and optimization of efforts to make the best out of scarce resources.

The aim of this chapter is to look in detail at the recent renaissance of Danish track cycling. However, we will also look at the century-long history of sustained success preceding the decline in the 1990s. The chapter is structured in the following way. First, the international competiveness of Danish track cycling will be documented through a historical review of results at the Olympic Games and the annual World Championships. This is followed by an analysis of the reasons for the sustained position among the best track cycling nations in the world. The next section provides a detailed account of the successful recent efforts to re-launch Danish track cycling as a medal winning Olympic sport. Then follows a section that discusses the reasons for this success by reference to the literature on comparative elite sport development and critical success factors. The final section outlines the future challenges and the lessons to be learned.

The chapter is partly based on secondary data. These include books and articles from journals and newspapers supplemented by data from archives and prior knowledge of the authors who have a long-time interest in and affiliation with cycle sport. However, the main source of data about the recent development, in particular, was collected through eleven in-depth interviews with managers, coaches, athletes and other experts.[1] The interviews were conducted in March/April 2010, and transcribed and analysed by means of generic methods for data reduction and data display (Lee and Lings 2008: 240–250). In this chapter the evidence will only to a modest degree be documented by means of citations, figures and text references. We have given priority to the presentation of a narrative, of which there is a general consensus among the core individuals involved without explicit citations from interviews. It will be noted explicitly in the few instances when there are divergent views and interpretations among the central participants in the process.

---

1 The following persons were interviewed: Lars Bonde (sports director [and national coach since March 2011], DCU, Danish Cycling Federation); Sven Meyer (national coach [until March 2011], DCU); Ole Kjeldsen (sports director, Dansk Bicycle Club); Henrik Elmgreen (president of the pro-track organizers organizations, UIV, and authors of several books on track cycling); Michael Andersen (executive director, Team Danmark); Michael Elleberg Pedersen (consultant, Team Danmark); Bo Overgaard (former consultant, Team Danmark); Mogens Jacobsen (journalist, Dagbladet Politiken); Michael Mørkøv, Niki Byrgesen and Rasmus Quade (Danish elite track cyclists). Each interview lasted approximately one hour.

Results in the Olympic Games and World Championships

Next to sailing, cycling is the sport where Denmark has won most medals in the Olympic Games. Out of 172 medals in total, cycling has won 22 (sailing has won 26 medals). Road cyclists have won their share, but most of the medals have been won on the track (15 in total). Furthermore, track cycling has won medals consistently since the early days of the Olympic Games (see table 9.1).

Table 9.1: Danish track cycling medals in the Olympic Games

Olympic Games	Gold	Silver	Bronze
1924		1	
1928	1		1
1932			1
1948			1
1964			1
1968	1	2	
1972	1		
1976			1
1980			1
1988	1		
1992			1
2008		1	
Total	4	4	7

Track cycling was one of the first sports that initiated annual World Championships with an inaugural event organized in Chicago in 1893. Danish cyclists won medals in three of the five first championships. Since then Denmark has consistently won medals at the World Championships (see table 9.2). However, three periods stand out as 'golden ages' for Danish track cycling.

The first Golden Age is associated with one of the all-time greatest Danish athletes. Thorvald Ellegaard won six professional Sprint titles (and four silver medals) in the period 1901–1913. This happened in an era when cycling was a major sport and professional Sprint was by far the most prestigious discipline. Thorvald Ellegaard was one of the most renowned international sports personalities before the First World War and he was able to maintain his dominant position for more than a decade. The second Golden Age was in the late 1920s and the early 1930s where cycling was by far the most successful Danish sports in international competitions. In the period 1927–1932, in total 10 medals were won in Olympics Games and World Championships. Willy Falck Hansen was one of the most prominent cyclists with a profile almost as prominent as Ellegaard's. The third Golden Age was in the 1960s and the early 1970s where Denmark was one of the best nations in the world track cycling championships almost every year. The Danish Pursuit team won the gold medal at the 1968 Olympics. Niels Fredborg, Mogens Frey Jensen and Peder Pedersen won several medals each, but the Danish prominence was broadly based and many athletes contributed to the strong overall performance.

Table 9.2: Danish track cycling medals at World Championships 1893–2010

Period	Gold	Silver	Bronze
1983–1900	1	2	2
1901–1913	6	4	2
1919–1930	2	2	2
1931–1939	2	1	2
1946–1950	1	3	2
1951–1960	0	1	2
1961–1970	4	4	3
1971–1980	2	3	0
1981–1990	5	5	8
1991–2000	1	4	3
2001–2010	4	4	2
Total	28	33	28

Denmark continued to win medals at almost all Olympic Games and World Championships until the mid-1990s. In the period 1964–1992, Danish track cyclists won medals in all Olympic Games apart from 1984. In the period 1980–1994, Denmark failed only once to win medals at the annual World Championships. This gives the impression of a sustained position in the very top of the international track cycling hierarchy. However, this is to some extent an illusion. The results represent a relative decline compared to the third Golden Age.

There are three reasons for this decline. First, one cyclist (Hans Henrik Ørsted) won a third (9 of 28) of all medals won in the period 1977–1994, so the medal tally reflects exceptional individual talent rather than broad-based excellence. Second, more than half of the medals were won by professional cyclists in a period when the level of competition among the professionals was relatively low. Third, the number of track cycling disciplines in both the Olympics and in the annual World Championships has expanded quite a lot in the last decades. Until 1964, there were only four disciplines at the Olympic programme. The number of disciplines had increased to 12 in 2000. At the World Championships a similar increase in number of disciplines and medal sets has happened. Until 1946, there were only four disciplines, and then until 1962 only six. Now, there are 19 disciplines. This means that the same number of medals reflects a decrease in the share of medals and accordingly a lower international competitiveness.

Then, in the decade 1995–2004 Denmark only won two medals. In the Olympic Games in 2000, Denmark only qualified in the Madison discipline, and in 2004 there was not a single Danish cyclist who qualified for the games. However, a remarkable resurgence occurred in the late 2000s. Since 2007, the Danish medal tally is as good as it has ever been. In the period 2007–2010, Danish track cyclists won 10 medals in total (3 gold, 5 silver and 2 bronze) Actually, Danish track cycling has never been as successful at any World Championships as in 2009 in Poland. The number of medals has never been higher – apart from the championships at home track in 1921.

The most important and significant success was achieved in the Team Pursuit discipline where Denmark won an Olympic silver medal in 2008 and medals at three consecutive World Championships culminating with the title in 2009. This is significant because this discipline is characterized by a very high level of international competition. It requires a broad base of at least five to six athletes at the top level rather than merely one top athlete as in the individual disciplines. Success in Team Pursuit is never coincidental, as it may be in other Endurance disciplines, but almost always a direct reflection of performance levels. Furthermore, it is also significant because success in this discipline has spillover effects on competitiveness in other Endurance disciplines such as Points race, Madison and Scratch. Actually, all the other medals since 2007 were won in these disciplines.

The recent success is partly the result of a deliberate niche strategy by Danish track cycling officials. The Danish Cycling Federation (DCU) has, in close cooperation with Team Denmark, given exclusive preference to the Team Pursuit project with its perceived spillover effects and has totally ignored the Sprint disciplines and the Individual Pursuit. However, this also reflects a long-term development trend. Sprint is the discipline where Denmark has won most medals (35 out of 105 medals in total). A further 11 medals have been won in other Sprint disciplines (1 km time trial, Keirin and Tandem). However, the last medal in a Sprint discipline was won in 1980. Since then, Denmark has not at all been competitive in the Sprint disciplines. All Danish medals after 1980 have been won in Endurance disciplines.

Denmark has also consistently won medals at the junior level. There have been organized track Junior World Championships since 1975 (see table 9.3). Danish results have improved significantly in recent years also at the junior level with several medals at the last two Junior World Championships. More than a fourth of all Danish medals in Junior World Championships have been won in 2009 and 2010. This demonstrates the broad based character of the recent revival of Danish track cycling, with a well-functioning recruitment of talents leading to excellence in the junior ranks in addition to a strong senior elite.

Tabel 3: Danish track cycling medals at Junior World Championships 1975–2010

Year	Gold	Silver	Bronze
1976		1	
1981–1986	1	2	5
1996–1998			3
2002			1
2006	1		
2009	1	1	1
2010	2		
Total	5	4	10

Three of the Danish track cycling medals (two senior, one junior) since 2007 were won by female cyclists (all in Points race). This is highly unusual. Apart from a single bronze medal at the 2002 Junior World Championships, no female Danish track cyclist has ever won medals in World Championships. This reflects the fact that female track cycling has never been strong in Denmark. Probably the recent success is a transient phenomenon. The two cyclists who won medals in 2007 and 2008 are no longer active in track cycling. There are only a very small number of Danish elite female cyclists and the best current riders are very far from the international track elite. The competitiveness of Danish track cycling is exclusively based on strength in the Endurance disciplines and only the male cyclists are competitive.

International track cycling was traditionally dominated by a relatively small number of Western European nations led by Italy and France. In recent decades, a large number of nations have invested far more resources than previously in track cycling success. This is partly a result of the increase in track cycling disciplines at the Olympics and the competitions have increased significantly. However, a few nations still win the majority of medals. Great Britain, Australia, France and Germany are the most successful nations. In the Olympic Games in 2008, Great Britain was the absolute super power in track cycling. Recent results indicate that Australia has taken over as the nation winning most medals. This is not surprising considering the strong long-term dominance of Australian athletes in the Junior World Championships.

A second tier consists of countries such as Holland, Russia, New Zealand, USA, Ukraine, Spain and, recently, also Denmark, whereas Italian track cycling has declined significantly in recent decades. Other countries win medals now and then, but this is a result of infrequent emergence of exceptional talents rather than consistent success based on strong systemic efforts. The other Nordic countries have no history of international success in track cycling, apart from the unique examples of Norway's Knut Knudsen who won Individual Pursuit gold medals in the Olympic Games and World Championships in the early 1970s.

Explanations for the long-term history of sustained success
From the early days of international track cycling competitions, from the late 1890s until the mid-1990s, Danish elite track cyclists consistently performed among the top nations in the world. There are several reasons for this.

One of the reasons is the unique role of cycling in Danish society in general. Cycling is a predominant means of transport in Denmark. Foreign visitors to Copenhagen are stunned by the extensive system of cycle lanes, the number of cyclists and the relative power of cyclists compared to other road users in urban space. The popularity of cycle sports is linked to this active cycle culture. Historically, this has resulted in a relatively high level of participation in cycle sports compared to other countries. The predominant position of cycling as a spectator sport with strong media interest is no doubt also linked to the strong tradition and culture of cycling in the Danish society. Cycling is the third most popular television-sport after football and handball in terms of both transmission time and viewing figures (Hedal 2006). Also the written media have traditionally had much focus on cycling as one of the major Danish sports. Media interest attracts money and, in the last decades, significant sponsor interest. Historically, the media have not only generated interest in cycle sports through their focus on top cycling competitions; they have also directly contributed to the recruitment of talent by organizing events such as 'Cycling for the Young'. These races for youngster with no prior experience of cycle racing were accompanied by significant media attention.

Cycle sport has also been part of the entertainment culture in Denmark. Since the 1930s, six-day races on temporary winter tracks have been a popular part of the entertainment scene and the night life in Copenhagen, and in some years also in Aarhus and Herning. A number of pairs compete in a competition lasting six days. Traditionally, this took the form of extreme Endurance contests. Nowadays it consists of a range of short separate races mixed with live music and other forms of entertainment. Although their significance as sporting contests is limited, the six-day races and other races on winter tracks have contributed significantly to the popularity of cycle sports and the recruitment of new talent.

Track cycling is not a sport with mass participation. This is partly due to the limited availability of cycle tracks. Furthermore, everyone who has experienced the challenges of negotiating the steep curves of a modern velodrome will know that this is not a sport for everyone. Road racing is far more accessible and there are far more active road cyclists. However, track cycling and road cycling are closely linked. It requires a certain level of specialization to become competitive at the top level on the track, but it is not only possible to combine track cycling with road racing. It is also a big advantage or even a precondition for track cyclists in Endurance disciplines to build capacity through participation in road racing competition. There are also many examples of road cyclists who transfer to the track or are able to combine the two forms of competitive cycling.

Conflicts and tensions in the relationships between track cycling and road cycling at the elite level will be discussed later. However, in this context it is important to note that Danish track cycling has thrived from a strong road racing culture in Denmark. Road racing has provided an invaluable talent pool for track cycling, and the popularity of road cycling has had positive effects on track cycling, and vice versa. For instance, the six-day races significantly strengthened the recruitment of road cyclists. On the other hand, the popularity of the Tour de France and other major road races have benefitted track cycling as well. Danish road racing has always had a good international level. An exceptionally talented generation of Danish road cyclists, with Bjarne Riis,

Rolf Sørensen and others, reached their peak in the decade from the late 1980s. This raised the profile of cycling significantly in the Danish public which is reflected in the increased exposure of professional road racing in Danish television and the high viewing figures for the Tour de France, in particular.

Road racing is popular in the other Nordic countries as well although it has never attained such a high profile in the national elite sport hierarchy as in Denmark. Track cycling, on the other hand, is in the Nordic context a unique Danish phenomenon. There are no international cycle tracks in Sweden, Norway and Finland. There is no tradition for track cycling, and historically there have been very few participants from the other Nordic countries in international track competitions. Interestingly, this is not because track cycling never existed in Sweden, Norway and Finland. In the early days of competitive cycling there were several cycle tracks in the other Nordic countries and regular Nordic championships in track cycling were organized before the First World War. However, track cycling only survived in Denmark. There was a brief attempt to re-establish track cycling as an elite sport in Norway in the early 1990s prompted by the hosting of the World Championships in 1993 on a temporary cycle track in the Olympic speed skating rink in Hamar, but the plans were abandoned shortly afterward.

The reason why track cycling survived and prospered in Denmark whereas it died and apparently cannot be revived in the other Nordic countries is partly the strong active cycle culture in Denmark. Longer distances have necessitated the use of other means of transport and cycling has never been as popular in the other Nordic countries as in Denmark. Probably, the strong winter sports culture in the other Nordic countries has also crowded out some of the space for cycling as a predominant sport. However, there are other reasons for the divergent development related to specific events in the early days of competitive cycling. In Denmark, the high profile of Thorvald Ellegaard is considered to have had important impacts on Danish track cycling in terms of media attention, attendance and economic resources (Elmgreen 2000). The celebrity professional sprinter also contributed to giving Denmark a central position in international track cycling.

The so-called totalizator betting is seen as another major reason for the strong tradition of Danish track cycling. This was introduced already in 1888 when the pioneers of Danish track cycling decided to copy the forms of betting used on horse racing tracks. This is a unique Danish phenomenon unknown in other countries apart from Japan where the Danish system of totalizator betting was copied in the 1950s. The betting system became a successful and stable business which provided Danish track cycling with an important source of revenue. Dansk Bicycle Club (DBC), who owned Ordrupbanen and organized track competitions and totalizator betting in Copenhagen, became one of the richest organizations in Danish elite sports. This made it possible for them to award significant monetary prizes. It also prompted organizational discipline and far more competition days than in other countries (more than 50 days of competition during the season lasting only from April to September). Problems emerged in terms of incentives for collusion as well as a practice of organizing many relatively short races with many participants. The latter is better suited for betting than the type of races which maximize the competitiveness of the elite in international championships. The commercial operation linked to one track also contributed to an organizational structure similar to a kingdom, with a powerful and affluent county with a lot of conflicts of interest between the Danish Cycle Federation and the formally subordinate but often more powerful DBC.

Finally, another factor explaining the long-term success of Danish track cycling is its embedded culture of excellence. Competitive cycling leaves no space for participants who are not fully committed. Not every active cyclist is at the elite level in terms of performance, but almost all participants train as if they are. Everybody trains hard and there are few conflicts between the interests of elite sports and mass sport. Cycling, and in particular track cycling, has always been almost unambiguously focused on the interests of the elite.

The revival – how did it happen?

The international competitiveness of the Danish track cycling elite deteriorated gradually from the 1980s and from the mid-1990s it was in free fall. The decline was caused by several factors. From the 1980s, track cycling had become a far more technology-intensive sport, and Denmark was falling behind in that respect. Until then a competition bike had been standardised and not changed much for decades. However, the UCI (the international cycling federation) opened up for innovation, which initiated a hitherto unseen race to improve design and materials. The most well known innovation is the bizarre, homemade track cycle built by the Scottish Individual Pursuit world champion, Graham Obree. He used material from various sources including a washing machine. However, the gradual improvement of the bikes – aerodynamic, carbon-fibre and scientifically tested piece-by-piece – had far more long-lasting impacts. In the 1990s, the UCI introduced limits to the technological innovation and the present improvements are more gradual; but innovation as a source of competitive advantage is still highly important within track cycling. Riders without access to the newest bikes and equipment are strongly disadvantaged, and in competitions where small margins are often decisive even small advantages in terms of material may decide the outcome. Danish track cycling was relative late in adapting to the new trends.

Another new development was the UCI's decision to transform track cycling from a summer sport to a winter sport. The calendar was revised. World Cups and World Championships were rescheduled to the winter season, and all major competitions were to take place on 250 m wooden indoor tracks instead of the traditional open outdoor tracks. The three traditional Danish outdoor tracks made of concrete had for some time suffered from decay and lack of investment. Now they became at one stroke completely outdated. Denmark had no permanent indoor cycle track and for some years there were no realistic plans for building such a track.

The situation changed in the late 1990s. The DBC decided to close Ordrupbanen and sell off the area for property development. The revenue from the sale and the DBC's accumulated capital were then invested in the construction of a new modern indoor velodrome. The new track was located in Ballerup (a suburb of Copenhagen, 20 km west of the city centre) with support of the local mayor who was then also chairman of the board of Team Denmark. The track was ready for use in December 2001 which was 13 months after the closure of Ordrupbanen. The new track got a good start, but the further decline of Danish track cycling as a result of the period without a track was evident. The World Championships were successfully organized in the Ballerup arena in October 2002 but the performance of the Danish riders was very poor. The Danish participants ended among the last in the few competitions they took part in. The Pursuit team ended last of all in a time (4:23 min) that was more than 20 seconds slower than the winning time.

Optimists saw this as the nadir from where only improvements were possible, but they were wrong. On 3 January 2003 disaster struck. The roof of the new velodrome collapsed as a result of a miscalculation in design. The entrepreneur refused to accept responsibility and engaged in a lengthy battle with the owners of the track about the liability issue. The legal battle ended with an out-of-court settlement. Little is publicly known about the character of the settlement because of the inherent pledge of secrecy. However, a new roof supported by cables was built, the DBC lost all its capital, and the local municipality became the new owner. The velodrome was reopened in January 2005 more than two years after the collapse. Meanwhile, the Danish track cycling elite barely survived. Some trained occasionally on a medium quality track in Frankfurt (Oder) and a few riders took part in six-day races in other European countries. The majority concentrated on road racing instead. The most important impact was lack of recruitment of new track cycling talent in the period of more than three years without a track.

However, the reopening of the track proved to be a new beginning. Now, the basic facility, the track, was of a quality that was second-to-none. Next followed the strategy. The DCU saw the potential in the form of raw talent, and in early 2005 an elaborate strategy was fleshed out in close cooperation with Team Denmark: the Team Pursuit project. The plan was to transform the Pursuit team into medal winners in the Olympics 2008. This was a tall order. In the interviews conducted for this article the initiators of the strategy recount how difficult it was to convince the riders that it was a realistic project. The aim was to improve on the Spanish bronze medal winners' time from Beijing 2004 (4:05 min). The DCU and Team Denmark considered this possible with the right support, but it was hard to believe for the riders who in the World Championships in March 2005 ended as the ninth best team, eight seconds slower than the bronze medal winners. It required some motivational efforts to convince the riders to focus fully on the project. The DCU and Team Denmark made it clear that they were willing to commit the necessary resources. The highly successful Danish lightweight four rowing team were used as inspiration. The riders were won over and their full dedication to the project is part of the explanation for its success.

Of course, it was crucial that the project was actually implemented in the intended way, with the necessary support and investment of resources. This process consisted of at least three important elements. The first was the acquisition of top quality cycles, equipment and other facilities. Prior to this investment the Danish team had used the cast-off bicycles of the Russian track cycling team. The newly acquired bicycles, in contrast, were of the best quality available. In all the 20 new bicycles, the so-called SRM system was installed. The system measures in watts the power transferred to the bicycle by its rider. It is one of the instruments used for performance analysis which have become an increasingly important factor in the efforts to ensure marginal improvements.

The second main element in the implementation of the project was the appointment of the experienced German coach Heiko Salzwedel as Danish track cycling coach in 2005. He originates from the former GDR and had earlier been highly successful as coach and team manager for the Australian and British track cycling teams. The new coach was committed, hands-on, uncompromising and authoritarian in his approach. He introduced a new regime with extreme demands in terms of training intensity, hitherto unseen attention to detail, and zero tolerance for anything less of full dedication. He was in-your-face and not afraid of creating problems. He rather saw problems as a means to move the project forward. This was an approach far from the normal democratic and participatory Danish approach. No dissent was accepted. The relationship with the riders was characterized by on-going tension and frequent problems. The sports director of DCU and the Team Denmark consultant with responsibility for cycling were frequently acting as mediators and problem solvers. However, the tensions were contained. Evident improvement of performance made the riders believe that the project would be successful and worth the efforts and ordeals.

A third important element in the implementation of the project was the increased transfer of financial resources from Team Denmark to the DCU. The support increased from 148,000 euros in 2003 to 480,000 euros in 2009. This allowed for a system consisting of full-time coaches, payments to athletes, systematic talent development, continuous upgrading of material and facilities, and serious participation in the ongoing efforts to achieve marginal improvements through novel training methods, performance analysis, dieting, etcetera. These factors will be discussed in more detail below.

The project quickly proved to be successful. In the World Championships in 2006 the Danish team was no better than no. 10, but they won the bronze medals already the year after. In 2008, the team won silver medals at both the World Championships and the Olympics. The year after, Denmark became world champions in Team Pursuit in a time (3:58) that was almost half a minute faster than the time of the Danish team achieved seven years earlier. This is an improvement seldom seen in top sports. It is equivalent of running a marathon 20 minutes faster or swimming the 100 m crawl seven seconds faster. Furthermore, in the years 2007–2009 the Team Pursuit project also had the intended derived effects in the form of medals in other Endurance disciplines.

The project had succeeded beyond expectations. It even survived the disruption on the coaching side. The engagement with Heiko Salzwedel was ended after the Olympics. The tensions and conflicts in his relationships with the riders could no longer be contained and Salzwedel's assistant coach Sven Meier was promoted to national coach. This was a remarkable shift in type of coaching and management style. Sven Meier was only 23 years old. He did not have the natural aura of authority of his predecessor. He had no prior experience of coaching, and his expertise was exclusively within the area of computer-based performance analysis. Anyway, the successes in the 2009 World Championships took place while he was the coach. The successful trend continued despite, or perhaps because of, a radical change in terms of coaching practice.

What explains international elite sport success in general?

In the next section we will elaborate on the explanations for the recent revival of Danish track cycling. We will discuss this by reference to the research literature explaining international sporting success. This section briefly reviews a few central contributions and outlines the conceptual framework which will be applied in the next section.

De Bosscher et al. (2008) distinguish factors explaining international sporting success located at the macro, meso or micro levels, respectively. There are macro level factors such as the social and cultural context that cannot be influenced by sport policy. An important micro factor is the talent pool including the genetically based capabilities of athletes. Other micro factors are the willingness to do what is required to become successful in elite sport and the influence of parents, friends and coaches. These factors can only be influenced to a modest degree, if at all. The factors that can be influenced by sport policy are located at the meso-level. These factors include financial support, participation in sport, scientific research, talent identification and development systems, athletic and post-career support, integrated approach to policy development, coaching provision and coach development, international competition and training facilities (De Bosscher et al. 2008).

Green and Houlihan (2005) have contributed two central books to the literature on international elite sport success. They identify four main factors contributing to elite success: support for full-time athletes; elite facility development; the provision of coaching, sports science and sports medicine support services; and a hierarchy of competition opportunities centred on preparation for international events. The same authors integrate these factors with factors listed in other contributions, including De Bosscher (2008) in a general conceptual framework consisting of a set of contextual, processual and specific factors (Houlihan & Green 2008: 4). In addition to the factors listed above, the following factors are included: an excellence culture, a media-supported positive sports culture, clear understanding of the role of different agencies, simplicity of administration, effective system for monitoring athlete progress, comprehensive planning system for each sport and lifestyle support.

What explains the revival of Danish track cycling?

The revival is of course partly based on the factors behind the long-term Danish success in track cycling. Factors such as strong tradition and a culture conducive to (track) cycling excellence are built over long periods or arise as bi-products of other societal phenomena. These factors can be seen as macro factors (De Bosscher et al. 2008). They are not depleted overnight even under adversarial circumstances such as a three year period without a track. The revival in the late 2000s can to some extent be seen as a return to normality. However, the revival breaks with a trend of gradual decline over two decades which cannot be explained by such macro factors. The revival can also to some extent be ascribed to micro factors in the form of an exceptionally talented group of athletes, in particular Alex Rasmussen, who has won three World Championships in other track disciplines (Scratch and Madison) in addition to the 2009 Team Pursuit title. However, the broad-based character of the revival, including the strong improvement of the international standing of Danish track cycling at the junior level, cannot be explained by such factors. It is evident that the factor explaining the speed and depth of the revival are largely located at the meso level. The most relevant factors primarily derived from the brief literature review in the preceding section are outlined below.

Financial support: Financial resources are no guarantee for sporting success. However, availability of the necessary financial means is a basic precondition for provision of many of the other factors explaining success as listed below. The evidence shows that the financial support of Danish track cycling has expanded significantly. Furthermore, it has been protected from the cuts in transfers from Team Denmark suffered by other sports as a result of diminishing government support for Team Denmark from 2009. Actually, cycling was the only sport that experienced an increase in financial support in 2009. Furthermore, track cycling was able to benefit from the new scheme for special support for projects aimed at strengthening the preparations for the 2012 Olympics. Two projects were supported: the establishment of a wind tunnel set-up for testing and aerodynamic improvement, and strengthening of existing advanced set-up for performance analysis. The support is still dwarfed by the financial resources available to principal competitors. The Australian budget for the junior track team alone is higher than the total Danish elite sport budget. Moreover, the available resources for the Danish track elite is less than a tenth of the budget of the British track cycling team (7.3 million euros). Still, the increased resources in Danish track cycling has made success possible with an efficient use of the available means in a niche strategy with exclusive focus on a few Endurance disciplines.

Elite facility development: The emergence of the Ballerup velodrome is one of the fundamental preconditions for the revival. The arena is of the highest quality at a level with the main UK velodrome in Manchester. A single track is still a relatively weak foundation. For comparison, there are more than 30 velodromes in the greater Melbourne area alone. The effect is that Danish track cycling has a basis only in and around the capital. This has partly been compensated by dedicated track cyclists frequently travelling to Ballerup for regular training sessions. However, it would improve the situation significantly if new tracks were established in the western part of Denmark. The building of new tracks is being discussed in Aarhus and (more realistically) in Odense, but the credit crunch has postponed the plans into an uncertain future.

Other important facilities in track cycling include the bikes, helmets, skinsuits, etc. There is a general consensus among the interviewees that these facilities are up to the very best standard for the Danish track elite. One of the Team Pursuit world champions compared the situation in 2010 with the situation five years earlier at the start of the project: 'It is far more professional now. It is similar to a professional road racing team where all the soigneurs, equipment and mechanics you need are available' (Jepsen, 2010). However, there is still some way to go to get to the level of the UK track cycling team. It has means for perfection in every domain from an obscure nut on a front wheel to computer-modelled prototypes for testing in a wind tunnel, using a model cyclist with movable legs (Fotheringham 2008a, 2008b).

Support for full-time athletes: Team Denmark introduced a basic payment to members of the national track team. In the beginning it was relatively modest (550 euros per months during the winter season). The amount has increased, but it still needs to be supplemented with other forms of income to make full-time focus on cycling possible. Most of the riders are also members of professional road racing teams. Although this has to be of secondary priority to being part of the track team, it makes full-time focus possible. Other riders earn supplementary income from relatively lucrative contracts for six-day races. Some of the younger members of the team are still living with their parents who contribute money and other resources in support of their cycling career. The basic payment from Team Denmark is modest compared to the support schemes among some of the competitors. In Denmark, the support is basically 'a security net for those who did not have (lucrative) contracts from road racing teams and six-day races'. Anyway, the payment has probably had a crucial impact. Without it the full-time dedication for a relatively long-lasting effort such as the Team Pursuit project would not have been possible.

Coaching provision, coach development and training methods: Top quality coaching was considered a crucial element in the Team Pursuit project from the very start. Team Denmark had to struggle with the sports federations for years to enhance professionalism in both administration and coaching, and full-time sports directors (sometimes called performance directors) and a co-ordinated structure of full-time coaches were conditions for support to federations. This was quickly put into effect in the DCU with a number of full-time coaches at different levels in a coordinated structure with a unified coaching practice guided by long-term strategic goals.

The role of the national team coach is of course central and the engagement of the experienced German coach Heiko Salzwedel was no doubt a crucial factor behind the success of the project. Under the Salzwedel regime new methods of training were introduced. Extreme quantity in terms of training passes lasting eight to nine hours was coupled with high intensity training at high altitude. Training camps lasting three weeks experimented with combinations of high and low altitude staying and training. Salzwedel was no doubt one of the very best coaches around. Despite tensions and conflicts with the riders it worked extremely well for a period of more than three years.

The new coach Sven Meyer was also the best possible coach available within his more narrow area of expertise. His area is computer-based performance analysis. The new coach was partly chosen by the experienced members of the Olympic Pursuit team. The logic seemed to be that the team was considered to be sufficiently self-motivated and knowledgeable to manage the whole project themselves. They needed no authoritarian coach to tell them what to do. What they felt they needed was the unique competence of Sven Meyer who would contribute the additional marginal advantage compared to the competitors.

At the 2009 World Championships he made an important, controversial and ultimately highly successful decision. After the preliminary time trial, where Denmark was only second best, he challenged the hierarchy of the team by substituting one of the most established members of the team with a less experienced substitute based on performance analysis. The gamble paid off and the rationale of the choice of new coach seemed to be confirmed. However, a new team was formed from the 2010 season with younger, more inexperienced cyclists. Some of the interviews expressed some doubts in March 2010 about whether Sven Meyer was to right person to lead the new young team towards medals in 2012. After coaching the new team to a place as number four in the World Championships in 2010, followed by a disappointing start to the season 2010/2011 Sven Meyer was fired in January 2011.

Sports science and sports medicine support services: The Danish track cycling elite have relatively favourable conditions in this respect. The emphasis on advanced performance analysis is one example of application of sports science. Sven Meyer is far from a conventional coach who primarily uses motivational skills and presumably excels in transfer of tacit knowledge accumulated in an active career. The former national coach is a theoretician with comparative advantage in knowledge and application of new research results within the field of sports science. He learns from new journal articles and draws from his network of contacts at various universities.

The track team has also taken full advantage of the support services provided by Team Denmark. They are among the most frequent users of Team Denmark's physicians and the physiotherapists, and some riders have also started to consult the psychologists. Another effect of this cooperation is the discovery by Team Denmark dietists that intake of bicarbonate, or baking powder, postpones the emergence of lactid acid in muscles during endurance sports. Bicarbonate pills are provided for the cyclists, and caffeine pills are also used. This has been raised as an ethical issue. The pills are performance-enhancing and are considered grey zone means, but no decision has been taken to restrict their use.

Mimicking the effect of high altitude training by means of tent-like altitude houses at sea level is another grey zone activity. The Danish track team has had training camps where they have either stayed or trained at high altitude. Altitude houses are discussed as a cheaper alternative which is more attuned to family life. The realities of international competition impose a pressure for adopting methods used by the main competitors which in this respect are mainly the Australians. Previously, it was a question of achieving enough power to compete with the other main contenders. After reaching this stage it becomes a question of marginal improvement through means such as wind tunnels, performance analysis, baking powder, and inventive forms of circumventing rules such as insertion of ice cubes in cavities of bikes during the weighing-in process to make possible marginally lighter bikes when the ice melts.

Well Well-structured competition programme: This is about competition opportunities and the structuring of domestic competition schedules to meet the needs of elite athletes who are preparing for international events (Houlihan & Green 2007: 4–8). The Danish track elite has ideal international competition opportunities. There are no limits to participation in all competitions that optimizes the preparation for international championships. Neither are there obstacles as a result of conflict with domestic competitions. The typical problems in this respect in other sports are between the interests of club versus the interests of national team. There are similar tensions and potential problems in the relationship between the professional road cycling teams and the national track cycling team. There is far more money in road cycling and the earnings opportunities for riders are much better. This creates a basic disincentive towards long-term involvement in track cycling. However, most of the interviewees argue that the relationship between road and track is fundamentally symbiotic. The potential problems are seen to be of minor importance and are being solved in practice. It is argued that Endurance track cyclists benefit from road racing, and road cyclists also take advantage of the speed and agility built on the track. The tensions between national and particular interests were no doubt more serious earlier when the particular interests of the DBC were very powerful compared to those of the cycling federation.

Integrated approach to policy development: To foster sporting success, it is important that the approach to policy development is integrated, that the planning system is comprehensive, and that administration is relatively simple. In this respect, cycling is seemingly close to the ideal situation. This is one of the factors explicitly mentioned by the executive director of Team Denmark, Michael Andersen, as a reason for considering track cycling a 'best practice' case. He views the political and administrative leadership of the DCU as very strong, ambitious, action-oriented and knowledgeable. The DCU lives up to the requirements of professionalism with a stable group of experienced leaders and managers. The DCU is seen as capable of developing ambitious and realistic long-term strategies as well as willing and able to prioritize accordingly. Furthermore, whereas other federations aim for unconditional financial support and arms-length relations to Team Denmark, guided by the principle 'we know best how to use the money', this is not at all the case with the DCU. The Team Pursuit project was planned and implemented in a highly integrated cooperation with Team Denmark.

Mass participation: It is remarkable that the revival of Danish track cycling has happened in spite of the lack of mass participation. Of course, the actual number of participants must be seen in relation to the conditions of each sport, and track cycling has always been a sport for the few. Even so, the number of active Danish track cyclists is remarkably low. The total is around 500 of which half are above 40 years of age and involved in recreational rather than competitive activities. There are around 100 children among the currently active track cyclists. Only 100–150 of the active track cyclists are between 10 and 30 years old and of potential relevance in relation to elite recruitment. The number of participants in Danish elite championships is around 35 but many of them are far from the top level. It is particularly remarkable that Danish junior track cyclists have been so successful in recent years despite the fact that the number of junior cyclists with licence as competitively active is only 120, of which around a third are active on the track as well as the road.

Talent identification and development system: In recent years as much as around 10 per cent of all active Danish junior track cyclists have won medals at World Championships. The DCU has full-time coaches for each age level. Detailed age-specific training guidelines and monitoring systems have been developed. The approach is science-based, structured and integrated (Kristensen 2010). Talent identification is relatively easy among the small number of active track cyclists. In addition, national road cycling coaches actively encourage Endurance talents to try the track as well as the road, as illustrated by the experience of the member of the current Team Pursuit, Rasmus Quaade, who was previously a road cyclist with no track experience. It was the national U23 road cycling coach who actively recommended him for the Team Pursuit team (Jacobsen 2010).

Effective system for monitoring of athlete progress and lifestyle support: All members of the national teams at the different age levels, including the senior elite, prepare daily on-line reports about intensity and amount of training as well as various lifestyle factors. The DCU provides lifestyle support as well as guidance and monitoring of training. Part of this takes the form of a follow-up on the analysis of the daily on-line reports combined with test results. In addition, advice about dieting and other aspects of a healthy lifestyle is provided by Team Denmark's experts.

Post-career support: Support for education or jobs, simultaneously with the elite sports career, has always been important for Team Denmark. This has been seen as the most important means of satisfying the requirements of the Elite Sports Act to provide elite sport support in a socially responsible way. Involvement in some kind of education, training or employment that facilitates civil career prospects after the end of the elite sports career has been interpreted as an explicit condition for provision of support. This is in conflict with the emerging reality of full-time athletes. The conflict has become acute in the case of cycling. Both track and road cycling are extremely demanding sports. The requirements for training and recreation are hardly compatible with studies for formal educational degrees or part-time jobs. Faced with these realities the requirements have been softened and the actual post-career support for elite cyclists is limited.

Team building: An important part of efforts to optimize the performance of intensely cooperating teams, such as the Pursuit team, is team building. The smoothing out of differences and mediation of conflicts within the team is an explicit philosophy in the British track cycling project (Fotheringham 2008a). Team building is also stressed in the Danish project. It has not only to do with motivation but also with establishing coherence and avoidance of destructive tension. This is reflected in the criteria used for selection of team members which are explicitly holistic rather than taking only performance level into account. Three criteria are used: the actual performance level; tactical capabilities and social role in team interaction; and individual behaviour, attitudes and actions in a moral and ethical perspective (Pedersen 2008). These criteria were applied in a controversial decision to exclude one of the members of the world champions from the Pursuit team in the 2010/11 season. He would certainly still be part of the team if performance level was the only selection criterion. However, he is significantly older than the other members of the new team and he was not able to follow the same training regime as the others because of family commitments. This was considered disruptive and not compatible with the holistic team building approach.

The challenges – is the revival temporary or sustainable?

In conclusion, the discussions shows that the revival of Danish track cycling can be explained by a combination of factors, old and new, that together create the basis for new success. It illustrates that a clear strategy, with a niche focus, can be highly successful even if competitors have great advantages in terms of talents and financial resources. However, future success is far from guaranteed. The present situation is vulnerable and there are huge challenges to overcome.

First, the narrow recruitment base makes it difficult to go beyond niche strategies and may make it difficult to maintain competitiveness. It has made the project highly vulnerable to injuries and individual withdrawals. After the World Championships in 2009, two team members withdrew from the team to concentrate on their road cycling careers. Another member had to stop his career because of recurrent injuries. The two remaining world champions achieved together with two newcomers a place as no. 4 in the 2010 World

Championships. Prior to the 2010/11 season, one of the remaining world champions withdrew and the other was excluded. The new team is young and inexperienced and could do no better than a place as no. 9 in the 2011 World Championships. Danish elite track cycling is also vulnerable to decisions to withdraw from an elite cycling career among top juniors. A study shows that more than half of all junior cyclists withdraw from competitive cycling within four years because they prefer an education, lack motivation or dislike the social consequences of an elite cyclist career (Kristensen 2008).

Second, the coaching practice and philosophy does not seem to be coherent and sustainable. The substitution of Heiko Salzwedel with Sven Meyer as national coach represented a radical shift. This was logical in the context of the previous team but hardly ideal with the new young team, which is reflected in the decision to change the coach. An in-house solution to the coaching problem was chosen instead, with redefinition of responsibilities of core personnel. The results in the season 2010/2011 were not promising and it is hardly a stable solution compatible with medal winning ambitions.

Third, the track cycling programme in the Olympic Games has been changed with effect from the 2012 Olympics. Two of the Danish priority events (Points race and Madison) have been removed. Furthermore, the only disciplines where Danish female track cyclists have won medals (Points race and Individual Pursuit) were also removed from the Olympics. There is good potential for Danish success in the new discipline, Omnium. However, this cannot compensate for events that have been removed. The Danish results will no doubt suffer and the removed events will shrink in popularity and prestige, as has happened with the 1000 m time trial that disappeared from the Olympic programme after 2004.

Fourth, although six-day races have lost some of their former public appeal, it will have a negative effect on Danish track cycling in general if there is no longer a commercial basis for such events. This is a realistic future scenario.

Fifth, Danish track cycling is totally dependent on the continued existence of the track in Ballerup. Without the Ballerup Super Arena, there would be no Danish track cycling. There are no immediate threats to its existence, but, unfortunately, its future is not guaranteed. At present, the arena is supported by the local municipality and Team Denmark. Both sources may dry up in the future, or will at least shrink, under the pressure of decreased overall budgets. The local municipality owns the arena with the permanent velodrome. It would be much easier to use the arena for other profitable activities if the track was not permanent. This would seriously diminish its value for Danish track cycling. The support from Team Denmark to Danish track cycling is hardly resistant to cuts either. There is at present an explicit commitment to long-term support independent of short term results. However, it is hard to believe that cycling would not suffer from future rounds of cuts if the recent performances are less brilliant than they were when cuts were implemented in 2009.

PART IV

Perspectives and priorities in national elite sports

Introduction

The present elite sport systems in the Nordic countries reflect the development presented in part II. The overall structure, institutionalized perspectives, built-in tensions among key actors, resources and priorities impact both ongoing efforts and the perceptions of future challenges.

In Sweden and Finland, the question about how to reform and restructure national elite sport efforts is a major issue. In Sweden, representatives of the two major actors, the national sports confederation (RF) and the national Olympic Committee (SOK), have for a long time been engaged in intense and disruptive discussions. They have strong, competing views on how to support elite sport efforts. The state has kept an arm's length distance, but has lately contributed additional resources. In Finland, in contrast, there is a lack of dominant actors. A multitude of actors on different levels are involved in elite sport. Their responsibilities and relationships are unclear, and at the same time there is a lack of coordination and integration in the system. Partly as a response to this situation, the authorities have taken a more active role in distributing funds throughout the system. However, there is no clear elite sport strategy.

In Denmark and Norway, national systems of elite sport frame more specific questions about resources, strategies and priorities. In Denmark there is a stable and well-functioning elite sport model supported by an elite sport law. However, the last year's public debates, involving both party politicians and broad societal interests, have questioned priorities and direction within national elite sport. In Norway the existing elite sport system represents a relatively stable framework for ongoing efforts. Unlike in Denmark, the state has a passive role, as a major provider of resources. Discussions about national elite sport are mostly about how the existing system works in relation to the requirements of international elite sport. There are recurring public debates about various aspects of elite sport, but the elite sport model seems to have a high degree of legitimacy both in the political system and in the wider society.

10

Swedish elite sport: contested terrain

Paul Sjöblom and Josef Fahlén

For quite some time a battle has been raging between the Swedish Sports Confederation (RF) and the Swedish Olympic Committee (SOK) over the design of the Swedish model for elite sport. The two organizations strive towards the same goal, but their mission and the resources they command differ. In recent years the battle has intensified, primarily as a result of the RF's and the government's initiative for a new joint support for elite sport.

At the RF assembly in 1999, a so-called Elite Sports Council was formed. It was commissioned to follow up elite sport support within the confederation and suggest measures for cooperation, development and adaptation of the support systems. The council's mandate was renewed in 2005, in close dialogue with the special sports federations (SF). The SFs requested better cooperation and increased lucidity. The government had promised to use part of the surplus of Svenska Spel, the Swedish gaming company, for elite sport (22.7 million euros). In 2008 the SOK and the Executive Committee of the Swedish Sports Confederation took a further initiative for a united elite investment for Swedish sport. A mediation team was appointed to produce a joint proposal for cooperation between the RF, SOK and the Swedish Paralympic Committee (SPK). All three parties accepted their mission of *giving elite athletes the optimal prerequisites for winning more gold medals in international championships* (Eriksson 2006: 4–7; RF 2008: 9–16; RF 2009a; RF 2009b; RF 2009c).

This chapter focuses on the Swedish sport movement's ideologies and strategies for international sport successes. Particular attention is given to the differences of opinion between the two main actors, their origin and consequences – why they find it so hard to work together. The study is based on interviews with leading representatives of the RF and SOK. It describes the actors' organizations, strategies and visions for elite activities, with particular attention to the following issues:

- How is the current elite sport system (or systems) in Sweden structured?
- What are the main actors' guiding values and interests?
- What future challenges can be envisaged for the development of Swedish elite sport?

The Swedish Sports Confederation (RF)

According to the RF, 'elite sport' refers to activities at an international top level and the levels immediately below. The confederation considers elite sport important because it reinforces the national identity, inspires children and young people to participate in sports, and gives them positive models. For this reason, the RF argues, there must also be an interest on the part of society in providing all sports containing elite activities with the basic resources required to keep up with international competition (RF 2009d: 25–26, 32–35).

Like other competition activities, the RF continues, all elite activities should take place under the responsibility of the special sports federations. Via the structure of the competition systems these federations guide the direction of club activities, even though each club decides what form its own activities should take, that is to say, which level of ambition they should have. There are two other central guidelines for elite sport included in *Idrotten vill* ('Sport wants to'), the overarching policy document. All sports for young people up to 18 years old should be operated from a children's rights perspective and follow the UN Convention on the Rights of the Child, and the sports movement should take its responsibility for fostering elite athletes as human beings, which means preparing them from the start for a life after the end of the sports career (RF 2009c: 26, 32, 35; RF 2010a: 5, 11, 15).

In support the RF approximately distributes a total of ca. 11.6 million euros per year (SOU 2008: 59: 321–323). The programme declaration *Utveckla eliten!* ('Develop the elite!') contains a more detailed description of how the RF wishes to implement its elite support. The support is directed to all special sports federations running a national team, which in return have produced or wish to produce a 'talent and elite plan', the objective being to answer to the special sports federations' requirements by offering management and support to the development. This is done within the framework of three activity fields:

- Talent and elite plan
  - Meeting requirements and offering development management and support
- Joint RF development
  - Elite sport and development
  - Network meetings
  - National team education programmes
  - Coaching education programmes (SISU Sport Education)
  - Development projects
- The special sports federations' own development
  - Financial elite support; talent and national team development
  - Competence support; tests, training, education, counselling and projects

The RF anticipates certain future changes for its elite support. Of the total elite resources the confederation wants to reserve 75 per cent for the specific elite activities of the special sports federations. Whether an activity is genuinely specific and, if so, to what extent, will be assessed on the basis of the following factors: ambition, results, potential and needs. The confederation also wants to invest more in 'facilitating the combination of sports investments with studies and/or jobs' via RIGs, the already established national sports upper secondary schools, via expanded post-secondary-school studies (scholarships), as well as via increased career counselling elements. The RF further wishes to develop coaching and management education at all levels supporting different types of experts. It wants more and better coordinated research and development (in cooperation with universities) and increased external coverage and feedback via a digital 'elite sport portal' (RF 2010b: 2–3).

Janne Carlstedt, operative manager of elite sport development within the RF, maintains that it is now high time to review current guidelines for elite support and produce new ones (the latest elite programme is from the 1980s) (Carlstedt 2010). In his opinion, an overarching problem is that the sports clubs, where the majority of the elite athletes spend most of their time, have not succeeded in creating 'elite sport environments' that are good enough, This is primarily due to lack of qualified coaches and coaching education. According to Carlstedt, SISU, the sports movement's own education organization, 'arranges fantastic programmes for parents/relatives and coaches on the most basic levels but does nothing for elite coaches.' Carlstedt speaks of an invisible wall between development and education work in Swedish sport.

Several federations successfully devote themselves to sport-specific talent development, but not to the more general training of athletes. This latter, in his view, is also necessary to achieve a continuous elite development. Carlstedt summarizes the RF strategy for talent development and of the deficiencies in the system in the following way:

> Talent development passes via the club to the district and upwards, with minor shifts towards regional and central power centres, and then it depends on what the national teams manage to do – where a lot has to do with money, since those who work with the national teams must have this as their profession…The individual path could in the future be the club,…alternatively a big club/federation and regional centre…as well as sport platoons during military service.…But today most things stand still while waiting for a joint elite effort – which will thus not take place since the RF and SOK cannot agree.

Carlstedt emphasize that the future issues of elite sport development concern *diversity problems*. There are within the RF about 250 different sports in 70 special sports federations operating elite activities. In terms of national teams for men, women, juniors and youths the total number amounts to some 1000. The task of the RF is to make the scanty elite resources suffice for everyone and to divide them fairly, with the primary objective of providing active talents in the various clubs with the right training, to the right extent and at the right age. He estimates that at least 40 out of the current 70 federations do not have an acceptable elite education of their own. The elite sport centre within the RF provides services for the federations. It has a total of 10 full-time positions, including administrators, developers and technicians/operative staff. They are too few for the task.

Another issue concerns all the talented who are neither included in the national team efforts nor receive any scholarships or RIG places. This relates to *broadening* of elite support. How do we capture, support and further develop late starters or those who are on the borderline, Carlstedt asks rhetorically. Most active elite athletes, except within a handful of commercial entertainment sports, have to pursue parallel sport and professional careers. Carlstedt is convinced that part of the solution is to achieve better cooperation with universities. The new elite sport programmes could then be led by joint councils with representatives from the universities as well as from the RF, SPK and

SOK. Thus, all interests would be met and joint competence and resources would be utilized. There already exist a few well-functioning examples of cooperation, but there is no overarching strategy. For the moment the issue is in the hands of SISU:

> SISU should really make sure that there is education all the way from the local study circle up to Ph.D. education in sport, both in regard of individual sport training and of a more general coaching education.

A third crucial issue concerns *cooperation about research* and *external analysis*. According to Carlstedt, the RF is badly informed both about current research and about what other countries are up to. This is due to lack of personnel and structural obstacles. The Elite Sports Centre, for example, has one person responsible for research, but that person's tasks do not include working close to the development departments. There are several people with a research background working at or in close connection with the Elite Sport Centre, but they are engaged in operative, day-to-day work. In Carlstedt's view, the RF would need both more people with the competence to gather essential knowledge, and to communicate this internally in the organization in a pedagogical way. The RF also needs forums for dialogue, where representatives of federations get the chance to meet and discuss with the best researchers and external analysts in the country.

A fourth issue identified by Carlstedt is to muster the strength of various sports. He advocates national sport centres, where coaches and active practitioners can take turns to partake of joint support resources and investments in selected big clubs where coaches and athletes from other clubs can apply for support. How the mustering of strength should be channelled depends on the actual sport and on the elite sport environments already available. In his view, there are far too few 'key persons' around elite athletes in Sweden, i.e. resource persons at club and district/special sports federation levels, primarily, who work professionally with elite sport development. There is a lack of coordination:

> National Team Support, Joint Support (to the federations) and Directed Support – those are the new forms of support, but we have no direction. Thus the system fails when it comes to allocating resources. We have the same discussions over and over again. [...] At present we do not do a good job vis-à-vis the federations. We help them here and now (often in an emergency), and often after many and long discussions, but we do not contribute to their development. There is too much top-down

work in Swedish elite sport. Each person does a splendid job individually, but we do not work together and learn from one another.

Summarizing Janne Carlstedt's reflections, they are about concentration of resources, expanding the education system, creating a new distribution system with increased lucidity and justice vis-à-vis the federations, purchasing and developing new technology, and improving research and external coverage. His overall explanation why the RF has such difficulties in achieving cooperation with the SOK, something that would definitely contribute to a better concentration of elite resources, is that it has to do with a struggle for power.

> Government and parliament wanted to see a better coordination, both to get the sports movement to speak with one voice about elite support and because better coordination achieves a better effect. The federations, too, thought that things had become messy, that you kept running both to Mum and Dad but never knew exactly what applied. RF, which received the commission, invited SOK for a wedding, but when it turned out that merging the organizations was no longer on, step two became trying to bring about a joint elite investment. All parties accepted, but since then nothing has happened except a lot of bickering.

Carlstedt puts a great deal of blame on the SOK, which in his view does not want to cooperate. The SOK has considerable competence and has succeeded remarkably well with sponsoring. The SOK has also been clearer about their objectives and requirements, and it has focused more than the RF on elite support. But the SOK, too, Carlstedt continues, has contributed to the problems of unsatisfactory elite sport environments. It has largely taken over elite development activities within the Olympic sports. As a consequence, clubs and centres have lost self-confidence and devoted less time, strength and resources to developing elite activities.

Karin Mattsson, chair of the RF, agrees (Mattsson 2010). According to her, it is above all leadership and coaching education that need to be strengthened, but the RF could and should also speed up its decision-making processes. At the same time the decisions have to be transparent, since they largely concern government funds. The most urgent problem to solve, she thinks, is the conflict between the RF and SOK.

> Our opinion is still that the best for elite sport development is to merge the organizations, because splitting the resources will not be feasible in the long run. But we no longer push the fusion issue actively. [...] If SOK does not want to compromise

on finding new forms of cooperation, we will unfortunately, which the management of SOK does not seem to realize, end up in a situation where the special sports federations and the government, who have given us the mission, will enforce a fusion anyway. And that will hardly favour SOK.

According to Mattsson, the basis of a sustainable Swedish elite sport structure is 'sport for all', because if all are included from the start the talents will also be there. Then you have to catch them and make specific efforts to develop them. Making demands will be important, in Mattsson's opinion, but it is even more important that athletes and their leaders have their own driving force. The task of RF is to strengthen these via supporting the special sports federations, so that they can and dare to take full responsibility for their own efforts. There is always an intermediate position between demand and control on one hand and spontaneity and self-determination on the other, Mattsson concludes, and the RF ought to become better at the former and the SOK at the latter.

Sweden's Olympic Committee

The SOK is Sweden's representative in the International Olympic Movement; its main responsibility is participation in the Olympic Games. This includes preparation work for the participation, the distribution and the follow-up of the so-called elite support, as well as for the resource team, which stands at the athletes' disposal. The SOK summarizes its mission in the publication 'Konkurrenskraftiga svenska OS-trupper ("Competitive Swedish Olympics teams")' (SOK 2010a: 1), the main tasks being:

- To organize and implement Swedish participation in the Olympic Games
- To prepare participants for the Olympic Games
- Development of elite athletes
- International work
- Marketing and sponsoring

The SOK looks upon itself as an operative support organization. At present it has four sports directors, who share the responsibility for the Olympic sports among themselves. Their task is to maintain a dialogue with the sports directors of special sports federations with Olympic sports, as with the athletes and coaches who partake in the SOK's support programme. The main responsibility for the development of each sport rests with the federations. The SOK's contribution is to reinforce the investments directed towards the international elite which are implemented by the federations themselves. The SOK currently consists of 36 regular member federations and 14 others, which are recognized by the International Olympic Committee (IOC), i.e. sports which have an Olympic potential but are not currently included in the Olympic programme.

The SOK distributes a total of ca. 6.4 million euros per year in support (SOK 2009: 20). The money for this mainly comes from the sponsors the Committee has managed to enrol. Most of the support consists of financial support, but also of competence and counselling support. These three forms of support are channelled via each special sports federation to athletes via the 'Top and Talent Programme', where athletes as well as teams may receive support based on their results (top) and their estimated all-round potential (talent) for reaching the world top in the next or next-but-one games. This is channeled via the 'Challenger Programme', which recruits promising young athletes to the Top and Talent Programme, and via the 'Support Programme', which consists of support of different kinds from specialists and resource persons. All these forms of support are primarily tailored to suit every individual effort and development plan. SOK's support for athletes and their coaches requires that the federation where the athlete's club is a member runs a so-called elite programme until the next Olympic Games and, in addition, has an annual national team plan. The federation is also expected to present a requirement analysis, a capacity profile, a training concept, a talent development programme and a follow-up programme.

The SOK's long-term objective is that the Swedish Olympic teams should have the capacity of winning 20 medals, five of which are gold medals, at both summer and winter Olympics by the year 2020. A prerequisite for achieving such a goal is that the support programmes are based on the joint responsibilities of the SOK and the Olympic sports federations (OFSs). The sports federations have the responsibility for the actual implementation. The SOK hopes that, over time, the experiences and the competence created can be utilized and spread further within each sport (SOK 2010b).Our mission concerns medals at the Olympic Games, not broad sport or, for that matter, entertainment sport. [...] We prefer total investment in a handful of talents rather than in hundreds who, in our judgement, cannot become the best. In this respect we are wholly professional in that we invest purposefully and for the long term (Reinebo 2010).

Peter Reinebo, one of four SOK sports directors, describes how he looks upon the role of the SOK today: An investment towards the Olympic Games must entail that an athlete is given the same chances as the best in the world. Hence, this limits the number of athletes that can be invested in. Currently, the budget of the Top and Talent Programme provides for 150 athletes, but Reinebo estimates that there is room for including twice as many. Money is the single most important factor in safeguarding future medals, Reinebo maintains. However, it concerns investments in individuals as much as in environments, cultures and infrastructures:

> If there emerge one or more athletes in an Olympic sport, we have to act to arrange matters for the best. [...] We build where it is possible to build and we endeavour to build up environments for elite sport which may benefit more athletes in the sport in the long run, environments that give transfer profits. [...] We'd rather do team building than build individuals.

This very idea of investing where there are talents, environments and a driving force seems to be a core idea with the SOK. Reinebo says that the strategies not only can, but also should be regarded as instrumental, while it is important to emphasize that all sport has to build on inclination. The SOK cannot control anyone or decide which sports athletes should choose. It can only make sure to enrol those who have the talent and the inclination to reach the international elite top level. The SOK does not make any distinction between poor and rich sports, or between 'nice' and 'ugly' sports, Reinebo continues. He also dwells on the demands that must be made on the Olympic sports federations. Since the support for athletes and their coaches is channelled via the federations, it is absolutely crucial that they face up to the requirement analysis, capacity profile, training concept, talent development and follow-up programmes. Athletes must fulfil demands regarding performance, capacity and results. In the tough competition that prevails everyone must act professionally, Reinebo points out. It is simply not defensible not to make high demands, with such a long queue of people wishing to get in.

The greatest difference between the current SOK-system and previous attempts, either in common with the RF or individually, is, according to Peter Reinebo, the investment management. The SOK has changed from just handing out money to individual athletes, to cooperation on a broader scale, with better continuity and greater commitment by OSFs and coaches. Another great difference relates to the SOK's efforts directed at young talents and other athletes on the level immediately below the top elite.

> We noticed that the top had developed while the pressure and refill from behind had ceased. We realized that we had to help the federations to go in for the young talents who fell just outside the Olympics investments.

The next step in the future development will be to focus more on the competence of the coaches. According to Peter Reinebo, there used to be too much focus on federations, federation managers and athletes, whereas the latter's personal coaches were left in the lurch. For this reason the SOK has tried in recent years to create opportunities for coaches to be more active in athletes' everyday activities. The resource team has also expanded and attempts have been made at intensifying cooperation with researchers to focus more on performance development issues. 'Today there are well-developed education programmes and research-based training development projects,' Reinebo continues. However, the SOK still experiences some problems in involving the coaches. 'Even though we often pay their salaries and offer them further education as part of their jobs, it is hard to make them understand the importance of the support that we can provide.'

Peter Reinebo's view is that the most important work in the future will be to create opportunities for more athletes to join the programmes run by the SOK. The equation is seemingly simple. If Sweden wishes to win more medals it is necessary that more athletes are enrolled. SOK must also invest more at the local and regional levels, and in certain sports it must rally all national forces. One key aspect of these investments for the future is to tighten up postsecondary education for both athletes and coaches. Another important part of the work is increased efforts in following up and evaluating all investments. 'Investments must be conducted with even greater precision, stricter follow-up, greater intensity and longer continuity', Reinebo concludes. The big challenge is the great differences between different sports and federations. Some federations need to develop their national team programmes. Others need to reform their national sports upper secondary schools. Others require central efforts, while others again require directed ones.

There is one thing, however, that all federations share, and that is the previously mentioned need for academic education for athletes and coaches. Reinebo is hesitant about general solutions that cut right across the existing practices. The SOK's philosophy is that all federations, or possibly sports that are similar, must find their partner and their forms of cooperation. He highlights the example of the Winter Sports Centre at Mid Sweden University, pointing out the importance of such cooperation being designed on the basis of the specific demands of each sport. For some sports a civilian education running parallel with a career to safeguard people's subsistence and career transfers is essential, for others it is research or coaching education. One has to consider both the prerequisites of the sport in question and the requirements of the individual, which is why Reinebo does not believe in general solutions.

Regarding the possible cooperation with the RF, Peter Reinebo's criticism of the prevalent order is evident. He thinks it is a pity that Sweden does not invest as much in non-Olympic sports, pointing out that this is due to the RF's behaviour. The SOK is willing to support new investments, at any rate where talents are to be found. However, the RF has made it clear that it wishes to be in charge of these sports and federations itself. From Reinebo's point of view it is not strange that the SOK's and RF's ideas of how to make elite investments differ, considering the different missions of the two organizations. The RF is a political organization serving its member organizations and distributing government funding. It is only natural that child and youth sports focusing on diversity take priority. But the SOK cannot think in such terms, not when winning international medals is the focus. 'We must invest where it is makes a difference', says Reinebo.

Because of the great differences, a merger of the RF and SOK would be devastating and contrary to the government's and special sports federations' wishes of a better utilization of resources ('joint elite investment'), Reinebo continues. On the other hand, he envisages an even clearer role distribution between the organizations. Both should concentrate entirely on what they do best and then coordinate the resources so as to complement one another. Then the duplication of work, which the RF uses as an argument for a merger, would stop being an argument altogether. Duplication is what the RF itself actually stands for, in Reinebo's view, since they have in recent years started to take very goal-oriented action in relation to federations and national team managements even in the Olympic sports. Instead, the SOK should take charge of the top investments in elite sports, with the RF continuing to support the national teams. The cooperation should at that stage be directed primarily towards the resource teams, which would then serve both the national teams and the 150–300 individuals in the SOK's support programme. However, an idea like this is based on the assumption that the RF first of all abandons the idea of a merger or takeover.

On the question of why cooperation on the joint elite support takes so long to work out, Peter Reinebo answers that it takes time to compromise in two such diverse cultures. The SOK cannot possibly give up its independence and its mission to prepare for the Olympic Games, since it is commissioned by IOC to be in charge of this. Unfortunately, he maintains, it seems as if the interest in the actual merger, not only from the RF, but also from the present government, is greater than in sports results:

> We have always experienced great support both from Social Democrat ministers of sport and from prime ministers. They have often, but not always, dared to invest even though the elite issue has been a sensitive one. We did believe that the present non-Social Democrat government would do the same or even invest more, as suggested by statements made in public. [...] But it has not turned out that way.

In Reinebo's opinion, The SOK is not against government intervention. On the contrary, such intervention has for a long time guaranteed that big money has accrued to sport. He is hoping, however, that more will be invested in elite sport from now on. In Sweden, sponsor money is still absolutely crucial for developing elite sport. To Reinebo, the problem with elite sport funding from the government, apart from being small compared to other countries of the same size, is the lack of management. The current principles of distribution via the RF directly to the federations (according to their size) lead to segmentation and stagnation. It causes those who receive resources to slacken and those who do not to give up. The SOK would welcome tougher auditing and clearer evaluations, elucidating how much is distributed, what are the objectives and what are the pay-offs. 'The lack of a national strategy might have worked historically, but we can no longer rely on the benefits we have drawn from our degree of industrialization, the diversity of our sports movement and the breadth of our government and municipal investments,' Peter Reinebo concludes, with emphasis. 'Sweden has lost what advantage it used to have. It is necessary to think anew, be more goal-oriented and more professional. This is required to win international medals. There are great values in elite sport, for athletes and viewers as well as for the general public – locally, nationally and internationally.'

Concluding discussion

The government and special sports federations are not satisfied with the development of elite sport, or how development resources are utilized. A united elite investment for Swedish elite sport has been called for and agreed upon, but cooperation is slow in coming. Why is that? Our explanation makes reference to certain ideological demarcation lines, which form the basis of a fierce struggle for power between, in the first instance, the RF and SOK.

The RF's and SOK's missions and objectives differ. The RF is a big confederation with independent member federations which have to make their own priorities. Major decisions are made jointly in connection with national assemblies every other year, where every member federation has a right of decision corresponding to its size: a weighted voting scale. The RF's mission from the government and the members is primarily to work towards 'sport for all', which means that investments are mainly directed towards the broad child and youth sports. The SOK, on the other hand, consists of a number of special sports federations, all with one vote each, and the mission and objective is to create competitive Swedish Olympic teams. Currently 149 individual athletes and five teams are supported (SOK 2009: 10). The SOK invests where the greatest chances of succeeding are supposed to lie. The RF, on its part, tries to distribute its support as fairly as possible between 1,000 national teams and 10,000 individuals. What is most important then is not to find and improve talents, but to make sure that as many as possible of those with the right prerequisites are given the chance to reach as far as possible; to encourage the athletes' own driving force as well as that of their coaches and leaders. The SOK's representatives talk more in terms of control and management. In order to succeed with the objectives the limited resources have to be managed carefully.

The differences of cultures, and the thinking influenced by them, also appear in the criticism the RF and SOK level at one another. The RF claims that the control which the SOK exerts has paralyzed the spontaneity and self-confidence of athletes and thus hindered development. The SOK asserts that it is the RF that blocks development when distributing money generally without control or, even worse, uses membership numbers as the only criterion for distribution. Both parties' self-reflection indicates that there is probably some basis for these criticisms.

The RF's president, Karin Mattsson, concedes that her own organization must speed up its decision processes and that their quid pro quo demands from those who receive elite support must be higher. The SOK's sports manager Peter Reinebo claims that the organization he represents has problems in getting coaches involved despite all the directed support. But how far from one another are they in theory? The RF wants stricter demands, greater efficiency, individually adapted efforts and more private sponsors. The SOK wants greater commitment and drive in those receiving support, more team-building and more government funding. It sounds as though they might complement each other fairly well, or, more correctly, that their specific cultures and logics could be complementary. It is evident that both parties agree on the objective that was set down in the government Sports Policy Proposition of 1999: supporting activities 'that strengthen the international competitiveness of sports practitioners' (Prop. 2008/09: 126: 1). But they do not agree on the strategies for creating such competitiveness, as is clearly demonstrated by our informants.

The problem at this very moment does not seem to lie in the differences as much as in the actual struggle for power. This struggle seems in many ways to be one for prestige: who will be praised for having developed the successful athletes and who will be blamed for the failures? It seems as if the notion of 'sharing glory and dividing blame', which has been discussed earlier on in this anthology, has been reversed. With two key actors partly representing different employers (the government and the member federations in the case of the RF, and the sponsors, above all, for the SOK) the question of responsibility naturally comes to the fore.

With respect to mission, overarching objectives and organizational models, and historical elite investments, the RF and SOK certainly differ somewhat. However, if we consider the descriptions of problems involved in the development of elite sport there are obvious similarities. These are related to ideas about what needs to be changed in the present system, as well as elite definitions and visions of future medals. The operative manager of elite sport development at the RF, Janne Carlstedt, identifies the 'elite environments', especially the lack of professionalism among coaches and leaders and the insufficient education offered, as the major problem. So does Peter Reinebo. As for the issues of the future, Carlstedt, like Reinebo, brings up the problems of having enough resources for all talents, of effectively supporting athletes both immediately below the top and those whose careers have just ended, as well as the problem of the disparity of sports and federations with their need of different solutions. They also emphasize the importance of concerted national efforts for different sports, of increasing competitive intelligence and cooperation with the research world, as well as of higher academic sport education programmes. The special sports federations have the main responsibility for elite development, with support from the RF or SOK, but a thorough follow-up and evaluation of their efforts is absolutely necessary for the development to proceed in the right direction. On this they agree.

In spite of this broad agreement the differences in actors' basic ideological assumptions have an impact. Even if organizations are moving closer to one another, towards some sort of ideological middle ground, the interviews reveal that they come from different directions. The RF approaches the middle from the point of equal opportunities for everyone, spontaneity and self-determination, while the SOK's starting point is investing in those who have the best chances of succeeding, with the support of management and control. The mistrust between the two organizations can be largely explained in reference to tradition and culture (see chapter 4). This shines through in our interviews. 'Is the SOK possibly striving to take over all elite activity', Janne Carlstedt ponders.

The starting point for further discussions of joint elite investment in Sweden is that the RF will never abandon the democratic decision-making process and the diversity perspective ('sport for all'), just as the SOK will not abandon its independence and mission to be in charge of the preparations for the Olympic Games. One would think that both parties could gain from burying their hatchets. However, it may not be enough to attempt to cooperate. Half-hearted joint investments and more drawn-out negotiations might risk causing further delays of a systems transformation of Swedish elite sport. Which reforms will serve Swedish elite sport development the best in the long run? A balanced conclusion would seem to involve trying to unite Swedish tradition with novel ideas. The social movement model may create broad support from society for elite sport and attract many talents to the sports. These two factors are seemingly crucial for any country with a small population and limited resources. Simultaneously, however, it is necessary to improve ways of catching and supporting talents as well as established elite level athletes.

National elite sport efforts seems to benefit from long-term strategic efforts with clearly formulated objectives. This is something all our respondents agree upon. How can this be achieved? It seems perfectly clear that the ongoing power struggle between the RF and SOK does not make any constructive contribution. It is also perfectly clear that even if it may have been Julin's 'Let a thousand flowers bloom' strategy , or the lack of a uniform elite sport strategy that contributed to Swedish sport successes in the past, international competition no longer leaves room for trusting to such coincidences as the ones lying behind this way of thinking (Julin 2007). Nor is it any longer possible, we maintain, in relation to the demands and expectations coming from financiers, employers and public opinion. With the new joint elite investments of in all ca. 27.8 million euros the demands for lucidity, predictability and stringency will increase, which does not necessarily lead to total conformity, but which will anyway enforce a much clearer choice of direction for the Swedish elite sport system. What will be interesting in the future is to follow these choices; to see if the Swedish tradition and culture can be integrated with that which is novel. In addition, international research indicates that a country's domestic elite sports discourse and debate need not necessarily converge with those of other countries or follow in the footsteps of other successful countries. Further, that historical comparisons lack relevance to the current international struggle for medals – the global sporting arms race (Bergsgaard et.al. 2007: 196–197; De Bosscher et.al. 2008: 134). The question remains, however, how much we are prepared to pay for the medals?

Finally, it is obvious that, centrally, the RF and SOK have a great influence on the Swedish elite sport system (although you cannot call the system coherent). However, their specific influence on Swedish elite sport development has not yet been investigated. Most elite sport takes place at the local level in clubs, involving single athletes, teams and coaches. In order to measure, describe and analyse these activities more comprehensive research is needed.

11

The anatomy of elite sports organization in Finland

Jarmo Mäkinen

This chapter continues the review of the Finnish sports movement started in chapter 5. The focus is on the period after the structural change of the early 1990s and on the current elite sports organizations. In the area of elite sports, discussions about strategic issues have been an ongoing concern in Finland. Discussions on the overall strategy were conducted in 1994, 1998, 2002, 2004 and 2010. Several working groups have also been established. The Finnish Ministry of Education and Culture and the national Olympic Committee established the first three strategic working groups jointly. The 2004 and the 2010 working groups were established by the Ministry of Education and Culture alone. The 2010 working group recently published its memo.

The memos of the five working groups evoke mixed feelings. Despite the 16-year time span, all the working groups list the same problems in the Finnish elite sports. The problems remain unsolved. The analyses of both the first (1994) and the last (2010) working group list the same problems: structural disintegration, lack of clear management structure, selfishness of the organizations and lack of cooperation between them. The suggested measures and plans to solve these problems have not been implemented. The 2010 working group titled its report 'From words to actions'.

The chapter is organized as follows: First, the most central elite sports organizations in Finland are introduced. Then each of them is discussed in some detail. In the 'Coordination and Coaching' section, the activities of the *Olympic Committee*, the *Ministry of Education and Culture* and the *national sport federations* are analysed. In the 'Training' section, the focus is on the *training centres* and *sport academies* located in various parts of Finland. The research and development activities in elite sports are discussed mainly in terms of the operations of *KIHU (Research Institute for Olympic Sport)*, which is the home organization of the author. Financial issues are, to a certain extent, discussed in connection with each organization. The last section summarizes the current structure of elite sports in the Finland from the organizational point of view. The chapter is based on a project carried out between 2008 and 2010 in the Research Institute for Olympic Sports in Finland (Mäkinen 2010; Mäkinen 2011).

Organizational chart of the Finnish elite sports

In some respects, the organization of the Finnish sports movement differs clearly from the neighbouring countries (see chapter 5). This also applies to elite sports. This section provides a short overview of the different organizations involved in elite sports. The organizational chart of the Finnish sport system is presented in figure 9.1. The elite sports organizations can be divided into organizations that belong to the sports movement and independent actors with which the sports movement cooperates in the area of elite sports (figure 9.1).

Vertical membership structures, typical of the Nordic sport movement, can to some extent still be found in the in the Finnish elite sports organizations. The elite sports federations recognized as Olympic sports are members of the Finnish Olympic Committee. The other national sport federations are not members of the Olympic Committee, even if the committee's sphere of responsibilities also covers non-Olympic elite sports. The members of the Finnish Paralympic Committee include the organization responsible for disabled athletes (VAU ry) and nine national sport federations. In the last few years, sports for the disabled have been integrated with national sports federations as in Norway.

Each national federation is responsible for elite athletes in its sport. In this respect, there are no major differences between the Nordic countries. However, there are differences in how the overall responsibilities have been implemented in elite sports. A few other differences can also be found in the roles that regional and local actors play in elite sports. In Finland, regional sport federations or the club levels do not play any significant role in elite sports.

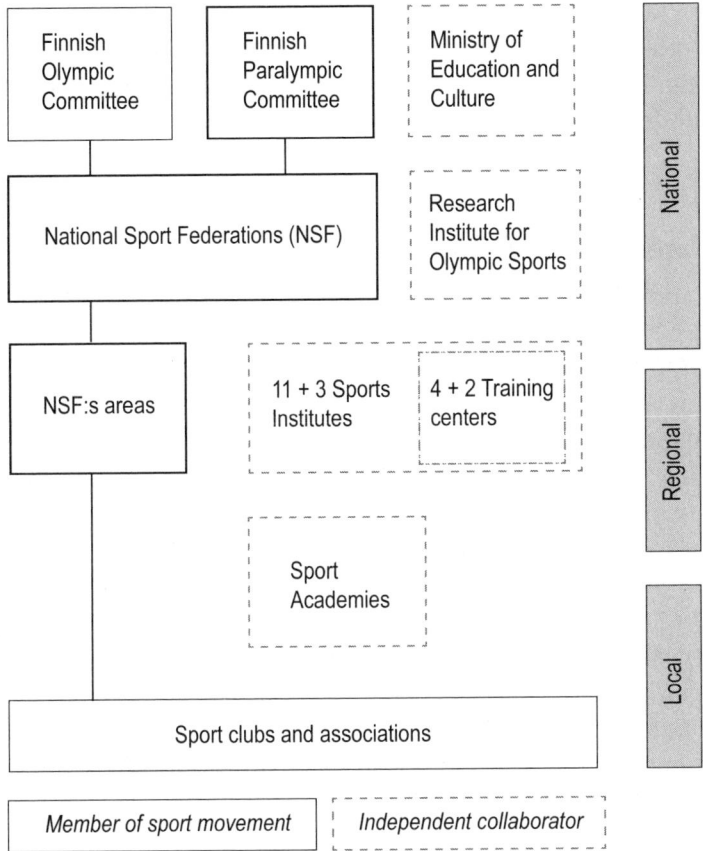

Figure 9.1: Organization of elite sports in Finland

The most important difference between Finland and the other Nordic countries is the existence of several elite sport organizations that are independent of the broader sports movement. The most important are the Research Institute of Olympic Sport (KIHU), sports institutes and their training centres, and local sport academies. Each of them has its own national mission in sports, but they also have considerable autonomy in carrying out their activities. The pluralism described here is an important reason why the overall coordination of elite sports has often been a challenge in Finland. For instance, the Olympic Committee cannot dictate to KIHU or the sports institutes what guidelines they should follow. As there is no shared top-level organization, coordination must be managed in other ways.

Owing to the disintegration of the field, the Ministry of Education and Culture exercises exceptional powers in Finnish elite sports. The Ministry is the only institution able to control all other elite sports actors. This is done through economic decision making power and a performance management system.

Coordination and coaching

The Finnish Olympic Committee (FOC) has an important co-ordinating role in Finnish elite sports. The state has delegated a considerable and exceptional role to FOC for the re-distribution of state subsidies. This section focuses on the means and resources it has to achieve coordination.

The responsibilities of the Finnish and Swedish Olympic Committees are quite similar. The Swedish Olympic Committee only supports Olympic sports, so the responsibilities of the Finnish Olympic Committee are wider than those of its Swedish counterpart. Compared to the Swedish Olympic Committee and especially the Norwegian Olympiatoppen or the Danish Team Denmark, the role of the Finnish Olympic Committee is more administrative. This is reflected in its personnel structure. There are 11 full-time employees and a part-time chief medical officer.

Only two employees are involved in actual coaching activities. Apart from being responsible for the arrangements related to the Olympic Games, most of the activities of the Finnish Olympic Committee concern elite sports subsidies and the development of the support system. Owing to insufficient resources, the Committee cannot assume operative responsibility for coaching.

The Olympic Committee and the national sport federations

In contrast to active coaching, the Olympic Committee's financial support is the most important instrument for managing elite sports. A considerable share of state support for elite sports is distributed through the Olympic Committee. Almost all the support for elite sports to national sport federations goes through the Olympic Committee. The Committee can decide who receives these subsidies, how much and on what conditions.

Lately, the Finnish Olympic Committee has been more active in directing the overall development of coaching. Nevertheless, the Finnish national sports federations bear the main responsibility for elite sports coaching. The Committee assesses the activities of the national sport federations through various methods. Still, it cannot be absolutely sure that the national sport federations implement the measures in accordance with the overall policy.

Most of the support from the Olympic Committee to the national sport federations is for coaching purposes. In 2007, coaching accounted for about 80 per cent of the total. After the Athens Olympic Games in 2004, the coaching support system was reorganized, linking the support policy to the coaching systems of the various sports. The level of elite sports coaching by the national sport federations started to influence the amount and quality of the support that they received. In the new support system, the national sport federations are divided into three categories on the basis of an assessment: system, top individuals, and development.

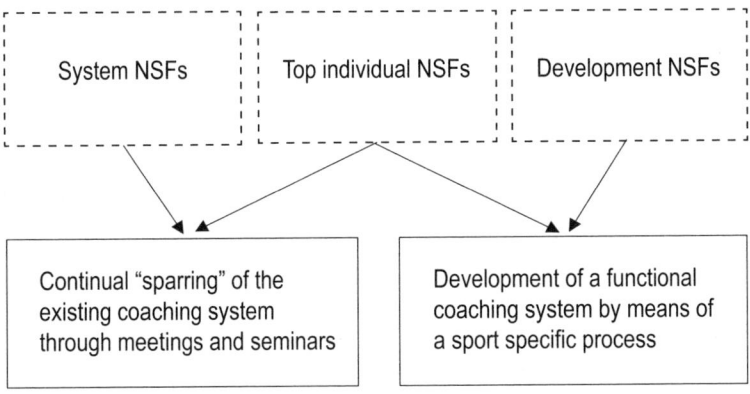

Figure 9.2: Coaching support system of the Finnish Olympic Committee

In the first category, the coaching system works, in the second it works partially, and in the third category the coaching system of the federations needs enhancement. In the first category, the federations prepare a coaching plan, and the Olympic Committee confirms the contents of the plan and grants a lump sum for its implementation. In the second category, the coaching plan and the support granted by the Olympic Committee are directed to individual athletes. Based on an agreement between the federation concerned and the Olympic Committee, part of the financial support can, however, be used to develop the coaching system. In the third category, the subsidies are used to develop the coaching system (Finnish Olympic Committee 2006).

The Olympic Committees' youth elite sports programme mainly consists of financial support for training camps. Camps are organized by the Olympic Committee. The national sport federation receives about 2,500 euros per selected athlete in the form of coaching support. The Olympic Committee also supports the costs incurred in hiring full-time special Olympic coaches for youth athletes.

National sport federations and coaching

There are 74 national sport federations in Finland. The number is higher than in the other Nordic countries. This indicates that some of the national sport federations are very small. For the most part, the financial situations of the Finnish national sport federations is, however, as good as those of the neighbouring countries. There are two major exceptions. The economic situation of the football and skiing federations is clearly weaker than that of their counterparts in Sweden and Norway.

The structural disintegration of the Finnish sports movement probably affects small national sport federations most. They do not have sufficient means to maintain a coaching system, and the shared coaching resources of the national sport federations are scarce. On the other hand, the weak cooperation between the national sport federations in the area of coaching affects all. In a recent survey carried out by the Finnish Coach Federation, a total of 88 per cent of 519 coaches said that there is not enough cooperation between the national sport federations in Finland (Sonera Next Generation ja Suomen Valmentajat ry 2010).

The national sport federations are responsible for elite sport camps and training arrangements, and for competitions in Finland and abroad. In most cases, the camps take place at sports institutes, and the national sport federations pay for this. The national sport federations contribute with coaches, but these coaches do not coach individual athletes directly. Coaching in Finland is still based on the personal relationship between the coach and the athlete. Several internationally recognised athletes have part-time coaches of their own. One cannot, however, say that there is a professional, integrated coaching system in Finland. When trying to find support for their sporting careers, individual athletes and their coaches often face difficulties in the maze of different organizations and actors.

There are lots of knowledge-based sports and coaching competence in Finland but it does not seem to reach the coaches and the coaching system. According to some critics, this knowledge is mainly biological-physical. Human/athlete oriented coaching has not made much progress in Finland (Puhakainen & Suhonen 1999). The problems may be related to the quality of both communication and knowledge. The focus of the Finnish elite sports organizations seems to be one step aside from individual athletes and their coaching needs. The current situation is that the Finnish coaching system cannot fully ensure the quality of coaching for even the best athletes (Niemi-Nikkola 2004: 391).

Ministry of Education and Culture and elite sports

The ways state sports funding are granted and allocated are not the same in Norway, Sweden and Finland. In terms of the allocation process, the Norwegian and Swedish systems are similar. The Finnish state-centred method differs significantly from the systems of these two countries. In Finland, practically all sports funds are allocated by the Ministry of Education and Culture, supported by expert organizations. In Sweden and Norway the whole state sports budget is granted to the umbrella organizations (the Swedish and Norwegian Sports Confederations) for reallocation. In these two countries, the umbrella organization carries out the reallocation to their member organizations and their various sectors.

The Finnish Olympic Committee is one of the few organizations that is still authorised to distribute state sports funding in the same way as neighbouring Nordic countries. The state has, however, retained the power to decide on and distribute, e.g. individual coaching and training grants, which are the largest forms of elite sports support in terms of money. On the other hand, the Olympic Committee is able to direct the support to the individuals it has chosen. It prepares the final proposal for the receivers of the stipends to the Ministry of Education and Culture in cooperation with the Paralympics Committee. Neither the Olympic Committee nor the Ministry of Education and Culture is able to decide how the receivers use their stipends. Like artists, athletes in Finland can decide on the use of their stipends.

The first sports stipends were distributed in the mid-1990s. In 1999, they became a regular form of support. The amount of the stipends has increased fast, especially after 2004. Since 2000, the amount has practically doubled, and the growth continues year by year. Sports stipends are tax-free. They can be given to an athlete whose annual income does not exceed euros 70,000. The total amount of sports stipends distributed in 2009 was euros 1,350,000. The number of receivers was 95. The largest was euros 15,000 and the smallest euros 7,500.

The largest stipends are awarded to athletes who can be expected to win medals in the future Olympics, Paralympics or World Championships. The smallest ones go to young athletes who have already been fairly successful in important international competitions and who may be expected to win medals in future elite competitions. Stipends may also be awarded to especially talented athletes even if they have not yet been successful in international competitions. The promotion of gender equality in elite sports is a factor that should be taken into consideration in distributing both large and small stipends (Opetusministeriö 2009).

Using performance management measures in the distribution of state support is a relatively new practice. The amount of support is affected by three target areas: children's and youth sports, adult sports and elite sports. The share of each area is one third of the total allocated to the national sport federations. Within the target areas, the quality of activities counts for 70 per cent and the number of participants counts for 30 per cent. The activities of each national sport federation are assessed and graded every fourth year by a special assessment group. The members of this group come from organizations that have an interest in the target areas, e.g. the Olympic Committee, Young Finland Association and Finnish Sport for All Association (Kunto). The Finnish Ministry of Education and Culture has established direct connections with the elite sports community. One reason for this is the fact that the Finnish sports movement is disintegrated. From time to time, the Finnish state has had to fill the structural gaps between the sports federations and raise issues that concern all the parties involved. Sometimes these interventions have not only dealt with strategic issues but have expanded to the core practices of elite sports. For instance, when the representatives of the ball games were unhappy with the support they received from the Finnish Olympic Committee, they turned directly to the Ministry of Education and Culture. After some twists and turns, the Ministry granted a special temporary subsidy past the coaching support system of the Olympic Committee to team ball games in 2004. This was not well received by the Olympic Committee, and in 2008, the support was transferred from the ministry to the Olympic Committee as part of the general system.

Training

There is a wide range of more or less independent training centres in Finland. *Sports institutes* are the traditional centres. Most of them were established in the first half of the twentieth century. *Sport academies* are network-like newcomers established in the past couple of years. Sports institutes are located in the rural areas and the academies in the main cities of the various regions. The academies have close links with the Finnish Olympic Committee. The sports institutes used to be linked to certain national sports federations, but today they operate quite independently. This section analyses this complex structure from the elite sports, and especially athletes', point of view.

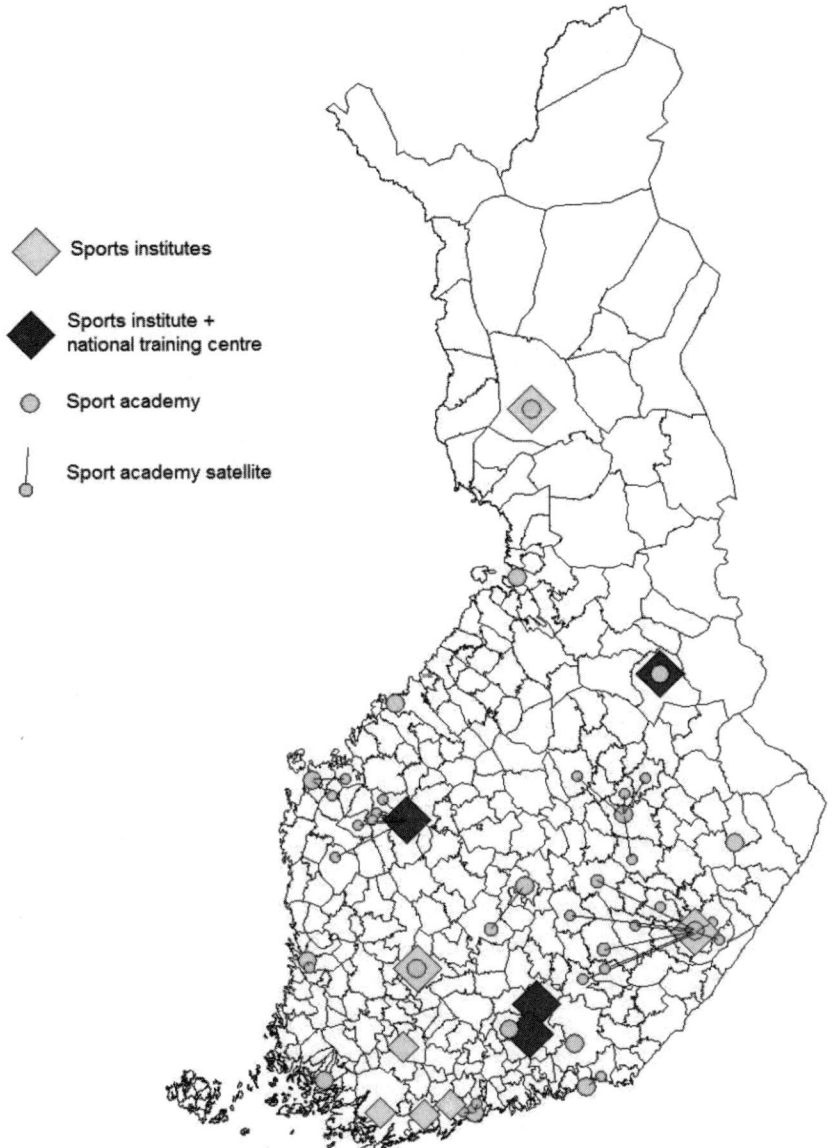

Figure 9.3: Training centres and sport academies in Finland

Sports institutes and training centres

Sports institutes represent a special feature of the Finnish sports system. There are 11 national and three regional sports institutes, all located in rural areas (figure 9.3). They were established by national sport federations or/and confederations in 1927–1977 to support their needs in education and coaching. Nowadays, sports institutes are important adult education centres in the field of sports and physical exercise, in liberal adult education, and in basic and supplementary vocational education.

In the course of the years, the sphere of the activities of the sports institutes has widened. Apart from providing education, they have become everyman's leisure centres for well-being, holidaymaking and training with well-equipped sports facilities and attractive outdoor recreation areas. They also offer hotel services and business and conference facilities for different kinds of meetings and seminars. These more or less business-driven activities have become an important source of income for the institutes.

Today, most of the institutes are run by an independent foundation or jointly by a foundation and a company. Their relationship to the sports movement is not as direct as it used to be. Sports institutes still serve the sports movement, but mainly on the basis of a service provider / customer relationship.

The liberal adult education that the national sports institutes provide is subject to performance-based support from the state. The support is based on an average unit price calculated from the number of student days. Most of it is paid from the state sports budget. The share of the sports institutes of the state sports funds is about 15 million euros, i.e. about 15 per cent. It is unlikely that the sports appropriations of any other Nordic country are used to support education to the same degree.

In their 1987 document, the Finnish Olympic Committee launched the term *(High Performance) Training Centre* (Suomen Olympiakomitea, 1987). The term referred to sports institutes, or more precisely to their extensive resources and knowledge concerning elite sports. The aim was to intensify the use of these resources as a means to promote elite sports' international success and to bring elite sports to selected national sports institutes.

The Finnish Olympic Committee proposed to the Ministry of Education that four national training centres be established: Kuortane, Vierumäki, Pajulahti and Vuokatti. Each centre would be responsible for the specific sport as defined in the 1987 document. A plan for further investments was also introduced. The Ministry considered the training centres important but, did not promise extra funding for this purpose. It was of the opinion that the establishment and operations of these centres should take place within existing state funding. In this way, the state left the decision to the discretion of the sports institutes.

The sports institutes established national training centres by themselves. In official documents, these institutes have been assigned duties and responsibilities concerning elite sports, but without specific support for these activities. In 2000, the Ministry of Education established a working group to reassert the overall national function of the training centres. The conclusion was that two sports institutes should have a special national function in certain sports. These institutes and sports were Varala in judo and women's volleyball, and Eerikkilä in football and floorball.

Since 1987 the question of the training centres has emerged in practically every official or unofficial document dealing with elite sports or sports institutes. The aim was (is) to build training centres that are able to strengthen abilities to compete at an international level. Further, there should be close collaboration between these centres and the Research Institute for Olympic Sport (KIHU). This collaboration has not, however, been fully realized. It is clear that the lack of state funding is an important reason for this. The last, unsuccessful, attempt to establish special funding for the training centres was made by the working group on elite sports set by the Ministry of Education in 2004.

At the moment, the training centres do not receive special state support. State support is based on the number of student days in the same way as with other sports institutes. In this sense all the activities of the institutes are equal. This model for state support discourages a focus on elite sports. In elite sports coaching, the numbers of the participants are small and costs high. So far, the state funds do not encourage the training centres to focus on elite sports.

The role of the training centres is unclear. Consequently elite sports cannot take full advantage of maybe the most significant sports resource and competence cluster in Finland. The combined turnover of the six sports institutes with status as a training centre was approximately 50 million euros in 2009. The total personnel were approximately between 350 and 400. They manage a significant number of sports halls and other training facilities. There is no exact information on the share of the training centre personnel of the total number personnel of the sports institutes. However, in 1999 it was 74 (Opetusministeriö 2000: 19). These employees are mainly hired by the institutes, but some receive their pay from national sport federations.

The scope of the activities of the sports institutes is also reflected in the job descriptions of the training centre personnel. These descriptions are flexible and the personnel perform several different tasks. Apart from elite athletes, the services of the training centres are also offered to keep-fit enthusiasts, various organizations and communities, and to foreign athletes and sports organizations. A recent example of innovative collaboration with foreign organizations is the cooperation of the Kuortane Sports Institute with the McLaren Formula 1 Team.

The sports institutes and their training centres are no longer direct members in the Finnish sports movement. They are independent actors, and it is difficult to estimate how much of their work is for the Finnish sports movement. Interdependence, however, exists especially in view of the training centres, in which the sports institutes have undoubtedly invested their own resources. More significant than the sports institutes' own immediately measurable investment in elite sports is perhaps the overall infrastructure that they maintain thanks to the wide scope of their operations. The question of a suitable steering/support measures to allow elite sports to utilize the infrastructure provided by the sports institutes in a more effective way is still unsolved.

Sport academies

Compared with sports institutes, sport academies are a fairly new phenomenon. They are local cooperation networks established after 2000. Educational institutes, sports organizations and various providers of support services in the same area cooperate to help athletes to combine their civil and sports careers. The Finnish Olympic Committee has coordinated and directed the activities of the academies since 2007. The systematic evaluation of their activities started towards the end of the same year. The Olympic Committee has granted a special elite sports status to the sport academies that meet its criteria (Suomen Olympiakomitea 2007; 2009).

At the moment, there are 15 sport academies in Finland. Most of them operate in major cities, such as Helsinki, Tampere, Jyväskylä, Kuopio and Lahti, i.e. cities that can also offer educational services to athletes. The network of sport academies covers the whole country and thereby supplements the network of sports institutes that operate in smaller towns and in the countryside. Sometimes the sport academies and sports institutes belong to the same network, e.g. Kuortane and Varala (in Tampere) (see figure 9.3). The operational models and networks of the sport academies have developed in different ways, depending on the local circumstances. They include foundations, associations and various kinds of agreement-based networks.

Since 2008, the Olympic Committee has provided special support to sport academies with elite sports status. The aim is to secure and strengthen coordination of the academies. In 2008 and 2009, the total amounts of subsidies were euros 117,000 and euros 155,000, respectively (Suomen Olympiakomitea 2009: 4). The funding received from other sources varies from area to area. The total finances of the 12 sport academies evaluated by the Olympic Committee in 2008 and 2009 amounted to about two million euros (Suomen Olympiakomitea 2009: 4). Owing to the network format of the activities, it is difficult to know the exact distribution of costs among the various organizations.

The activities of sport academies resemble the system of elite sports support currently being developed in certain major cities in Sweden. One example is Malmö Idrottsakademi (MIA), which operates as a cooperation network of the City of Malmö, Malmö University and the Skåne Sports Area (see http://www.malmoidrottsakademi.se). The Malmö network is one of the pilot projects implemented by the Swedish Sports Confederation (RF) to promote the local network that help athletes combine sports and studies. The most central actor in the Swedish sports, the Swedish Olympic Committee (SOK), has not been mentioned in the context of these local networks. So far, the activities of the Finnish sport academies seem to be more organized than their Swedish counterparts.

Research and development

In Finland sport sciences are in general well supported financially through the sport budget. This also holds true compared with the other Nordic countries. Most of this financial support is directed to academic research. KIHU is the only organization that fully focuses on elite sports research. Moreover, there are about 25 organizations (mainly universities and sports institutes) that conduct research or development connected with elite sports. This section deals with the co-ordination problems that originate from insufficient interaction between academic institutions, and from the needs of the elite sport actors

Research Institute for Olympic Sport (KIHU)

The Research Institute for Olympic Sport (KIHU) is located in Jyväskylä, Central Finland. The University of Jyväskylä is the home to Finland's only Faculty of Sport and Health Sciences. Therefore Finnish sports research is concentrated in the Jyväskylä area. The KIHU Research Centre was founded in 1990. At first it was one unit of the Finnish Foundation for Promotion of Physical Education and Health (LIKES). The independent KIHU Foundation was established in 1999 by LIKES, the University of Jyväskylä, the City of Jyväskylä and the Finnish Olympic Committee. The purpose was to promote elite sports research and to apply research results to practical coaching and education. The Board of the KIHU Foundation is nominated by the University of Jyväskylä (3), the Olympic Committee (3), the City of Jyväskylä (1) and the Board itself (2). The Olympic Committee has to consult the University before nominating their board members. In 2010, the number of KIHU's staff was about 35.

KIHU's role is as a relatively autonomous research institute. It is not the R&D unit of the Finnish Olympic Committee. It is more academic by nature, and its sphere of research topics often goes beyond that of the research unit of an organization like the Olympic Committee. KIHU is not directly responsible for coaching and training athletes, either. An athlete is not a common sight in the corridors of the KIHU's office. In summary, KIHU's sphere of activities, responsibilities, working methods and structural position are not similar to, e.g. Olympiatoppen.

KIHU influences practical coaching indirectly through projects. There are three different types of projects. Firstly, the outcomes of the research projects have to meet scientific criteria. The funding decisions of the projects are usually made by the Ministry of Education and Culture on the basis of peer-reviewed scientific applications. Secondly, the aim is to develop equipment, methods or programmes that benefit athletes, coaches or sports in general. These projects are mostly supported by Tekes (the Finnish funding agency for Technology and Innovation), the Finnish Olympic Committee or the Finnish Paralympics Committee. Thirdly, KIHU implements service projects at the request of customers to satisfy their needs and demands. KIHU's customers include sports associations, training groups, sports institutes, testing centres and private companies. As the above indicates, KIHU is not an organization that sets goals for elite sports and thereby an interested party. KIHU's framework of activities is defined by the objectives set by the customers that order projects or by scientific goals.

Conclusion

The Finnish Olympic Committee bears the main responsibility for developing and coordinating elite sports. It sets guidelines for the development of elite sports in the national sport federations through shared planning and economic incentives. The responsibility and the control of the Olympic Committee do not, however, extend to the operational level. The Committee is not able to provide tools or a workforce for coaching and training athletes. The national sport federations are responsible for the goals they set for themselves, and most of them also have coaching resources to reach these goals. Elite athletes are also provided with coaching support, training camps, and high-quality testing and training facilities by sports institutes and their training centers.

The sports institutes are independent operators, and their relationship with national sport federations is that of provider-client. The Research Institute for

Olympic Sport (KIHU) also offers support related to coaching. The Institute bears the main responsibility for implementing national elite sport projects. KIHU, too, is an independent foundation, and its relationship with the Olympic Committee is a provider-client relationship.

Elite sports coordination, development, coaching and training resources are dispersed in several independent organizations. Each of these organizations is funded by the Finnish government through the Ministry of Education and Culture.

Unlike in the other Nordic countries, the earmarking of government funds is more organization-based than task-based, without consideration to the overall efficiency. Funding is distributed to autonomous organizations that focus on different elite sports areas. This kind of dispersed model needs cooperation and specialization. This, however, is not the case in the Finnish system. For most of the organizations that receive elite sports support, elite sports are just one field of activities among others. As there are several independent systems and organizations operating in the same area, the result is overlapping tasks and a waste of resources. The roots of this dispersed system go back to the reorganization of the Finnish sports movement in the early 1990s.

One consequence of the dispersed structure and funding of elite sports in Finland is that the organization responsible for elite sports only receives a small share of the funding. The key organization is not able to demand financial accountability of the other organizations or safeguard the interests of elite sports. Compared with the neighboring countries, the problem in Finland is not so much the scarcity of resources as their efficient use to support elite sports. The effectiveness in the use of resources is weakened by the fact that Finland does not have a similar 'watchdog' like the Norwegian Olympiatoppen. Elite sports funding comes from several sources, and the activities are not evaluated in view of the overall interests of elite sports.

The lack of coordination and concentration is by no means due to lack of criticism. As pointed out above, all the elite sports strategies that have been drawn up during the past 20 years have criticized the structure as dispersed and ineffective. This means that the actors on the Finnish elite sports scene were aware of the need to make changes at the time when e.g., Opympiatoppen started to develop from a project into an organization. In spite of several attempts, the implementation of the changes expressed in strategies has not succeeded in Finland in the same way as in Norway. However, the most extensive effort since the early 1990s to improve the structure and working methods in Finnish elite sports is currently taking place in Finland.

12

Danish elite sport and Team Denmark: new trends?

Rasmus K. Storm

Team Denmark (TD), established as a kind of public welfare institution in the Danish universalistic welfare state, has changed its organizational strategies of elite sport development over a short period of time. Following an international trend of targeting financial resources toward a smaller number of elite sport disciplines, TD is increasingly incarnating the shift towards new public management that spreads out through the public sector from the 1970s/1980s and onward (Knudsen 2007: 57, 244; Hansen 2008; Gjelstrup & Sørensen 2007: 21). Attempts to introduce market incentives and raise efficiency in this way have modified the Danish welfare state. This has also affected the Danish elite sport policy, leading to a stricter focus on international success in the daily operations and rhetorics of TD.

In terms of sporting results, this development seems to be positive – at least so far. In 2009, Danish elite athletes achieved their best international results to date, thus offering moral support to TD's strategy. Regardless of these international successes, however, a network of federations, which have faced cutbacks or exclusion from financial support due to Denmark's new elite sport program, is now challenging TD's operations. They claim that the newly established practice of elite sport support is inconsistent with the political intentions behind Danish elite sport policies in general. The members of the network – entitled 'Elitekurs' – want to regain their status as members of the Danish elite sport family.

Focusing on this growing controversy in Danish elite sport, this chapter deals with the tensions between the traditional Danish elite sport policy and new international trends. A central question is whether the targeting approach to elite sport support is an appropriate solution to current challenges facing Danish elite sport.

The chapter is structured as follows: The first part presents an overview of the organization of Danish elite sport, its finances and concept of support. This section also includes a brief introduction to recent developments in Danish elite sport policies since the revision of the Danish Act of Elite Sport in 2004. The second part focuses on international elite sport developments, as a context for the Danish trends and arguments for taking a new path ahead. The third part discusses specific challenges to Danish elite sport. The last part sums up and provides some reflections on how the Danish elite sport system is likely to develop.

Organization and development

The Danish elite sport model has traditionally been characterized by decentralisation and cooperation within a formal hierarchy. Private associations and clubs at the lower levels make up nation-level sports federations that are part of umbrella organizations, such as the National Olympic Committee and Sports Confederation of Denmark (DIF). Since 1984, this model has been modified and supplemented by Team Denmark (TD), a public organization responsible for elite sports development.

A Danish act on the improvement of elite sport (Lov nr. 643 af 19. december 1984 om eliteidrættens fremme) was passed in 1984. Even though it was proposed to the parliament by a conservative central government – it can largely be viewed as the institutionalization of social democratic welfare state ideals of equality and social concern (Bøje & Eichberg 1994: 72; Nielsen 1996: 109, 117; Ibsen, Hansen, & Storm 2010). The left-wing parties saw the initial proposal as controversial. It was specifically aimed at supporting elite sport, and this narrow view on elite sport did not mirror the principles of equality that characterized socialist parties at that time. However, the political process that followed introduced additional concerns; including the possible consequences of leaving elite sport developments to be dictated mainly by market forces. The inclusion of such wider concerns eventually won support from the socialists as well (Løvstrup & Hansen, 2002: 85). It seems clear that without addressing these wider concerns, the act probably would not have gained the necessary support enabling it to pass.

Although the act gives TD a major responsibility for elite sports development, the central elite sport institution is highly dependent on the federations responsible for elite sports disciplines. The Danish federations are also heavily dependent on the financial resources provided through TD's concept of support. In fact, most federations could not uphold their engagements in elite sport if they were left to fund it alone. Small federations outside mainstream media coverage are especially dependent on TD's funding as sponsors primarily stick to disciplines that are exposed to large audiences. Denmark's municipalities are also seen as important partners for TD. They provide facilities for top level sports as well as mass grassroots participation. However, as TD is responsible for the overall framework and planning, as well as distributing financial support to the federations, it is the principal actor in Danish elite sport (Løvstrup & Hansen 2002; Storm & Nielsen 2010a).

Key financial numbers

When controlled for inflation, TD's revenue has slightly decreased from 2001 to 2009, having peaked in 2006 and ended at its lowest point so far in 2009 (see figure 12.1). In 2009 the state provided 69 per cent of TD's revenue, the DIF (whose main source of income is also the state, e.g. lottery money) 16 per cent and the remaining 15 per cent came from sponsors and television rights. The bulk of TD's expenses go directly to the federations' activities for their top athletes, while the remainder is spent on a range of activities organized by TD itself. The latter includes partnerships with municipal authorities, costs of special testing and training centres for elite sport, research funding, expertise in anti-doping and sports medicine, funding for events and management and communications costs.

TD's spending, however, only represents a small proportion of the total budget in Danish elite sport. A 1999 study estimated that elite sport accounted for approximately 60 per cent of the sport federations' total expenditure in the broadest understanding of the term (see KPMG Consulting 2002: 3.). Based on these figures, which are based on uncorroborated data provided by the federations, it is estimated that the federations' total spending on elite sport is approximately twice that of TD. Consequently, the total budget for elite sport at the national level is estimated to approximately euros 60 million p.a.

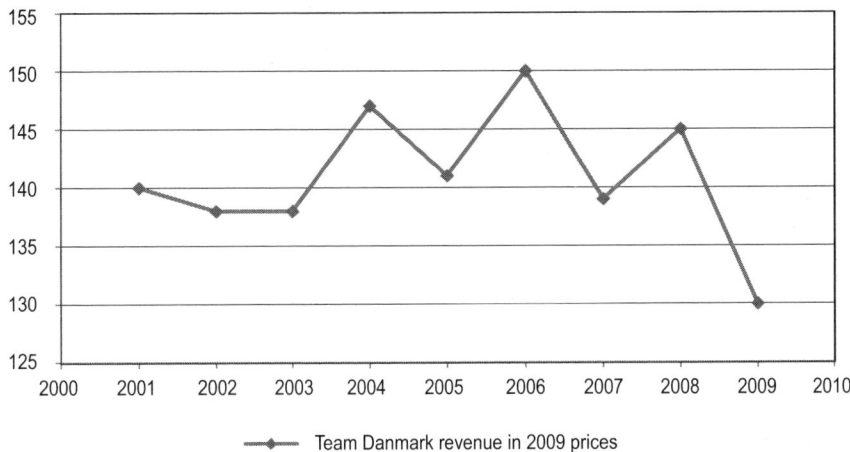

Figure 12.1: Team Denmark revenue in 2009 prices in million Danish kroner (140 million DKK equals 19 million euros; 130 million DKK equals 17.5 million euros)

To calculate the spending on elite sport in local sports clubs, the resources from municipalities and the costs associated with commercial sports would need to be added to this figure. However, reliable data are not available for either of these factors.

How does Team Denmark support elite sport?

TD distinguishes between three levels of elite sport. International elite sport consists of athletes judged as capable of winning medals at European championships, World Championships and the Olympic Games. National elite sport consists of athletes who represent their country or club in senior international competitions, as well as talented youngsters with the potential to reach the international elite as seniors. Club elite sport consists of athletes who compete at the highest competitive level in Denmark. TD aims its support at the international elite and talented youngsters at national level (Team Danmark, 2009).

As mentioned above, almost two-thirds of TD's funds are earmarked for financial support to the individual federations' work at the elite level. To be eligible for such funding, a federation (e.g. football, athletics or rowing) must draw up an analysis of the discipline's potential in terms of development and results. This analysis, which is conducted in collaboration with TD, includes – among other things – a study of the international results achieved by Danish athletes or teams, of the quality and quantity of the training, and of the level of professionalism of the trainers. It also includes the federation's objectives and strategies for recruiting talent, and takes into account the elite athletes' education/training, nutritional and financial conditions, and so on. Finally, it identifies organizational, financial and facility issues deemed to impact the capacity for elite sport development. Based on this broad analysis, TD evaluates whether the federation qualifies for elite support.

A new and targeted approach to elite sport support

Over the last couple of years the number of federations (i.e., sports disciplines) supported by TD has been narrowed. The scope of this chapter does not allow for a detailed analysis of the processes behind this, but it is related to the impact of new public management in the Danish public sector (see Knudsen 2007: 38; Gjelstrup & Sørensen 2007). For TD, the outcome of this has been the establishment of a 'performance contract' with the Danish Ministry of Culture for the period 2006 – 2008 regulating the goals of the organization.

One of the main objectives of this contract, which was a direct result of a revision of the act on elite sport in 2004, was to clarify the relations between TD and the Ministry of Culture. Another central objective was to ensure a better record of medals in the 2005–2008-period than in the foregoing 2001–2004-period (Storm, 2008).

The funding for TD has remained at almost the same level in both periods (measured in 2009 prices). In average TD received 18.8 million euros in revenue per year in the 2001–2004 period and 19.3 million euros on average per year in the 2005–2008 period. The last years TD has pursued stricter priorities to keep the pace internationally, given the increased focus on medal capability stressed in the performance contract. The necessity to prioritize and target financial support was emphasized in TD's concept of support, as well as in comments to the final law document, which in turn regulated TD's goals (Storm 2008: 54.).

An implementation of the concept of support was planned to follow the 2001–2004 period. At that time, powerful sources in TD had already tried to narrow down the number of federations entitled to financial support. A 'political riot' among the federations that felt excluded started a political debate among a range of stakeholders and decision makers in Danish elite sport policy. The plan was never fully executed. Instead a new plan was developed, which reallocated TD's resources in more moderate ways. It was still, however, in favor of a smaller set of federations.

In 2009 another step was taken towards stricter performance-based criteria of support. On the rhetoric level this step was viewed as a necessary move due to decreasing sponsorship and lottery revenue following the credit crunch crisis. However, this step was also an excuse to continue ahead on the path that was only moderately altered a few years before.

The changes in TD's strategy can in short be summarized as follows: In the 2001–2004 period, 16 federations lost their financial support from TD, whereas in the 2005–2008 period 17 federations had their funding reduced. In 2005–2008, 16 other federations (primarily federations with athletes categorized as internationally elite) received more support than they did in 2001–2004 (Storm 2008: 68). However, in 2010 two more federations were excluded from financial support. In addition 14 federations had their funding reduced; 10 of them by more than 20 percent. Three federations received increased funding, while another 10 federations received special funding targeted at medal candidates in the 2012 London Olympic Games.

The development described above can be viewed as a symbolic shift from a more universalistic 'public service' approach, previously conducted by TD, to a more performance orientated model: 'Money in exchange for medals'. Thus, instead of allocating its resources more broadly to a large set of federations, TD is increasingly focusing on Olympic medal disciplines and candidates. A growing number of federations, however, do not have short-term medal potential in these prestigious disciplines, and are therefore left to run their elite sport programs without or with decreasing financial support.

The consequence of this policy change is that a range of elite athletes are not covered by the ideals of social awareness and responsibility originally laid down in the 1984 act and upheld in the 2004 amendments. It has been argued that the targeting process is inconsistent with the overall Danish tradition in the field of elite sport policy. Some Danish federations contend that it is an outright illegal development, as the narrowing of priorities leaves a growing number of elite athletes outside the scope of the law on illegitimate grounds.

This controversy has arisen because the 2004 act appears to be unclear about the relationship between international medals, social concerns and talent development. On the one hand it stresses the social aspects of elite sports, together with TD's general responsibility for ensuring talent development.

But on the other hand it also stresses the need for TD to prioritize its resources in more efficient ways to increase the Danish medal portfolio.

In practice, TD links the goal of securing more international medals to its funding. Higher efficiencies are viewed as its primary concern. This goal also can be said to be in line with the overall political environment. Since the 1970s, shifts between conservative/liberal and social democratic governments have led to several new public management reforms. The objective has been to ensure a greater foothold for market incentives and efficiency in the Danish public sector by placing greater focus on investment output (Gjelstrup & Sørensen 2007; Sørensen 2007; Knudsen 2007). This trend can also be found in other Western countries (Green 2007; Green 2009), but Denmark stands out in a Nordic context.

On a symbolic level the liberal government that came into office in 2001 emphasized this policy, not only regarding the public sector, but also in the Danish society at large. The slogan was: 'We will renew Danish society so that it is natural to reward those who set themselves ambitious goals and achieve them.' The newly elected Danish Prime Minister, Anders Fogh Rasmussen, claimed that by rewarding the best, Danish society would be better off than if it followed the socialist doctrine of equality, which was previously a solid pillar in Danish society and politics. In a broader perspective, the prime minister's statement represents the ideals that have been applied to both elite sport and life in general in the new century (Ibsen et al. 2010).

The arguments used to justify elite sport policy are in line with arguments more generally used when reforms of the Danish welfare state are passed: As macro-trends, such as globalization, increasing global competition among nations, reforms securing efficiency and high work ethics are necessary in order to secure future growth and prosperity of the Danish nation (Kaspersen 2008: 213.). As several scholars have identified a new international trend, described as a 'global sporting arms race', that is threatening nations' abilities to stay competitive in elite sport (De Bosscher, 2007; Houlihan & Green, 2008; Oakley & Green, 2001; see also: Houlihan 2009: 64), these trends give weight to the arguments mentioned above.

Despite the argument that stricter priorities are needed, a closer look at the development of Danish international sport results does not confirm that Denmark is falling behind. There is evidence that Denmark has lost ground, thus calling for a new strategy, but in 2009 the Danish results peaked unexpectedly.

Thus, an interesting question is whether the new performance-oriented strategy has favored this positive development? Or, could it be that the more universalistic strategies pursued prior to the recent targeting strategy were sufficient in keeping up with international developments? We will return to this question after a closer look at the developments of Danish sporting success.

Denmark's standing in the international sporting arms race

Denmark may not seem as successful in elite sports as the other Nordic countries. Due to natural conditions, Denmark has mainly been engaged in summer sports. In this domain it does not have as glorious a past as the former Olympic superpowers, Sweden and Finland. Even Norway has recently, dwarfed Denmark's Olympic Summer Games medal portfolio in addition to its dominant position in the Olympic Winter Games. Still, Denmark has held a strong position in its two major team sports, football and team handball. Denmark is the smallest nation that has ever won the European Championships in football (1992). It has also won the European Championship (2008) in handball for men, and it has also won three successive Olympic gold medals (1996–2004) in handball for women. In addition, Danish elite athletes have consistently had top level international results in sports such as badminton, sailing, rowing and cycling.

At the Olympic Summer Games, Denmark's medal portfolio has been remarkably stable (Storm & Nielsen 2010a: 9): Denmark has won six to eight medals in 10 out of the 16 Olympic Games after the Second World War, including the last five games. No other country has experienced similar stability. If the total number of Denmark's medals is divided by its inhabitants, Denmark has consistently been placed among the top 10–15 nations in the world. In fact, Denmark has slightly improved its standing in the last two Olympic Games with eight and seven medals respectively (Storm 2008; Storm 2009; Storm & Nielsen 2010a).

Denmark's medal portfolio in World Championships, or Olympic sports events in the years between the Olympic Games, has not been so stable. The average total number of Danish medals has decreased in the three last periods between Olympic Games (1997–1999: 12 medals; 2001–2003: 7 medals; 2005–2007: 5 medals). Denmark's standing in the top 8-points scale shows a similar trend. The latter includes rankings from no. 4 to no. 8 in addition to medals. It is used as an indicator of how capable nations are of competing at the highest level, since the top 8-points scale is more reliable than a tally of medals. The total sum of Danish top-8 points in the Olympics Games decreased between 1996 and 2008 (1996: 108; 2000: 92; 2004: 98; 2008: 87).

The decrease in total top-8 points in World Championships or similar events in the Olympic sports disciplines in the years between the Olympic Games is even more pronounced. This overall trend represents a deterioration of Denmark's international standing in most sports where it has traditionally won most of its medals; in the Olympics and other elite competitions. This is in particular pronounced in sailing and badminton. Denmark has only been able to maintain its standing in team handball and rowing (Storm & Nielsen 2010a). In 2006 and 2007 Danish sport was considered to be in a dire situation, but soon after success peaked in 2009.

The 2009 year of success

2009 stands out with dramatic improvements of results compared to the decreasing trend of the preceding years. What is significant is the tremendous increase in top 8-points from 87 in 2008 to 146 in 2009 (+59). The 2009 figure represents top international results in a large number of disciplines, including track and road cycling, swimming, rowing, team handball and badminton (Nielsen & Storm 2010). Not even the previous best year, in 1996, comes close to this. Only four other nations have made a more successful move up the top 8-points table from 2008 to 2009: Germany (+176), Spain (+82), Azerbaijan (+65), and Hungary (+64). However, the German and Hungarian improvements are not so extraordinary, as these nations more or less returned to their respectively high levels after notably unsuccessful years, especially at the 2008 Beijing Olympics.

Denmark's success in 2009 can also be viewed in relation to its population and Gross Domestic Product (GDP) per capita compared with those of other nations. A regression analysis of performance, taking into account differences in population and GDP, reveals that Denmark's performance is ahead of what one would expect. This relative measure of success (see De Bosscher, De Knop, & Heyndels 2003; Kuper & Szymanski 2009; De Bosscher 2007), reflects to what extent a predicted output value, calculated on the basis of the correspondence between a given dependent output (in this case the respective nations' top 8-points) and given independent factors (here: the nations' population and GDP per capita), correspond to real empirical observations.

In short, a nation that obtained a higher score than predicted (from the model) is considered successful in relative terms. A nation that performed below is considered to have not taken sufficient advantage of its available macro-resources, and is therefore unsuccessful in relative terms (De Bosscher et al. 2003: 114). This measure of relative success is a supplement to the absolute measure of success presented above. Taken together these measures may provide a more nuanced impression of elite sport success.

Factors behind the Danish 2009 peak

What are the reasons behind the sudden peak of the Danish athletes, both in absolute and relative terms, in 2009? More research is necessary to fully understand this development, but it seems very likely that a range of parallel developments have an influence. In short these can be distilled to the following: (1) in the 2001–2009 period TD gave its largest payout to Danish sports federations; (2) public funding allocated for Danish elite sport grew in general; (3) municipal involvement in Danish elite sport development became stronger; (4) TD resources were used more efficiently; and (5) there was a post-Beijing 'relaxation' among some of the most powerful sporting nations.

1) Largest numerical TD payout to federations in the 2001–2009 period

As described above the funding available for Danish elite sport through TD has more or less remained on same the level since 2001 to 2009, with a slightly decreasing trend (controlled for inflation) hitting a low in 2009.

This suggests that the 2009 results came out of lesser resources than in previous years. However, a closer look at accounting data reveals that TD used a larger amount of its revenue on the supported federations each year in the 2005–2009 period – ending in a culmination in 2009 (despite the falls in revenue in that particular year). Taking this overall targeting process into consideration, the amount allocated to the top federations – mainly aimed at winning medals in favored Olympic disciplines – was higher than ever before. Even though the year-by-year increases – according to the available data – were incremental, it is reasonable to assume that this financial build-up had an effect on the 2009 success.

2) Growing governmental funding for Danish elite sport

Besides the financial build-up provided by TD, other public sources of funding grew, in line with the growing governmental interest in sport since the Danish elections in 2001. First, the Danish government launched an 'Action plan to attract major sporting events to Denmark', for which 265 million DKK (33.3 million euros) has been earmarked for the years 2008–2011. Around 40 million DKK (5 million euros) of this total was given to TD, to be spent on improving talent recruitment and development.

Furthermore, a significant amount has been provided for new facilities for events and elite sport through 'Elitefacilitetsudvalget' – administered by the Danish Foundation for Culture and Sports Facilities – giving the municipalities incitements to build new elite sports facilities. Finally, the Danish 2009 'year of sport' – initiated as a part of the above mentioned action plan (and in which the IOC Congress and Session was held in Denmark) – resulted in several international sporting events and championships being hosted in Denmark. In at least two cases, this seems to have had a positive effect on Danish results. In the Finn dinghy sailor class Denmark, somewhat against expectation, won the gold medal. Similarly, in the 2009 World Wrestling Championships – held in Herning – Denmark won one silver and one bronze medal. As pointed out by Johnson and Ali (2000), home advantages often affect the host's capabilities of becoming successful.

3) Stronger municipal involvement in elite sport

Supplementing the growing state-focus on elite sport described above, a new formal cooperation between TD and Danish municipalities was initiated. This was a consequence of the revised act on elite sport in 2004. Today 18 municipalities (expected to become 20 during 2010) have a formal corporation with TD that entails various demands on sports organization at a local level. This has released financial as well as organizational resources focused at elite sport development not previously seen in Denmark at the municipal level.

Furthermore, the development of local elite sport funds – often under municipal administration or with significant municipal support – aimed at coordinating local efforts and raising sponsorship revenue for local elite sport projects, has increased in the years following the 2004 elite sport act revision (Storm & Brandt 2008: 115).

4) Efficient use of resources on the level of TD

Another factor behind Danish success may be the effective use of resources, partly linked to the organization and strategies of TD. Such factors are difficult to measure in an exact way. As pointed out in Storm and Nielsen (2010a) and Storm (2008), TD is more able to pursue strict priories based on potential for international performance. Even if there is room for improvements in certain areas, the overall impression of TD, with regard to efficiency and organization, is very positive. This may explains some of the achievements in last decade, including the 2009 peak.

5) Post-Olympic 'relaxation'

A final explanatory factor for the historic Danish results could be that other nations have relaxed their sporting efforts in the 2009 post-Olympic year. For example, the Danish gold medal in track cycling for teams at the World Championships in Poland must be seen in relation to the fact that Great Britain, which dominated the Beijing Olympics, did not bring their best team to this event. In addition, the Danish gold in the Finn dinghy sailor class was won when Ben Ainslie, the best sailor in ten successive years, did not participate.

China also took a year off after Beijing. It did not participate in a number of disciplines at world tournaments, and in others it sent new and inexperienced athletes instead of established stars. It should also be noted that American and Australian results also declined measured in absolute terms. The same goes for Norwegian athletes, following their peak in summer disciplines in Beijing. The weaker results of these nations, to a certain degree, contributed to the impressive increase in Denmark's top-8 point total in 2009.

Concluding remarks and perspectives: leaving the universal welfare state model of elite sport support?

Discussions on the development of Danish elite sport prior to and following the Beijing Olympics have been centred around two main questions: First, whether the level of public funding available for TD is sufficient for keeping up with the pace of the international sporting arms race; and second, whether TD should continue the trend of supporting only the (most internationally competitive) Olympic sports – resulting in a more narrow and performance-oriented approach to elite sport development.

The two questions are closely connected. As indicated above, Denmark actually comes out as an over-achiever over the examined period, thus simultaneously improving its standings in absolute as well as relative terms in 2009. This finding brings into question the strategy of increasingly prioritizing resources, focusing on a narrower set of sports. The related question is whether Denmark needs to take the threat of a growing international sporting arms race more seriously.

One may argue that a growing international competition is imminent, thus giving weight to a never-ending optimizing of resources to prevent other nations from closing in or moving ahead. While preliminary results indicate a return to a more normal level of overall performance by Danish athletes in 2010, some argue that further action is needed. However, as Denmark is doing quite well, and there are no significant signs of a current or coming performance crisis, why continue down a path that increasingly focuses on narrow performance goals? This brings us to the second question.

Seen from an international perspective, TD is following the international trend of targeting its resources (Oakley & Green 2001) in order to adapt to the environmental development and utilize scarce resources. Presumably, such an approach makes it possible to exploit available financial resources more efficiently. Consequently, it would increase the probabilities of winning medals, as the available resources are pooled on disciplines with short-term medal chances. However, the direct consequence of this approach is that the smaller and not-so-popular sports in Denmark are left to themselves without any (or with very small) chances of building or maintaining an elite sports program. In response to this concern, several Danish federations have formed a network aimed to challenge TD and appeal to Danish politicians about the future elite sport policy.

Representatives from the network argue that the new approach is inconsistent with the act on elite sport. It discriminates athletes based on their respective disciplines, leaving them without the 'welfare state' elite sport rights so fundamental to the intentions originally pursued in the act.

Whether narrowing down the number of federations and athletes covered by TD support can be considered outright illegal is not clear. Much is pointing to the conclusion that that is not the case. However, it can be argued that recent developments have moved TD away from its position as an institution supporting certain universal welfare state ideals in Danish elite sport. Conversely, it can be argued that the observed development is consistent with the demands from the general political environment. The implementation of new public management reforms characterizes the Danish welfare state in many areas. The result is an increasing focus on (quantitative) performance output.

Dependent on whether one finds this development fair and necessary or inconsistent with Danish tradition, the new path can be seen both as positive and outright destructive. This is not for this author to decide. What seems clear, however, is that the question of who should be entitled to support will become a cornerstone in the debate over Danish elite sport in the future. Exactly how the debate turns out remains to be seen, but it is likely that it will involve a fierce battle between the supporters of the new elite sport policy and the federations in line of exclusion. It is along this fault line that the future of Danish elite sports model will be formed.

13

Olympiatoppen in the Norwegian sports cluster

Svein S. Andersen

Norway, as all sports nations, has had its ups and downs. The results in the Winter Olympics of 1980 and 1984, as well as the Summer Olympics of 1984 (Norway boycotted the Summer Olympics in 1980), were particularly disappointing. In late 1984, Project 88 was created to support elite sports. The project had a particular focus on the 1988 Olympics, but short-term results did not materialize. In the 1988 Olympics, for the first time, Norway did not win any gold medals in the winter games. However, it was decided to build on and extend the central elite sport effort. The Olympic Top Sports program was created in 1988 (see chapter 2). A centre for top sports, built in 1986, was integrated into the Olympic Top Sports program in 1993. Norway had been awarded the winter Olympics for 1994. This provided increased funding for a special effort. The 1994 results were far beyond expectation. It is quite common that Olympic hosts experience improved results. However, the Norwegian case is exceptional in that improvements have been lasting, both in winter and summer sports.

Attempts to learn systematically from experience are a central feature of all elite sports. Reliable learning is dependent upon good judgement in ambiguous situations. The challenge is to apply, develop and adjust knowledge to the special needs of athletes and teams. In accordance with this, the activities of the Olympic Top Sports Program from the start had the ambition of being 'knowledge-based and leading in the systematization and application of knowledge from research and training activities'.

The key question here is how the leadership and organization of the Norwegian Olympic Top Sports program supports a model for reliable experience-based learning across different sports. The way this learning model is practised may vary within the program itself, and also within different sports. However, the systematic support for reliable learning seems to be a major factor behind significant improvement of Olympic results over the last 25 years. Marginal differences in reliable learning may, over time, have a major impact on results. In the words of the head of the program: 'We focus on the details, without letting the detail steal the focus from us'.

In the international context, the organization of Norwegian elite sports is characterized by a high degree of cooperation and active exchange across sports. In this sense the Norwegian elite sport system can be viewed as a cluster, an inter-organizational structure characterized by rivalry and cooperation stimulating the development and application of competences and capacities that may be exploited by the different sports (Porter 1990; Maskell 2001). Olympiatoppen is the core organization that support such processes though formal authority and as a competence-centre that also serves as shared learning arena. Breaking down the barriers between specialist cultures has been central in building a national elite sports culture. The active challenge of specific plans and approaches in individual sports, based on experiences from many different sports, is often said to be the most important task (Kaas et al. 2007).

When breaking new ground, things never go exactly as planned. Small deviations from what coaches and athletes hope and expect are inevitable, even when things go well (Jones & Wallace 2005). Deliberate exploitation of such deviations to learn and adjust training is a key to reliable learning. In the words of an OTS coach: 'Everything is about causes and consequences. No-one initiates a plan without thinking about expected results and how to evaluate and adjust it in the near future.'

Such an attitude to learning is in line with Sitkin (1992) who advocates a strategy of learning through small intelligent failures as the best way to learn from experience. It is also important to look behind big successes and failures in terms of results in competitions. Great performances are rarely perfect, and major failures may be very close to success.

The focus of this chapter is how the overall organization and leadership of elite sport modifies and strengthen efforts of elite sport development that traditionally took place almost exclusively within the national sports federations.

Almost all everyday activities still take place within various federations, but the special national elite effort, with Olympiatoppen in a key role, has added new capacities and dynamics to these efforts. Before we enter the more detailed discussion we will, however briefly describe the Norwegian systems and the research design.

The role of the Olympic Top Sports Program in learning and development

The Olympic Top Sports program has an overall responsibility for the development of Norwegian elite sports. It is the operative organization for elite sports within the National Federation of Sports and the Olympic and Paralympic Committees. In terms of employees and budget, the program is a modest organization. In 2008 it had 26 full-time employees, but there is a considerable number of people involved on part-time contacts and as consultants. The total is about 75, many of them specialists in their area. The budget was about 12.5 million euros, including the cost of participating in the Olympics and Paralympics.

The program's direct support to the federations was in 2005 estimated to 11 per cent of their total financing. Federations receive about the same amount from sponsors, sports arrangements and media rights. There are, however, considerable differences between federations. They use between 20 and 40 per cent of their budget on elite sports. In smaller federations, the contribution from the program is a major part of the total budget for elite sports (Augestad & Bergsgard 2008: 197). This is the case for the rowing federation, which has about 0.5 million Euro euros for such activities. In contrast the skiing federation has about almost 12 million euros. This is about four times as much as the handball federation, which has the second largest budget for elite sports. However, it is not only the amount of money, but the values and demands that follow the money from Olympiatoppen which are important.

The program serves as a linchpin between different elite sport efforts in different sports federations. It has transformed a loose and fragmented network into a cluster. A cluster is a special type of inter-organizational network. This concept has been introduced to explain why some national economic sectors have been able to develop and sustain international competitiveness (Porter 1990; Lazonick 1993; Maskell 2001). A national elite sport system includes great variety across different sports. What makes it a cluster is the ability of its members to identify and exploit the underlying similarities related to relevant resources and the creative use of such resources in different settings within the domain of elite sport.

Clusters create opportunities for exchange of ideas, information and experiences across boundaries. This can happen in different ways; by simply observing what others do, through mobility of key personnel, or systematic gathering and sharing of experience. Such a learning context makes it possible for others to see what is needed to succeed internationally when sharing many of the same local conditions. Although competitions take place in different arenas, there is indirect competition and rivalry related to status, internal resources and external sponsors. Porter (1990) pointed to the motivational effect related to the emotional aspects of local rivalry in such settings, but sharing of experiences can also increase the feeling of security.

We sometimes find organized facilitators that improve coordination and distribution of knowledge within a cluster. This would be a typical function for economic branch organizations. In elite sport, national federations and Olympic Committees may serve as linchpins, but often with limited capacity and scope for exchange and learning. Team Denmark is an active coordinator and supporter of development in different sports. However, the number and types of contacts are more limited than those between Olympiatoppen and various Norwegian sports federations. The latter is characterized by more intense and cross-cutting relationships. The Top Sports Centre also serves as an informal arena where athletes and coaches meet and share experiences.

The program has competence and capacity for direct influence of learning and development processes in elite sports (Gotvassli 2005; Augestad & Bergsgard 2007). However, the contribution to the success in various sports varies considerably, and it cannot be measured in an exact way. Even the best will not always succeed, and there is always someone who wants to do things his own way despite advice to the contrary. Some successful athletes have not participated actively in the program. Cooperation with individual sports may also vary over time, depending on resources, results and individuals. Small federations need resources. The larger ones can be more independent. The Norwegian Skiing Federation is an example of the latter. However, disappointing results for ski jumpers and cross-country skiing in the 2008/2009 season led to closer cooperation with the Olympic Top Sports program in preparation for the 2010 Olympics.

The program has an informal working style, and experience-based knowledge and documented success has a strong standing in the culture. Decisions are made quickly and implemented with vigour. Leadership is partly about influencing policy and priorities in individual sports, partly about challenging and supporting development processes involving individual athletes and teams. The generalist coaches in the program play a key role through actively challenging and supporting coaches, athletes and teams in individual sports. Both the leader and assistant leader of Olympiatoppen use part of their time in such operative activities. Bjørge Stensbøl, who was the leader until 2004, had a different leadership style than the present leader Jarle Aambø. Still, there is considerable continuity in perspectives and approaches. Several of the generalist coaches responsible for the follow up of athletes and teams have been in the organization since the early 1990s.

Cooperation between the Olympic Top Sports program and national sports federations also contains a certain degree of tension and disagreement about 'best practice' and who should take the credit for success (Hanstad 2002; Steen-Johnsen & Hanstad 2007). The overall development model is practised in various degrees within the program and in different sports. Still, the overall success of Norwegian elite sports to a large extent seems to rely on a dominant model for experience-based learning. It is a model that draws upon cooperation between different sports in an effort to exploit the many small failures that are inevitable when breaking new ground. The context for and main relationships in this process will be developed in the rest of the article.

The national elite sport cluster with Olympiatoppen in a central role is the context for learning. This structure creates connections across sports and allows for flexible exploitation of information and ideas. Shared vision creates attitudes that provide direction and focus for learning. Olympiatoppen represents active leadership and specialized competence that contributes to a continuous emphasis on reliable learning. Successful use of comprehensive and robust knowledge in the analysis of unique situations and events contributes to more accurate judgements in development processes. This, in turn, contributes to the further development and legitimacy of the program's organization and learning model.

Before elaborating characteristics of the Norwegian elite sport system, we shall briefly describe the research design and methodology.

Research design and method

The study was conducted over a period of three years. It started with a broad explorative perspective, but gradually the role of the Olympiatoppen in complex and uncertain learning processes emerged as the focus. This case definition reflected what seemed to be the major concern of key actors in the program, in the way they presented themselves and in their everyday priorities. It also reflected a fairly stable context with respect to some overall issues and priorities regarding available resources, the legitimacy of elite sports within the sports federations and in society. Another stabilizing factor is the program's formal role and competences supporting a model for reliable learning and development. These factors are important preconditions for elaboration and refinement of perspectives, roles and tools that support reliable learning.

The study uses different sources of data, as schematically presented in figure 13.1. They contribute to the overall arguments in different ways. Written sources (documents, newspapers, and existing studies) were the starting point for description and categorization of the Olympic Top Sports program. The program has many different facets. However, the emphasis on continuous development through systematic application and use of knowledge pointed towards a learning organization. It appeared to be a pioneering effort in creating a dynamic learning organization in the Norwegian context. At the same time, it had a special role in a national sports systems characterized by exchange of experience and cooperation, but also tensions between the program and different sports federations.

Written sources, including a couple of books by top coaches, provided general descriptions of approaches and working methods in learning and development processes. Repeated conversational interviews were conducted with key persons, mainly leaders and generalist coaches in the program, to develop further details and understanding of such accounts. Such conversations started as open, but increasingly focused, interviews that also involved more active testing of preliminary interpretations of cognitive models and their theoretical implications (Kvale 1996; Holstein and Gubrium 2002). Although informants did not always share my interest for management theory, and sometimes expressed scepticism towards it, they were thoroughly acquainted with a wide range of the practical challenges in modern management.

Developing in-depth knowledge though conversational interviews is an iterative process, where preliminary interpretations of key facts, relationships and theoretical significance are tested in conversations of increasing detail. As in statistical methods, constructing and structuring data is a complex process consisting of many steps of data reduction. Unlike in statistical methods, there are, however, no simple procedures for summarizing the underlying logics and presenting data that support the analysis. The conventional way to deal with this is to use typical examples of approaches, practices and arguments to illustrate essential elements of data structure and interpretation. This is also what is used here (Silverman 2005).

Data	Objectives	Analysis	Indicators/documentation in text
Written sources (documents, newspapers, existing studies)	Establish main characteristics of organization, leadership principles and everyday practices	Description and categorization in relation to known organization models	References
Informant interviews and conversations:	Develop understanding of organization and leadership practices	Establish relationship and consistency between actors' understanding and external description and interpretations	Typical examples of approaches and practices in learning and development processes
	Develop understanding of main model for experience-based learning	Show how structure, leadership principles and practice strengthen intelligent learning from small failures	Typical examples that illustrate relationships
	Critical exposure of facts, descriptions, interpretations and possible relationships. All direct quotes and the way they are used have been accepted by informants.		

The study uses pattern matching as a main procedure for qualitative data analysis (Campbell 1975; Yin 1989: 119). It applies both to preliminary interpretations of facts and relationships, and to overall interpretation and explanations. All interpretations imply additional, and increasingly detailed, empirical observations. As the analysis matures, assumptions and interpretations are validated in relation to ever more comprehensive empirical patterns to eliminate other interpretations and explanations. In this way it is possible to establish systematic relationships which exploit numerous observations in the case. However, in contrast to statistical analysis, it is not the number of observations that provide analytical control. It is the congruence between a rich set of implications that follow from assumptions and interpretations, on the one hand, and observed empirical patterns, on the other (George & Bennett 2005).

Below we will develop the argument that the Norwegian Olympic Top Sports program can be viewed as the central actor in a national sports cluster.

Olympiatoppen's role in the Norwegian sports cluster

In the Norwegian elite sport system sports federations, coaches and athletes are part of an organized network. A simplified illustration is presented in figure 13.1. It pictures a national cluster with Olympiatoppen in a central role, where different sports also are linked to international networks. Only a few sports federations are included in the illustration, but the system is in principle open to all 55 sports federations. Some sports, like male soccer, have been reluctant to participate actively. Not all federations have the international results that are required to get priority in the system due to limited resources. In the periods leading up to Olympic Games, resources are concentrated on sports and athletes with medal chances. Still, in 2008, before the Beijing Olympics, generalist coaches from Olympiatoppen actively worked with 38 sports.[2]

As a linchpin, the Olympic Top Sports program strengthens learning processes in Norwegian elite sport. However, everyday developments are mainly the responsibility of individual sports federations, where contact and exchange with international within-sports expertise is essential. Nevertheless, the program has an important influence due to its formal position, budgetary power, special competence, and as a meeting place for athletes and coaches from different sports. Exchange of experience and involvement across sports contribute to reliable learning. This is widely regarded as a key factor behind improved international results. Until the mid-1990s, the Olympic Top Sports program was pushing for professionalization within special sports federations. Over time, the competence in individual sports has made them important contributors to the collective knowledge pool.

---

2 Yearly report, Norwegian Sports Federation, 2008: 20.

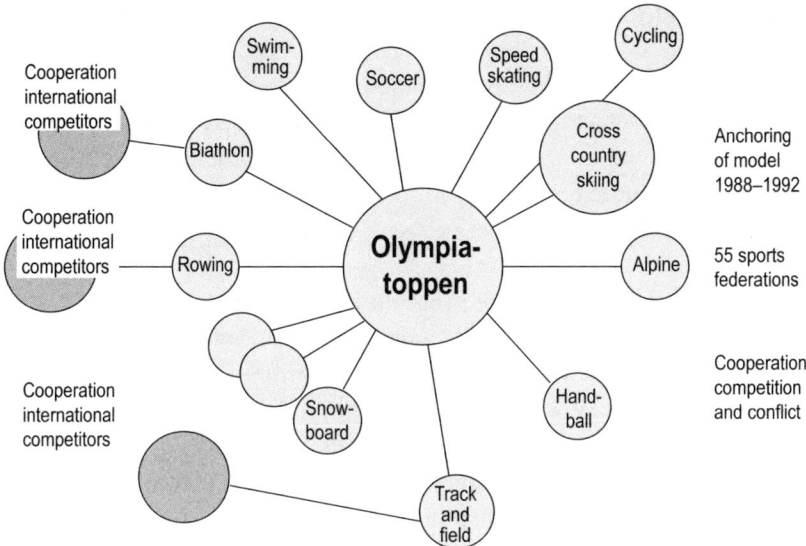

Figure 13.1: The Norwegian sports cluster

From the outset, the key to success has been to create an understanding of the benefits from cooperation and knowledge-sharing across sports (Kaas et al. 2007). This was considered necessary to achieve critical mass in a small country with relatively few talents within different sports. Linking of separate learning horizons and experiences creates a potential for more efficient learning and better judgement, particularly through richness of ideas, information and conceptual variation. Such an approach is consistent with modern ideas about learning organizations, but had a much weaker position in the management literature at the time. Ideas were borrowed from theories on special pedagogic and social interaction (Befring 1977; Schou-Andreassen & Wadel 1981).

The former leader of the program, Bjørge Stensbøl, actively challenged the sports federations and used his authority to strengthen common culture and cooperation. However, Anne Grete Jeppesen, one of the Olympiatoppen coaches, emphasizes that he was very receptive and had a coaching leadership style when meeting coaches and athletes. Breaking down barriers between special cultures and knowledge in individual sports encourages exchange and sharing of experiences. This increases the number of observations and experiences that knowledge development can exploit, while creating increased attention to assumptions that are often taken for granted in individual sports.

This philosophy, which is often repeated, is reflected in the following statement:

> "One of the most important success criteria in Norwegian elite sport is the transfer of experience and competence between training groups in different sports. The challenge is: We must even 'tear down the pyramids'; that is continue to develop transfer of experience and competence between sports.[3]

The key people brought into the program had already proved themselves as world class coaches in their sports. Olympiatoppen offered new career opportunities, to further develop competences through contacts and experiences within different sports. They became generalist coaches. However, their educational and professional background was often outside sports (Kaas et al. 2007: 10). Proven leadership and practical experience, rather than formal competence in sports related disciplines was emphasized. These coaches knew of each other, but did not know each other. They became the core in the new overall model for elite sports development. They represent a competence that is complementary to what is found in individual sports. With few exceptions these coaches have had part-time positions, and often been involved in leadership development in both private and public sector as consultants.

The relationship between Olympiatoppen and individual sports consists of a multitude of crosscutting relationships:

Economic support is based on strict priorities. They focus on teams and individuals that have already achieved or are in the process of reaching international top level. The principle is 'first results, then support'. To get an A-stipend of 15,000 euros, athletes have to belong to the highest international level. In cross-country skiing only four athletes receive such a stipend for the 2010 season. The requirement is that they have won at least one World Cup competition. B-stipends of 9,350 euros are for those on the next level. Also, promising young athletes can receive stipends of 6,250 euros. A total of 44 A-stipends, 53 B-stipends and 36 stipends for young athletes were awarded. In addition 5 teams received support 25 and 85,000 euros.[4] Support for sports federations presupposes that athletes or teams are qualified for Olympiatoppen support.

Generalist coaches at Olympiatoppen are engaged with the different sport. Their role is not to be an additional coach within the sports. They observe, interpret, summarize and communicate lessons learned across sports. An important part of this is to challenge and support plans, as well as various ac-

---

3   Internal report, Olympiatoppen 1999, cited in Gotvassli 2007: 147.
4   www.Olympiatoppen.no, November 30, 2010.

tivities and projects. In this way they act as coaches for the national coaches within the different sports. They may also be directly involved with specific athletes and teams. They may stimulate or require exchange of experiences, documentation of plans and criteria for evaluation. Such demands are in accordance with a development oriented training culture. There is a close link between words and actions. 'What distinguishes the Olympic Top Sports program from most other organizations is that they do what they say they are going to do', says the former leader Bjørge Stensbøl.

From the perspective of individual teams and athletes, the relationship to various sports science specialists may be most important. All athletes and teams receiving economic support also have the right to take advantage of such resources. Medical staff, physiologists and mental trainers provide support, planning, implementation and testing, supplementing the capacities in individual sports. These personnel are located at the Top Sport Centre, and they are part of various projects and often follow athletes on training camps. While most contacts are coordinated through national coaches within the federations, there is also room for individuals to initiate contacts.

So far we have described the overall structure of the Norwegian elite sport system, the role of Olympiatoppen and its relationships to various sports. In the next section we shall take a closer look at the internal structure of the Olympiatoppen and how it contributes to learning and competence development within the cluster.

The internal structure of Olympiatoppen

Olympiatoppen represents ambitious goals and persistence. 'A major objective is to communicate what it takes to compete successfully on the international level', says Finn Aamodt, the main coach for technical and tactical sports within the program.[5] Marit Breivik, coach for the women's handball team which won gold in the Beijing Olympics. who is responsible for team sports in the programs, puts it like this: 'What I like with the Olympic Top Sports program is that that people do not complain about the conditions for a small country that wants to achieve international success. They set ambitious targets, and then they do what is necessary to get there'.[6]

From the mid-1990s, the Top Sport Centre offered training facilities and specialized sport science expertise to support and challenge efforts in indi-

---

5   Conversation, 25 August 2009.
6   Conversation, 16 June 2009.

vidual sports. A matrix structure establishes connections between established experience-based and scientific knowledge. Actors with different roles make sure that important questions are asked and acted upon (Gotvassli 2005: 40, 158–59). This is explicitly stated in the formal presentation of the Olympic Top Sports program:

> The specialist departments shall provide the best competence in their fields. This competence shall be implemented in the sports. In addition, the specialist departments have an obligation to be updated on best international practices as part of their effort to continuously develop their competence. Consequently, specialists should challenge individual sports and coaches in their field, while the coaches should make sure the input is optimal in relation to the specific need of individual sports.[7]

The organizational structure is presented in figure 13.2. This provides an overview over the resources available, but it does not reflect the various processes through which resources are developed, mobilized and used. Such processes may be research-based activities to acquire new competences and capacities, but quite often development is best described as mundane incremental refinements that extend existing capacities.

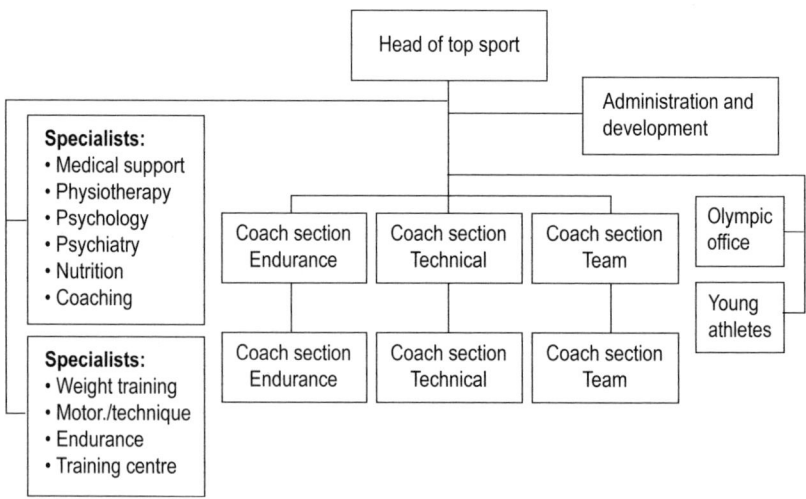

Figure 13.2: The organization of Olympiatoppen

---

7   Olympiatoppen's home page, www.olympiatoppen.no/om_olt/oppbygning/page725.html, 27.2 2008.

The generalist coaches play a key role also in internal processes. They play a key role in making sure that good as well as bad experiences in various sports are shared and reflected upon as part of ongoing learning and development. They also engage in dialogue and cooperation with the specialist who represents scientific knowledge. In this way they have a central role in integrating many different types of formal knowledge as well as experiences from various sports. By watching, discussing and comparing somewhat dissimilar solutions to similar challenges, often emerging from everyday practices, they become sensitive to important details in development and learning.

Learning across sports means that insights and correction may be identified at an earlier time. It is hard for a single sport to replicate internally the process of parallel experimentation and testing of a variety of approaches that take place within the different sports (Maskell, 2001: 928). Experiences from one sport can also be exploited in other parts of the system. The twice Olympic champion Andreas Thorkildsen is, like all javeliners, exposed to the risk of shoulder injuries. However, insight from gymnastics, which has considerable expertise in this field, has contributed to devising training methods that can reduce the risk of such injuries. This has been an important success factor.

Another example of cross-sports learning is reflected in the improvements achieved within Norwegian swimming over the last years. Norwegian swimmers had many important success factors in place, but had been unable to create an international breakthrough. However, the introduction of new elements, based on experiences from successful rowers, was a key factor behind medals in the Beijing Olympics in 2008 and continued international success. These elements related to mental factors and analyses of training methods which supplemented the existing competences within the sport.

In addition to the organized efforts to stimulate learning and transfer of competence, there are also a lot of informal contacts within the networks that add to this. Such contacts are stimulated by the fact that the Top Sport Centre serves a meeting place for coaches and athletes from different sport:

> It is clear that a lot of unorganized transfer of competence takes place, for instance related to cooperation in training...where they train every day and get to know each other very well. Such exchange may include everything, from...technique to discussions about short or long breaks...to general training regimes. That is what they are interested in, discussing training, and athletes do that a lot.[8]

---

8   Leader in Olympiatoppen, cited in Gotvassli 2007: 151.

Although Olympiatoppen does not work only with Olympic sports, it has a special focus on the Olympics. In 2009 such efforts to optimize preparations for the Vancouver Olympics (and Paralympics) was the key priority. This relates to coaching within winter sports, setting ambitious objectives, in terms of both results in competition and training goals, as well as identification of and use of relevant competence in various national sports teams. In addition Olympiatoppen, based on nominations from individual sports, formally decides who should participate, and they have the overall responsibility for organizing all practical aspects related to Olympic participation.

The program emphasizes that everyone has a one hundred per cent responsibility on all levels. Also individual athletes must take responsibility for their own development. An important part of this is their contribution to the development of others. In the words of one elite athlete:

> I know that none can reach excellence alone. To improve myself I have to help others. I demand a lot from other athletes and other persons involved, as they do from me. I try to help others, so that they improve themselves. …In such a culture of extended egoism progress will reflect what everyone is able to learn and exploit in a continuous open process, not in relation to what individuals keep to themselves. [9]

The interconnectedness of Norwegian sports is supported by a strong elite sport culture. The shared culture emphasizes resistance towards simplification and generalizations from individual experiences, critical attention to ongoing processes and expectation based evaluation. In the words of the head of the Olympic Top Sports program: 'We must never believe that we found a recipe. …There must be considerable space for fresh discussions. …Disagreements are necessary to achieve developments.'[10] Comprehensive shared, accumulated and tested knowledge increases the potential for precise communication and more detailed understanding of conditions for its adaptation and use. Such factors reduce the chance that observations and relationships are accepted without strong support.

The presentation so far shows how the Olympic Top Sports program systematically supports exchange of information, ideas and experiences across sports. The richness of information and perspectives creates an institutionalized counterweight to what is often a problem in experience-based learning, namely the tendency to develop too much confidence in judgements based

---

9   The Top Sports Program home page, www.olympiatoppen.no/om_olt/prestasjonstilstanden/page905.html, February 27, 2008.
10 Conversation, 3 June 2008.

on a narrow set of observations. In such a learning environment it is possible, over time, to develop shared perspectives and a rich repertoire for learning under uncertainty. The next question is how the overall structure and culture is linked to everyday learning processes. Below we will show how institutionalized perspectives, leadership roles and tools support a practical methodology of reliable experience-based learning.

The learning model: perspectives, leadership roles and everyday focus

The vision of the Olympic Top Sports Program is to 'to train better than anyone in the world'. This effort can build on comprehensive and reasonably certain knowledge, but to stay ahead it is necessary to continuously develop new knowledge. Practical knowledge is combined with scientific knowledge in experience-based learning under uncertainty. However, even in successful performance development processes there will always be something that does not go exactly as planned. In this sense successes also contain small failures that provide learning opportunities (Sitkin 1992).

In our first meeting one of the senior coaches, Johan Kaggestad, summarized the working methodology in the following way: 'Everything is about causes and consequences. No one initiates a plan without thinking about expected results and how to evaluate and adjust it in the near future.'[11] When experience is evaluated in light of clear and detailed expectations, such small failures are more readily detected and acted upon. Failures can be exploited in an intelligent way. It is possible to achieve big success through small intelligent failures. Such a mindset also represents a counterweight to overconfidence due to repeated success.

The learning model in Olympiatoppen emphasizes a cycle of planned action; expectation-based evaluation that leads to new insights and modifications of existing knowledge. It encourages systematic exploitation of the learning potential in small failures, within a culture that is worried about overconfidence. In the word of Finn Aamodt, a senior coach: 'If something goes well, I become nervous. In such situations we have to work even harder.'[12] Planned action creates expectations that guide evaluation and learning. 'When you train hard, it is important to know that you do it right. It is important to measure whether what you do actually leads to what you want to achieve' (Kaas et al. 2007: 111). A high

---

11 Conversation, 29 November 2007.
12 Conversation, 25 August 2009.

degree of accuracy in the implementation of every training session turns out to be a general success factor in performance groups that succeed over time. [13]

Within the Norwegian sport cluster, key actors share a basic conceptual framework. What would otherwise lead to too much complexity and confrontation can build the *conceptual slack* that supports a strategy of learning through small failures. Schulman (1993:364) defines conceptual slack as divergence in analytical perspectives among members of an organization over theories, models, or causal assumptions pertaining to its production process. This divergence is not over *what* the organization is doing, but *how* it is doing it.

Key actors exercise active leadership in ambiguous situations, acting as translators (Røvik 2007) or brokers (Wenger 1998: 109). Coaches make connections between different sports and situations. They keep processes on track, and remind others about lessons learned. In the words of an informant: 'We spend a lot of time translating experience and reminding people about lessons already learned. These things are of critical importance'.[14] There is a continuous search for small improvements that may increase the capacity for top performances, increasing the likelihood for success in major competitions. The starting point is a systematic mapping of all factors that can influence performance. This includes physiology and psychology as well as technique and equipment. From the perspective of an athlete:

> I work systematically to control an increasing number of factors that may influence my performance. When I get 'used to' control over certain factors, I try to achieve control over more. How much I am able to control depends on how far I have come in my development.[15]

In the words of the head of the Olympic Top Sports program: 'Our work is characterized by a continuous process, where the perfect always can be even more perfect'.[16]

An important difference between elite sports and other organizations is the ability to identify and systematically pursue a few prioritized areas of improvement considered to contribute most to improvement. Such an approach has many similarities to value chain analysis; emphasizing benchmarking of various partial processes (Porter 1985). In the Olympic Top Sports program it is

---

13   Yearly Report, Norwegian Sports Association and Olympic and Paralympic Committee 2002: 16.
14   Conversation with Dag Kaas, 13 June 2007.
15   The Top Sports Program home page, www.olympiatoppen.no/om_olt/prestasjonstilstanden/page905.html, 27 February 2008.
16   *Svenska Dagbladet* 17, May 2009.

sometimes called factor analysis, and an important difference is that benchmarking of partial processes does not necessarily focus so much on what competitors do, although this may be a part of it. It is primarily a tool for development within individual development plans. It is considered vital to focus the energy on what is considered most important for each individual. A generalist coach gave examples where too much focus on competitors had undermined faith in athletes' own plan and methods.

The methodology described emphasizes an unbroken learning cycle, where a focus on improvement of partial capacities dominates everyday efforts. Some efforts, like weight training, have indirect effect on results. However, many training objectives are brought into competitions, just as competitions become part of the training effort. Training requires full concentration on the tasks at hand. If an athlete does not realize how to achieve his best in training, it seems unlikely to happen in stressful competitive situations. In competition, athletes focus on the execution of tasks. This provides a certain feeling of normality in situation where they experience a high level of tension. This is the background for the slogan by the internationally successful ski jumping coach Mika Kojonkoski: 'Normal is enough' (Gangdal 2004).

Process objectives dominate not only in training. Too much focus on overall objectives may threaten focus and even limit the capacity for performance in competitions. Johan Olav Koss, who won three gold medals in the Lillehammer Olympics in 1994, experienced that he could finish a race without being able to give everything, because he had aimed for the wrong finishing time. His coach, Hans Trygve Kristiansen, one of the senior coaches at the Olympic Top Sports program, remarked: 'I thought you were giving all you have, it is after all an important competition.'[17] Eventually, they decided that it made more sense to let Koss focus on his technique, to skate well. If he managed that, it would go faster. And, as it was jokingly added, if the result was a record, it could not be helped. Such an attitude does not only lead to better results, it also makes it easier to see what needs to be corrected for after the competition.

Judgements under such conditions will always include an element of uncertainty. They are best guesses in situations that are not, and cannot be, fully understood. Coaches have a pragmatic view of causal analysis. It is better if it helps produce better results. It is a clinical orientation in line with Starbuck's (2004: 1249–50) report on a physician's view:

> There are many more combinations of symptoms than there are diagnoses…and there are many more treatments than diagnoses. Doctors may make more depend-

---

17 Introduction at the presentation of the book *Fra ord til handling* (From words to action), Oslo, 21 June 2007.

able links between symptoms and treatments if they leave diagnoses out of the chain... Good doctors pay attention to how patients respond to treatment. If a patient gets better, treatments are headed in the right direction.

This learning logic draws upon comprehensive and complex experience-based knowledge. In this way, the Norwegian system for elite sport development represents a context that supports learning through small failures, allowing for mindful learning. This finding is consistent with Weick (2006: 1724) who argues that rich cognitive models and repertoires of action may reinforce learning: '[W]hen people expand their repertoire, they improve their alertness. And when they see more, they are in a better position to spot weak signals which suggest that an issue is turning into a problem, which may well turn into a crisis if it is not contained.' Such relationships strengthen the deductive element in experience-based learning, although it may sometimes be experienced as strong and reliable intuition. Also the literature on expert knowledge (Hodges, Starkes & MacMahone 2006) emphasizes that rich expectations stimulate a sharper eye for details in complex processes. This strengthens the capacity for reliable cause-effect inferences in experience-based learning.

In the preceding sections we have concentrated on elements of the Norwegian sports cluster that contributes to learning and competence development, and through this to the competitiveness of Norwegian athletes and teams. However, working of the system is also dependent on legitimacy and support from the broader sports movement and from societal interests.

The Norwegian model – celebrated and controversial

The Norwegian sports cluster is characterized by across-sport cooperation and systematic efforts to exploit learning and transfer of competences within the system. The system has produced major and lasting improvements of results in international competitions over the last 20 years. It is widely celebrated as a success. In sports, success can be achieved in many different ways. Also, there is often a surprising degree of similarity between those who succeed and those that do not. Marginal differences may have major impacts on results. Over time, successes are vulnerable to erosion through small and unnoticeable variations that are not fully understood. However, it appears that the organization and leadership model in Norwegian sport is quite effective in exploiting limited human and economic resources.

The Norwegian sports cluster is the outcome of an institutionalization process where the view on elite athletes, how to achieve world class performance and the position of elite sport in society has gone through dramatic changes. In significant ways it represents a break with a historical path. The present system reflects a new paradigm; i.e. a set of values and assumptions that make up a fairly coherent frame for evaluating efficiency and legitimacy of organization solutions, activities and results (Andersen 2009). The success and viability of the Norwegian elite sport system rests, therefore, not only on willingness to cooperate at the level of elite sports. It is also dependent on acceptance and active support in the wider sports movement and in society.

There are continuous discussions and controversies relating to the relationship between elite and mass sport, the relationship between Olympiatoppen and sports federations, and how the logic of efficiency should be weighed against the general values of the sport movements and the Norwegian society.

The early development of elite athletes mostly takes place within the sports federations, and the club level is most important. This is where age limitations on competitions among children become an issue. As talents reach a level where they can be expected to compete successfully on the international level, they still spend most of their training within their sport. However, at the same time they become part of the central elite sport system. Elite sport is, therefore, to a large extent part of the broader sports movement.

The relationship between Olympiatoppen is characterized by cooperation, but also disagreements about forms of cooperation, what is best practice within their sport and, not least, who should take the credit for success (Hanstad 2002). The intensity and content of such discussions may vary, but for the most part it may be viewed as healthy and productive (Augestad & Bergsgaard 2007). Some of the bigger and most resourceful sports federations have wanted more autonomy than smaller ones that need the resources that Olympiatoppen can offer. Relationships also vary over time, reflecting specific challenges as well as personal relationships.

Elite sport celebrates the continuous transcending of boundaries. Scientific knowledge is essential in developing new knowledge about new training methods and how much training athletes in different sports can absorb. The possibilities that open up may come in conflict with general values and concerns about health and long term effects. Also, optimal training efforts require that athletes organize their life around this in a very disciplined way. This may involve sacrifices in other areas of life, at an age where others are taking an education or building a family life (Augestad & Bergsgaard 2007).

The controversies mentioned above are not in any way special for Norway. However, the legitimacy of Norwegian elite sport in the wide sports movement and in society depends on how such controversies are dealt with. The reorganization of elite sport that started in the 1980s strongly emphasized that the new system would be based on core values in the sports movement and in the Norwegian society. This is expressed in a yearly report from the Norwegian Sports Federation (2003: 8):

> Norwegian elite sport should, through…performance inspire others to explore their possibilities and potential, it should represent Norway in a positive way, it should reflect the values of sports…

In a recent yearly report (2008: 9) these views are developed further:

> The professional basis for elite sport must be of high quality to ensure that athletes are given the opportunity to realize their ambitions and develop sport skills on the highest international level in an environment where the common sport values; joy, communality, health and honesty dominate, providing Norwegian elite sport with a shared identity and close ties with the rest of the sport movement.

It appears then, that the stability and sucess of the Norwegian elite sport system rests upon a number of trade-offs between different interests and values. Such tensions have to be dealt with on a continous basis. The fact that elite sport in Norway continues to be a contested terrain may well be an important explanation for the overall stability and dynamics of the system.

Concluding remarks

The Olympic Top Sports program has played a major role in the sustained success of Norwegian elite sports. It represents an organizing core in a national elite sport system. At the same time, the successful development and application of tested knowledge is linked to a learning strategy that attempts to exploit the diversity of experiences and competences across sports. This enhances the capacity for precise and self-critical learning from experience in a way that improves the quality of best guesses under uncertainty. It is like playing with loaded dice. The main arguments are supported by general insight from theories about cluster organizations and conditions for reliable experience-based learning.

PART V

Same ambitions – different tracks

14

A comparative perspective on Nordic elite sport: filling a gap

Svein S. Andersen and Lars Tore Ronglan

As pointed out in the introduction, there is a surprising lack of studies that focus on the actual organization and management of modern elite sport in Nordic countries, both at the national level and at the level of individual sports. In contrast, there is a considerable body of recent research on other topics related to sports in the Nordic countries. It includes the organization of sport as a mass movement (Eichberg & Loland 2009; 2010; Helle-Valle 2008; Skille 2005; Støckel et al. 2010); voluntary organizations (Carlsson & Lindfeldt 2010; Ibsen & Seippel 2010; Norberg 1997; Ottesen Skirstad, Pfister & Habermann 2010; Seippel 2010), and sport policy focusing on the societal effects on health and welfare (Bergsgard & Rommetvedt 2006; Bergsgard & Norberg 2010; Enjolras & Waldahl 2007; Skille 2004; 2009). However, also in these areas there is a lack of comparative studies. The fourth issue (vol. 14) of *Sport in Society* (2010) dealt with sport in Scandinavia, but the comparative elements were sketchy and unsystematic. In the domain of Nordic elite sport, comparisons have been almost non-existent.

The SPLISS studies ('Sports policy factors leading to international sporting success') is a popular comparative research program on national elite sport. It focuses on the relationship between rough macro-structural indicators and various measures of international sport results (De Bosscher et al., 2008). Such studies 'skip' the organizational level that influences the actual efforts that may lead to world class performance. In contrast, Boelke (2006; 2009) compared organization of Swedish athletics and Norwegian cross-country skiing, with a specific focus on the role of coach education. In line with the overall argument made here, the study showed that the practices applied in the two systems contradicted, at times, the idea of an overall convergence in international elite sports. Various national systems, or systems with different national sports federations, offered a similar set of support services expectations. However, it was the way support service was organized and how the interaction between athletes, coaches and support staff members was managed that constituted the decisive factors for overall results of the elite sport system (Boelke 2007: 50).

We have identified one study that attempts to compare elite sport in what is considered to be a typical Nordic social democratic country with elite sport in a neoliberal country. The study compared Finland with Australia (Green & Collins 2008). The conclusion drawn from the study was that elite sport lacks legitimacy in Nordic countries, because it violates social democratic values. Australia, in contrast, is considered an example of the opposite, something that is explained by a neoliberal shift in the 1990s. However, the study does not recognize that Finnish politics also experienced a neoliberal shift in the same period. Consequently, as the reader of the preceding chapters will know by now, such a conclusion misrepresents the Finnish case and the Nordic countries as a group.

As mentioned in the introduction, this book focuses on elite sport within a set of countries that represent 'most similar systems' (Meckstroth 1975; Gerring 2007). The four countries are quite similar with respect to size, geographical region, societal and political institutions, and welfare state arrangements. In the domain of sport they share a basic model emphasizing a broad voluntary sport movement and the utilitarian values of sport participation. These similar characteristics are the context of the comparative analysis in this chapter. Since empirical details are well documented in preceding chapters, we will not repeat specific references here.

Our discussion is organized within an institutional framework. One key dimension is the relationship between convergence and divergence. During the 1990s, studies of elite sport emphasized the growing convergence between national systems. They focused on the rationalization, professionalization, scientific research, and the role of elite sport in promoting national pride. The concept of totalization (Heinilä 1984) was used to characterize this trend. Strong international competitive pressures dictate quite similar national responses (Digel 2002; Green & Oakley 2001; Houlihan 2009). However, such responses are also likely to be influenced by local traditions and conditions (Houlihan & Green, 2008: 290).

Although some have pointed to the importance of local variation within the broader trends, there are few studies of these variations and how they come about. Our comparison contributes in two ways. First, it emphasizes the role of the national context in shaping modern elite sport arrangements within the broader trend of convergence. Second, the fact that the Nordic countries represent most similar cases makes it possible to capture sources of local dynamics within similar local contexts. It illustrates how situational contingencies and institutional entrepreneurship reinforce or modify historical paths.

Below we will explore similarities and differences relating to elite sport among the Nordic countries. The comparison builds upon the individual chapters. However, as mentioned in the introduction, we have also carried out independent research for the purpose of conducting a comparative analysis. The discussion will follow the overall organization of the book. We start with the historical development of Nordic elite sport systems. This is followed by a comparison of success stories from particular sports in the four countries. The final section highlights similarities and differences in today's national elite sport systems.

Historical foundation - paths of divergence

The institutionalization of modern sports, including elite sport, in the Nordic countries after the Second World War created a rather similar overall foundation for sports in the Nordic countries. The overall picture of the development of the last decades is schematically presented in figure 14.1.

1950s and '60s: The historical foundation

During the 1950–'60s elite sport was not organized as a special domain. It was part of a broader mass sport movement, in the context of social democratic values and the development of the welfare state. When Norway and Finland took on the task of hosting the Winter and Summer Olympics in 1952, the two countries were relatively poor and marked by the Second World War. However, these events were also part of a welfare state strategy to stimulate the interest among ordinary people to engage in sports. The games created popular enthusiasm, and strengthened efforts to develop infrastructure for sports.

At the time, elite sport in the Nordic countries was the responsibility of individual sports federations where mass sport dominated. Only the national Olympic Committees had a strict international elite sport perspective, by virtue of being subunits of the International Olympic Committee. The developments in the 1950s and '60s became a common point of departure for the elite sport developments that followed in the next decades. Despite such similarities, the four countries have pursued quite different paths to excellence in elite sports over the last 30 years. They all reflect a broad trend towards professionalization and rationalization of elite sport, but all three parts of this book also tell a story about increased divergence. The timing, the political processes, and nature of changes, differed. Below we will compare and discuss these developments in more detail.

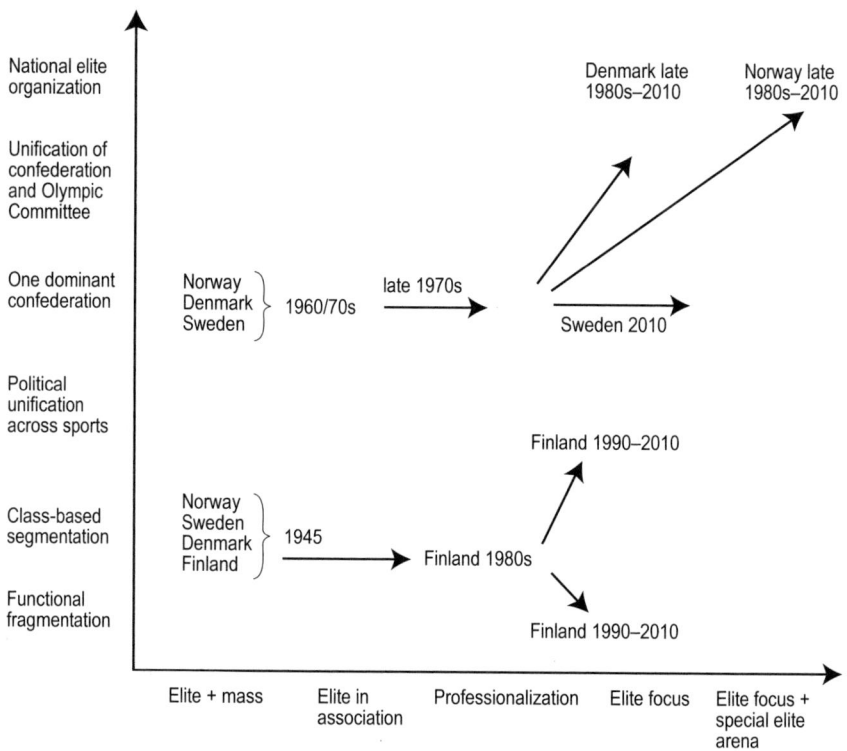

Figure 14.1: Overall organization of sports in Nordic countries 1950s–2010

Denmark and Norway in the 1970s and '80s: Stagnation and reform

During the 1970s and '80s both Denmark and Norway experienced setbacks in major international sports competitions. In Denmark, results in the 1972 Summer Olympics in Munich were especially disappointing with only one medal, and a striking contrast to an average of six medals over the preceding decades. In Norway, both the Summer Olympics in Los Angeles and the Winter Olympics in Sarajevo in 1984 were experienced as great disappointments, despite the fact that the number of medals was about the same as the historical trend. In Los Angeles, Norway won three medals, but no gold. In Sarajevo three of the nine medals were gold, but only one in cross country skiing, a sport with a huge symbolic value in the Norwegian society.

In both countries, central actors interpreted disappointing results as signs of systemic problems. This triggered initiatives to strengthen special elite sport efforts. These involved redefinitions of what elite sport was about, the amount of resources required to stay in this increasingly tense competitive race, and how elite sport efforts should be organized. However, the central actors in such processes, their concerns and the solutions offered, differed.

In Denmark, lack of agreement within the sports movement led party politicians and civil servants to play a key role. Their motivation was only partly directed towards the internal efficiency of the elite sport systems. Political discussions were framed as an extension of a welfare state perspective. A major concern was that the elite athletes engaged in the extreme efforts of modern sport would sacrifice health, education and opportunities in later life. The elite sport law from 1984 was a response to this. It constituted a framework for the new central elite sport agency, Team Denmark, which was state funded, but formally organized as a foundation with a separate board that, in addition to the organized sports, also represented broader political and societal interests.

In Norway, concern was related not only to the number of medals in the Olympics, but the failures of particular sports, especially the national sport cross country skiing. In contrast to Denmark, it was the leaders within the sports movement that introduced new initiatives. They focused on how to strengthen the competitiveness of elite sport, and wanted such challenges to be solved within the sports federations. The state should contribute with funds, but at an arm's length distance.

The first initiative in 1984, called Project 88, had a four-year perspective. It was an effort to strengthen cooperation across sports to improve results in the 1988 Olympic Games. Results in the Seoul Summer Olympics were well above the historical trend. However, the results in the Calgary Winter Olympics were disappointing. For the first time Norway did not win any gold medal in cross country skiing. Lack of short term results in winter sports, and particularly skiing, made it clear that not only more resources, but also stricter priorities, more competence, and stricter training requirements, were needed. This became the basis for the permanent national elite sport institution, Olympiatoppen, created in 1988.

Sweden and Finland in the 1970s and '80s: Still doing well

Sports in Sweden and Finland also experienced their ups and downs during the 1970s and '80s as measured in Olympic results. Compared to Denmark and Norway they had been great powers in elite sports during the 1950s and '60s, especially in summer sports. During the 1970s and '80s they continued to do better than their Nordic neighbours.

In winter sports, Sweden had weak results from the mid-1960s to the mid-1970s, but recovered in the mid-1980s, before losing ground in 1988. Finland also experienced some problems between the mid-1960s and 1970s, but less so than Sweden. During the 1970s they recovered and climbed to a new peak in the mid-1980s before settling on the historical trend by the end of the decade.

In the Summer Olympics both countries experienced dramatic setbacks compared to the preceding decades. Sweden won 35 medals in 1952 but only 5 in 1960. With the exception of the 1972 Olympics, where they won 16 medals, the number of medals varied between 4 and 8 from then until 1980. The 1980s represented a new era of success, peaking with 19 medals in 1984. Finland won 23 medals in 1952 Olympics and 5 in 1960, which introduced a new trend. During the next decade the number of medals varied from 4 to 8, with 12 medals in the 1984 Olympics as the peak.

Still, compared to their neighbours, both Sweden and Finland were doing well, and perhaps equally importantly, prestigious national sports were largely successful. In Sweden, the exceptional results in tennis, and later golf, contributed to the country's image of itself as a successful modern elite sport nation. In Finland successes in new sports, like Formula 1, and the growing professionalization of the national sport ice hockey, modified the impression of decline. Thus, the variations in Olympic results were not interpreted as a systemic issue neither in Sweden nor Finland. As a result, there were no serious discussions about changing the overall system of sport to accommodate the special needs of elite sports. Important changes took place, but within the established structures.

Denmark and Norway 1990–2010: Consolidation and institutional elaboration

The 1970s and '80s led to the introduction of special elite sport organizations at the national level in Denmark and Norway. This modified the segmented system where individual sports had the sole responsibility, as part of a broader effort where mass sport was the basis. The organizational changes in the two countries shared some similarities, but in many respects they were also quite different. This became increasingly apparent during the next two decades, which saw a consolidation and elaboration of the two national models for elite sport. They differ with respect to formal arrangements, roles, working methods and priorities.

Team Denmark has created a more unified elite sport system, strengthening common policies, cooperation and general support for elite sport development. As an independent foundation it is only indirectly influenced by the Sports Confederation of Denmark (DIF). When the Danish Olympic Committee (DOK) merged with the DIF in 1993, the DOK was in a weak position. Team Denmark had already taken over many of its core functions.

The new central elite sport organization is staffed with personnel with a background from sports sciences. It supports various types of development work to improve conditions for elite sport; like research, coaching competence and strengthening of organizational capacity in federations and clubs. Individual grants provide direct support for elite athletes. Team Denmark sets conditions for support, but it has limited capacity for direct involvement or intervention in actual development processes. However, in terms of Olympic results, Denmark has been able to defend its historical trend, with an average of six medals, with a low of three in the 2000 Olympics, and a high of eight in 2004. Also, in other international championships Danish athletes have achieved excellent results.

In 2004 a new elite law was passed. It represented a strengthening of Team Denmark's mandate, but also a strengthening of the state influence. Under the new law, Team Denmark is a sort of independent state agency, with its own board. Although indirectly, the Danish state has taken a more active role in elite sport than in any of the neighbouring countries. The formal status of Team Denmark also influences administrative procedures and working methods. Since 2004 the projects are governed by the principles of new public management, with contracts as a major governance instrument. Hiring of personnel has to fulfil requirements that emphasize open competition and formal competences.

An important part of any elite sport effort is to prioritize between sports and athletes based on potential for international results. In team Denmark this process is also influenced by general political values and views represented at the board level. How, and to what extent, priorities shall be based on strict criteria for international results has been a major public controversy in Denmark over the last years, where party politicians have played an important role. Attempts to pursue strict criteria for elite support based on international results are met by arguments about the need to preserve a broader elite concept that also includes national level elites. One of the board members put it this way in a board meeting we attended (July 2009): 'We get more of the best, rather than making the best better'.

In Norway, the loose structure of cooperation that characterized Project 88 was replaced by centralization and stricter priorities. The creation of Olympiatoppen in 1988 coincided with Norway being granted the 1994 Olympics. This provided a strong support for the further development of the national elite sport system in the years to come. The coming Olympics created a coordinated effort within all winter sports with a considerable increase in available resources. In this situation, the new leader of Olympiatoppen worked closely with the president of the Norwegian Sports Confederation (NIF) and the Norwegian Olympic Committee (NOK). In 1996 the NIF and NOK were merged into one organization, but in contrast to Denmark, the NOK was merging from a position of strength. Olympiatoppen became the operational instrument for all elite sport in Norway.

The changes in Norway represented a more far-reaching modification of the segmented sports model than in Denmark. Olympiatoppen had a stronger formal position in relation to individual sports, and the organizational changes reflected the concern of central sports leaders about conditions for international success. There was no interference from the state or party politicians. However, through their support for the Lillehammer Olympics they provided resources that supported the institutionalization of new perspectives on elite sport, athletes and their role in society. Elite sport as inspiration for mass sport activities was still important, but the efforts that went into the creation of an elite sport system differed dramatically from how the Oslo Olympics in 1952 was used politically.

In the early 1990s, Olympiatoppen was a modest organization. It consisted of a group of senior coaches that had proven themselves within their own sports, and eventually the administration of the NOK was merged into the organization. In contrast to Team Denmark, it had a relatively autonomous position, and at the same time considerable discretion over the direct state support for elite sport. They were free to hire people on merit, without worrying too much about formal qualifications. The working style was informal and anti-bureaucratic. Informal contacts and relationships were viewed as essential in strengthening cooperation and exchange of knowledge and information. Priorities were strict, and often support was linked to direct intervention to influence leadership, organization and training methods in individual sports. As in Denmark there was a general improvement of international results in many different sports. Compared to the preceding decades, the average number of Norwegian Olympic medals has increased from an average of 2.5 to 8 in summer sports, and from 9.8 to 23 in winter sports.

Sweden and Finland 1990–2010: Stagnation and institutional stalemate

The development over the last two decades in Sweden and Finland differs quite a bit from what happened in Denmark and Norway. Development in the two countries also differs dramatically, both in terms of results and in terms of how the organization of elite sport has been debated and changed.

During the 1990s, Sweden did quite well in the Summer Olympics, with an average of 10.6 medals, but experienced a setback in winter sport to an average of 3.3 medals. After 2000 the situation was reversed. In the Summer Olympics the average fell to 6 medals, while the average in the Winter Olympics rose to 10.3. Finland, in contrast, was characterized by general stagnation. In the Summer Olympic the average for both decades was about 3 medals. In the Winter Olympics, the average for the 1990s was 8.3, falling to 6.6 after 2000. Despite these differences in results, the growing perception in both countries was that reforms were needed to keep up with international competition. However, tensions and conflicts developed over what to do, and they have become more intense over the last years.

Despite an on-going debate about the need to change, the overall Swedish system has remained remarkably stable during this period. Important changes have taken place, but mainly within the traditional segmented structure. Growing tensions and polarization between the Swedish Sports Confederation (RF) and the Swedish Olympic Committee (SOK) has undermined broader reform initiatives. As documented in chapter 10, the perspective of central actors in these organizations regarding the nature both of the challenges and of each other reflects basic cleavages in the Swedish sports movement.

The Swedish system of allocating resources through the RF to different sports federations based on local membership activities is reinforcing the tension between mass and elite sport. The RF has a broad perspective on elites. In contrast, the SOK represents an exclusive elite perspective, but only for Olympic Sports (35 out of 80 competitive sport federations). Also, within the SOK all sports have one vote, independent of membership. For this reason the system also has a built-in tension between big and small federations. The RF is funded by the state, while the SOK, which owns the Olympic logo, is primarily financed through sponsorships. This arrangement tends to reinforce the tensions between the voluntary and the commercialized sports.

In contrast to Sweden, Finland has experienced dramatic changes in the organization of sports. However, these changes to a large extent reflect broader societal and political changes unrelated to the challenges in elite sport. Finnish sport was divided along class and ethnic lines until 1994. The breakdown of the Soviet Union led to a political reorientation in Finnish society and politics. Part of this was to establish a new unified sports federation, the SLU. An important element behind this compromise was that it should be a coordinating mechanism, but without centralized authority. At the same time it should provide various services and support to federations.

By the end of the 1990s, two things happened that came to change the existing structure of Finnish sports in a dramatic ways. First, in 1993, the SVUL, the dominant sports confederation that had served as an organizing core actor within the field of sport for almost a century, went bankrupt. Soon thereafter it discontinued its operations. This meant that the overall capacity of the sports movement to act in a coherent way was seriously weakened. Second, the doping scandals, particularly in the Nordic Ski World Championships in Lahti 2001, lead to strong criticisms and loss of legitimacy for elite sport in general. The forces of fragmentation became too strong. The Finnish Olympic Committee has neither had the capacity nor the resources to influence this development. Although Finland in this period experienced a political turn towards neo-liberalism, the reaction was a return to traditional mass sport utilitarian values related to a welfare perspective.

Elite sport is still mainly the responsibility of federations and some elite clubs. The Finnish Olympic Committee is weak. Public money to sport is distributed directly from the ministry to federations and clubs. Commercial sponsorship has tended to dry up. Specific sport federations have been losing out to new more specialized ones. Cross-country skiing created its own federation in 2009, and a number of regional and often non-competitive associations have been established. There have been several reform initiatives. Although it is recognized that the system needs more central authority that can influence structure, priorities, and support of elite sport, very little has come out of it so far. No one has had the authority or ability to effectively intervene.

The variety of success stories: more than one way to Rome

The four success stories presented in part three of this book provide a glimpse into different paths to success. Rather than trying to identify a general recipe for sustained success in elite sport, the comparison highlights differences and similarities between the stories about Swedish tennis and golf, Norwegian women's handball, Finnish men's ice hockey, and Danish track cycling. Having read part three of the book, it should already be clear to the reader that success means different things in these cases. Not only do paths to success differ, but also the context in which these developments took place. In the team sport examples from Norway and Finland the main stories are about successful implementation of strategies decided on a central level to improve and maintain the competitiveness of the national teams. In contrast, the story about Swedish golf and tennis pictures a powerful bottom-up process leading to a remarkable increase of both performance level and number of elite players. In contrast to this, Danish track cycling is an example of how specific infrastructure and competence in combination with strict priorities can foster long term success despite a shrinking recruitment base.

The divergences of the four stories might help to kill the myth that 'one size fits all'. There is no such thing as *one* way to excellence. Even within a quite homogeneous Nordic context, obvious differences regarding strategies and initiatives emerge when we take a closer look at the success stories. It seems clear that societal, organizational and sport-specific contexts must be taken into account when trying to understand why particular initiatives and efforts succeed or not. Strategies that may be efficient in one context may be counterproductive in another. However, despite significant differences between the four success stories, there are also similarities. Below, drawing upon an institutional framework, we have identified six dimensions that will be used to characterize the cases, as presented schematically in table 14.1. These are (1) mass sport foundation, (2) sport specific facilities, (3) strategies and key actors, (4) team building as an organizational strategy, (5) international influence, and (6) interaction with the national elite sport system. The further discussion is organized around these dimensions.

Mass sport foundation

There is a saying within the world of sport that 'mass sport produce elites', implying that a broadening of the recruitment base almost by necessity will lead to a higher elite level among the best. However, research does not confirm such a causal link between elite sport performances and mass sport participation (Hanstad & Skille 2010; Horne 2007). The same goes for our analysis of the four success stories. Nor do our cases support the assumption that successful elite sport as such will generate mass sport. Nevertheless, in particular situations the relationship between mass and elite sport may be relevant. For example, the stories from Swedish tennis and golf indicate that the broadening of the sports on grassroots level, turning them from 'upper-class' to 'folk sports', was one of the important changes prior to the elite sport success. But, evidently, other factors played an equally important role in actually producing, and not at least reproducing, elite performances at the highest level.

Table 14.1: Key dimensions in elite sport development – four cases

	Swedish tennis and golf	**Norwegian women's handball**	**Finnish men's ice hockey**	**Danish track cycling**
Mass sport foundation	Increasing mass participation prior to success period	Stable mass sport base prior to and during success period	Stable mass sport base prior to/during success period	Shrinking mass sport base during success period
Facilities	Massive building of courts prior to success period	Gradual improvement prior to / during the period	Massive building of courts prior to success period	The one essential track modernized and reopened
Strategies and key actors	Bottom-up process. Local/regional mobilization driven by coaches and athletes	Top-down process. Strategy to extend core competence driven by leaders and central coaches	Top-down process. Strategy to extend core competence + infrastructure driven by leaders and central coaches	Top-down process. Niche strategy, strict priorities, and infrastructure, driven by leaders + central coaches
Team building focus	Team based: Players developed within teams	Team based: National team	Team based: National team	Team based: Individual athletes + team
International influence	Foreign coaches, more international participation, US colleges	Foreign club coaches, intensified international contact, exchange of players	Foreign coaches, implementation of new training models, exchange of players	Foreign coaches, implementation of new training models
Interaction with national elite sport system	Modest	Increasing	Non-existent	High

In the three other cases the link between mass participation and sustained elite sport success seems to be even more ambiguous. Norwegian women's handball and Finnish ice hockey were both widespread and popular mass sports in the national context for a long time prior to the success at the international elite level. The number of players did not increase prior to or during the rise to international excellence. Other factors have to be taken into account to explain this. In the Danish track cycling story the relationship between mass and elite was even more problematic. The recruitment base, measured as the total number of track cyclists, diminished during the success period. However, it should be noted that also Danish track cycling is based on a widespread sport activity in the country, namely road cycling. Also the number of competing road cyclists shrank during the success period of Danish track cycling, but the sport has kept its position as a folk sport and a prestigious competitive sport among the Danish population.

Consequently, a common feature across the stories is that all the four sports had a broad foundation within the population, both as mass sport activities and in terms of public interest. Not all of them can be considered 'national sports', but they definitively were popular in the respective countries. In this way, all the four stories are examples of elite successes founded in sporting activities with a broad support. An important factor seems to be the relatively low level of controversies between elite sports efforts and mass sports efforts during the success periods. In general, conflicting priorities between elite and mass sport are an ongoing concern within Nordic sport, both on the societal level and within the sports organizations. However, this was not a central issue in our cases. On the contrary, such conflicts were reduced during the success periods of Norwegian handball and Swedish tennis and golf, and almost non-existent in the cases of Finnish ice hockey and Danish track cycling. These observations suggest that the elite efforts took place in a context of high organizational and public legitimacy.

Facilities

In road cycling, athletes need efficient equipment, but there is no need for a specific arena. However, track cycling, as well as tennis and golf, require special facilities. Also in team sports there is a need for this if elite athletes and teams are to develop. Thus, both the capacity and quality of facilities are relevant to develop elite sport.

In each of our four cases improved facilities were part of the success story, but to various degrees and in different ways. The importance of such infrastructure is most clearly demonstrated in the cases of Swedish tennis and golf and Finnish ice hockey. Here, a massive building of facilities in different parts of these countries took place in the years ahead of the success period. Undoubtedly, this contributed to improved training conditions for athletes and local teams. Particularly in Sweden, this development may be regarded as a decisive factor in facilitating the broadening of tennis and golf.

Danish track cycling is a quite different story. Here, the crucial factor was not the number of tracks, but to rebuild the one track that was essential to regain international hegemony. Because of the recruitment base found in road cycling, and the centralized niche strategy employed in developing elite track cyclists, only one top modern track was needed. The example illustrates how a sport by reinstating one 'missing link' in the chain can regain international competitiveness. Other key factors such as necessary competence, elite sport traditions, and a dedicated talent base are already present. In contrast, in Norwegian women's handball, the relationship between infrastructure and elite success is less obvious. The building of courts was a gradual process both prior to and during the success period.

Strategies and key actors
The cases of Norwegian handball, Finnish ice hockey and Danish track cycling reflect top-down strategies. The sports federations were important driving forces behind the successes. Specific performance units (national teams) were prioritized, and strategies were chosen to create optimal conditions for these teams. In contrast to this, the stories of Swedish golf and tennis are about an evolving bottom-up process.

Danish track cycling represented the most narrow and focused strategy, as the federation adopted a strict niche strategy to facilitate the development of a number of carefully selected athletes, participating in particular track cycling events (e.g. Team Pursuit and Points race). A vital part of this strategy was to get support for re-establishing modern training and competition facilities. Central leaders in the cycle federation, in close cooperation with facilitators from Team Denmark, were the entrepreneurs behind this strategy. In this way, the track cycling case also appears as a success story for Team Denmark, as it demonstrate how its priorities, resources and relationships with actors outside sport were crucial to the track cycling success.

In Norwegian women's handball and Finnish ice hockey the strategy had a broader scope, but it was developed by central leaders in the sports federations. These targeted strategies adopted by the federations aimed at developing and extending core competences, improving infrastructure (Finland), and optimizing talent development. Both in Finland and Norway the centralized strategies gave priority to national teams rather than the elite clubs. Hence, national team performances were not just reflections of improved performances at the club level.

Leaders and national coaches employed in key positions in the federations acted as vital entrepreneurs in establishing long term strategies for national team development. Such strategies included allocation of increased resources, clarification of defined playing styles, consistent training methods and coaching philosophies, and the implementation of talent development programs linked to the national teams. Particular strategies were initiated and carried out by federations in order to facilitate national team success, but also with positive effects for the organizations in a wider sense (like increased participation and media attention).

In Swedish tennis and golf, in contrast, there was no federation or central elite sport body that operated as a driving force for world-class performance. Initially, the primary agenda for federations and clubs was to broaden the sports. This transformed rather narrow upper-class sports to broad popular sports. This was made possible through massive building of courts and expansion of 'open' clubs. The result was an explosion of new players prior to and in the early phases of the elite success periods. The increase of young players was not primarily part of any elite sport strategy.

However, when world-class results started to come, the relatively small tennis and golf federations took some actions to nurture the continued success. Such actions included improved coach education and talent development in general, rather than direct intervention in the elite milieus. These milieus, being organized within a variety of partly private funded teams of top players, contribute to the picture of the Swedish cases as examples of decentralized rather than centralized success stories.

It is important to bear in mind that the four stories represent 'successes' in quite different meanings of the word, in different sports and within quite different settings. The Danish and Swedish stories seem in many ways to be opposites in terms of strategy and scope. Nevertheless, both the centralized strict niche strategy adopted by central leaders in the cycle federation in Denmark and the evolving wave of elite tennis and golf players nurtured within a more decentralized Swedish sport model resulted in sustained international success. The different strategies chosen; top-down versus bottom-up processes, can be seen as efficient and well adapted to the particular organizational and environmental situation in a specific period of time.

Team building as an organizational strategy

A common feature of the four cases was that *teams* constituted the core unit where the daily performance work took place. While this is quite obvious in team sports like handball and ice hockey, it is not as obvious that teams should play a vital role in individual sports. Nevertheless, this was clearly the case also in Swedish golf and tennis and Danish track cycling. In Danish track cycling Team Pursuit was prioritized as one of the core events, with day-to-day activities organized within the framework of the team as a consequence. In both tennis and golf in Sweden special teams, constituted of three to four players and their coach, travelled together to tournaments and competed, trained and boarded together.

Within the context of international elite sport such team organization may have several advantages; creating team spirit, fostering exchange of knowledge and competence, lightening competition pressures perceived by the individual, and offering social support. In Swedish tennis, one of the most significant manifestations of the country's hegemony was their Davies cup success, reaching the world finals seven years in a row. This was the most prestigious national team tournament of this sport and subject to huge attention worldwide as well as in the Swedish society. This particular success contributed to the perception of the 'Swedish tennis miracle' as a team based achievement.

Also in Norwegian handball, the team-based organization appeared as a more profound way of structuring the performance development than usually found in team sport. The coach role was deliberately broadened. In addition to sole 'hands-on' coaching on the court, it also included 'orchestration' of relationships between youth and senior teams, between coaches on the different teams, and between different parts of the support staff. In this way, a team-based organizational strategy was adopted both within the national team as such, and as a strategy to link different parts of the broader 'performance system' closer together.

Within the national team, 'sub-teams' – e.g. position teams, defence teams, and keeper teams – were established to strengthen group based performance development. Across different units surrounding the senior and junior national teams, linkages were created to strengthen the integration (coaching teams, medical teams, and recruitment teams). The overall idea behind this emphasis on team organization was to optimize knowledge exchange and coordination within a unifying philosophy. Such a strategy was easier to pursue due to the remarkable stability in leadership positions within the handball federation in this period.

International influence

International influence was clearly a part of all four stories. Such influence was promoted through a growing exchange of persons and ideas. Recruitment of foreign elite coaches represented one aspect of this exchange. Another was the growing number of domestic players going abroad for training and competitions. These developments were not just a reflection of increased internationalization of elite sport during this period. The intensified exchange seemed, in all four cases, to be a deliberate strategy to strengthen competitiveness.

Particularly in the early stages of the success periods, carefully selected and distinguished foreign elite coaches played a major role. These coaches probably were important in introducing and establishing the quantity and quality of preparations and training needed to meet the demands of international elite sport. In a break-through phase, such international influence may be decisive. Also, players going to excellent milieus abroad to train and compete in the initial phase, like Finnish ice hockey players and Swedish tennis and golf players, contributed to 'setting standards' relevant for the domestic elite sport milieu. The same goes for the Norwegian handball team, seeking the most respected foreign countries as sparring partners, particularly when establishing itself as an elite nation. It seems that the international influence in the early stages of development was necessary to get to know 'the state of the art', that is; to become familiar with the level, demands and competencies needed.

In order to have sustained success, international influence is necessary, but far from sufficient. Copying what others do is not enough if the aim is to exceed them. A striking similarity across our four cases was the gradual creation of a 'success formula identity' specific to the sport in question. That is, increased international influence was followed by developing their 'own way' in the preparation and performance of the sport. As already mentioned, one common aspect of this was the team-based organization adopted in the Nordic cases. Other aspects were distinctive to each case, like specific training methods (Sweden), playing styles (Sweden, Finland), coaching philosophies (Norway) and a carefully selected niche strategy (Denmark). These local emphases do not imply that the performance work was completely different compared to elsewhere in the world. However, tendencies towards convergence with international trends were supplemented by the exploitation of local factors that could create competitive advantages. Moreover, the distinctive success formulas in each case contributed to the institutionalization of the success. Coach education programs and talent development models were also part of this.

Interaction with the national elite sport system
The four Nordic cases differ significantly in terms of how closely they were linked to the national elite sport systems. The interaction with the national system can be characterized as high in Danish track cycling, increasing during the Norwegian handball success, modest in the Swedish tennis and golf cases, and almost non-existent in Finnish ice hockey. To a certain degree this variety reflects the particularities of the four countries' general elite sport systems.

Danish track cycling can be seen as a success created by the Danish cycle federation in close cooperation with Team Denmark. Team Denmark played a crucial role. In many ways a small sport (e.g. track cycling), in the need of a particular and defined form of support, is an 'ideal case' for a centralized elite sport body like Team Denmark. In such cases strict priorities, specialized support and relatively small but highly targeted investments are likely to pay off, given that other necessary factors are already in place. In Norway, Olympiatoppen has played a similar role in other small but dedicated elite sport milieus, for example rowing and kayaking. Like in the Danish track cycling case, Olympiatoppen in Norway is a closely integrated part of these internationally competitive elite sport milieus on a daily basis.

The relationship between Olympiatoppen and the case of Norwegian women's handball evolved somewhat differently. The institutionalization processes of the handball success during the 1990s developed parallel to the professionalization of Olympiatoppen as the central node in the national elite sport network. Thus, the handball federation's interaction with Olympiatoppen increased during the period, including a growing exchange of competence which both parties benefitted from. This process reflects how the central elite sport body (like Olympiatoppen and Team Denmark) may play a different role in relation to bigger and more resourceful milieus than what was seen in the track cycling example. Regarding Norwegian handball, Olympiatoppen offered funding and specific expertise, but the initiatives and basic strategies were instigated by the sport itself.

In the cases of Swedish tennis and golf, in contrast, the national elite sport system played a modest role. The creation of these 'sport miracles' was first and foremost a result of societal and sport-specific developments, not at all initiated or coordinated by the Swedish Sports Confederation (RF) or Olympic Committee (SOK). Given that neither golf nor tennis were Olympic sports during the success periods (tennis became an Olympic sport in 1988), the sports were not included in the SOK's efforts. Furthermore, the RF's policy at the time was to keep an arm's length distance to elite sport developments. It offered coach education programs relevant to elite sport, but otherwise it did not interfere in sport-internal affairs.

In Finnish ice hockey, the elite sport progressed despite the lack of any support or interaction with the elite sport system in general. The Finnish ice hockey federation managed to keep up good results during a period marked by near collapse within other parts of the national system. The example illustrates how a strong single-sport organization through close relationships with public authorities, semi-public sport institutes, and private sponsors can provide the resources and competences needed to succeed in elite sport, even within a fragmented national sport system. Clearly, this presupposes a strong and well organized federation. The fact that ice hockey can be regarded as the national sport in Finland is an important backdrop for understanding the case.

In sum, the four Nordic cases progressed with different relationships to the sport organizations constituting the overall elite sport systems in the four countries. In this way they reflect important characteristics of the national systems as such.

Elite sport models – responses to international challenges

Outcomes – organizational models

The discussion about the historical development of Nordic elite sport systems emphasized the overall pattern of organization, the role of elite sport within a broader sports movement, and the relationship between elite sport and the wider society. The timing of change, the type of actors involved and outcomes vary considerably, but all four countries have gone through major changes. In Denmark and Norway, initiatives for change came early and succeeded in creating major changes in the overall structure of national elite sport. In Finland a major shift came about as a result of an external shock due to the fall of the Soviet empire, but no one had the capacity to recreate a unified structure. In Sweden, changes have taken place within a stable overall institutional structure.

We have identified four dimensions that can be used to characterize the systems, as shown in table 14.2. They are: (1) the role of a broad voluntary movement, (2) degree of unified structure, (3) legitimacy of sport elites, (4) centralization of authority and support and funding. Below we will discuss similarities and differences between the present national systems of elite sport organization along these dimensions.

Table 14.2: Dimensions of the current Nordic elite sport systems

	Norway	Denmark	Sweden	Finland
Role of broad voluntary movement	Yes	Yes	Yes	Yes
Unified structure	High	High	Low	Weak
Legitimacy of elite sport	High	High/Medium Contested-contested	Medium contested	Weak
Centralization of authority and support	Authority Funding Project support Expertise Active intervention Training centre	Authority Funding Project support	Segmented structure	Segmented, decentralized structure

The role of broad voluntary movement

In all four countries, both mass and elite sport has had a broad voluntary movement as its basis. This is something that gives Nordic elite sport a unique character. Clearly, several trends related to modern elite sport may be regarded as threats to such a model. The role of professional and scientific knowledge, full-time paid athletes and commercialization, where sponsorship and advertising leads to commodification of sports, teams and athletes are just examples. Still, however, the backbone of all the Nordic elite sport systems is the local clubs with volunteers, often parents. This is where young talents are identified and developed, and where they keep a lasting affiliation and presence even as they become international elite athletes.

The state has traditionally kept an arm's length distance to the voluntary movement. However, increasingly the financial support from the state plays a key role. There are several reasons for this, and an important one has been to avoid that the impact of commercialization and private sponsors should be too strong. There are of course tensions between the values of the broader sports movement and the values, requirements and external supporters of modern elite sport. However, the ways they are handled vary. This is related to the overall organization of sports in the four countries.

Degree of unification of national sports

In Norway, the elite sport organization is the operative arm of the National Sports Confederation (NIF) and the national Olympic Committee (NOK). In Denmark, the national elite sport organization, Team Denmark, is a state institution. It is directly financed by the state and with an independent board where the national sport federations participate together with representatives for various societal interests appointed by the Ministry of Culture. In both cases the state is a major source of funding for elite sport, supplemented by private sponsors that may vary with the popularity of different sports.

The tension between the Swedish Sports Confederation (RF) and the national Olympic Committee (SOK) is partly related to mass versus elite sport. The RF is mainly financed by the state and responsible for how the money is used in all parts of the sports movement. The SOK mainly relies on private sponsors and targets special athletes and teams with international elite potential in Olympic sports. In contrast to Denmark and Norway, this structure seems to recreate and intensify the underlying tensions between mass and elite sport as well as that between public and private funding.

In Finland, the overall sports movement has become increasingly fragmented over the last 20 years. The bankruptcy of the dominant sports confederation SVUL led to a loss of capacity for central coordination of the system. This happened at the same time as the Finnish society and politics went through a period of comprehensive change, casting off the constraints of the Cold War period and the historical heritage from the civil war 70 years earlier. The result is a curious mix of organizational autonomy, decentralization and fragmentation, on the one hand, and a more direct and centralized state role where the ministry is distributing funds directly to various federation and clubs on different levels, on the other hand.

The legitimacy of sport elites

The notion of sport elites covers different aspect that may be viewed differently within the Nordic countries. Sport elites may be defined as those that have been successful in national and international competitions. In this sense the celebration of sport elites seems to be a quite universal phenomenon, and the Nordic countries have been no exception. Another aspect of sport elites has to do with how they achieve excellence. The means applied in this process, where the resources come from, how such efforts relate to other aspects of life and societal values may be important for how success in international competitions is viewed. The status of elite sport in Nordic countries has to be discussed in this broader perspective.

In the 1950s and '60s, sport elites were celebrated as heroes. However, in contrast to today's sport elites they were amateurs who had to make a living through a normal job. In this sense they belonged to the masses (see chapter 2) in a way that was consistent with a social democratic view of society. Present day sport elites represent something quite different. Elite sport is a full-time and paid activity, supported by professional expertise, pushing physical and mental as well as ethical boundaries. In this sense modern elite sport represents an extreme activity for the few, funded and celebrated by the many. Athletes are heroes, but also brand names. It is no wonder that the role and status of sport elites create debates within the Nordic countries.

In Denmark the concern for the athletes in the pursuit of extreme performances was an important motivation for the first Elite Law (1984) and the creation of an elite sport organization in the mid-1980s. In this sense it was an extension of a welfare state strategy, pushed by party politics. This was important in creating a legitimate frame for elite sport, based on a holistic perspective on the athletes. This became the basis for efforts to support performance development, with a broad definition of sport elites that included both national and international level. Such a broad definition of elites is the backdrop for public discussions the last years over stricter priorities aimed at maximizing international results.

In Norway, there has traditionally been a strong scepticism towards elites in all parts of society. The status of modern sport elites represents a remarkable exception. Like in Denmark, initiatives for an elite sport organization also stressed a holistic view on human development and the link to national values, but there were important differences. From the beginning there was a stronger emphasis on strengthening of international competitiveness, and the strategy was initiated and created by the sport movement. Major improvements in international results have reinforced the general support for an elite sport system based on strict priorities. Representatives of the elite sport system have, to a large extent, been able to influence the way society views modern elite sport.

As pointed out above, the tension between mass and elite sport in Sweden is partly build into the national confederation (RF), and clearly a source of lasting tensions between the RF and the Swedish Olympic Committee (SOK). While elite sport is celebrated, the system is set up in such a way that it is difficult to arrive at national priorities for elite sport development. Such priorities are set by individual sports federations, sometimes with support from the SOK, but resources and capabilities vary considerably.

In Finland the status of elite sport is highly contested, despite strong and celebrated traditions in international sports. The fragmentation of the national sport systems means that resources are spread out in a way that does not support systematic elite sport development. At the same time doping scandals have undermined the support for elite sport, leading to problems of state funding as well as private funding from sponsors. There are great differences between various sports. However, it seems that that a national sports policy has taken up and strengthened the traditional utilitarian aspect of sports related to health and wellbeing. Efforts to reorganize the Finnish elite sport system have proven very difficult.

Centralization of authority and support

For small countries, there is a recurrent debate about the need to concentrate limited resources. This may be necessary to successfully compete with countries that have many times the population and economic resources. This issue is related to the questions about centralization of authority and support. The argument for decentralization is partly related to the need for diversity, partly to the autonomy of sports federations and clubs. The argument for centralization is linked to efficiency, often discussed in terms of costly investments in infrastructure or the need to concentrate competence to achieve critical mass. We also find that Nordic elite sport systems vary considerably with respect to these dimensions.

Team Denmark represents a formal and legal concentration of both authority and funds in national elite sport. An independent board appointed by the Ministry of Culture, with representatives of the national sports federation sets general policy. The specific funds for Danish elite sport are awarded directly over the state budget. The budget is used to support various projects in different sports. Initially, the support and follow up for such projects were based on administrative procedures. However, with the introduction of new public management in Danish state administration, such projects are mostly governed by contractual obligations. This means that Team Denmark has a limited mandate, competence and capacity for intervention in performance development in specific sports.

The Norwegian elite sports organization, Olympiatoppen, is part of the national sport federation. It reports to the board of the confederation through the general secretary, but with considerable autonomy. State funding for elite sport is not formally earmarked for Olympiatoppen, but transferred from the national confederation. In this sense the formal autonomy of the Norwegian elite sport organization is not as strong as in Denmark. However, in practice

Olympiatoppen has a stronger position in influencing what goes on in various sports. It represents a concentration of national expertise in coaching and sports science, with an elite sport training centre that also serves as an arena for informal exchange of experiences between coaches and athletes. In addition to giving out stipends and supporting development projects, Olympiatoppen is also directly involved in challenging and supporting performance development in different sports. The system is open for all sports, but there is a special emphasis on preparations for Olympic competitions.

In contrast to Denmark and Norway, neither Sweden nor Finland has a central elite sport organization with an overall responsibility for developments in all sport. Elite sport development is mainly taken care of by specific sport federations. Resources and strategies differ considerably between sports, and there are also variations with respect to what is done on central and local levels. In both countries the national Olympic Committee has an independent and supportive role, despite open tensions between the Swedish Sports Confederation and the national Olympic committee (SOK). The SOK has a limited staff, but it plays an important role providing support and funding for various athletes, teams and development projects based on strict priorities. In Finland, the national Olympic Committee has few resources and capacities for active support.

Concluding remarks

The prestige related to international success in elite sport is a driving force behind the increased investments and state support in this domain. The SPLISS research program attempts to explain national results in international competitions as the outcome of variations in the nine pillars of national elite sport systems (De Bosscher et.al. 2008). Others look for causal explanations in the relationship between GNP per capita and the number of medals won in major competitions (Morton 2002; Bernard & Busse 2004). In contrast to such studies, general causal modelling has not been the main concern in this book. Rather, we have tried to capture the more detailed structures as well as intentions and processes behind national elite sports systems. Research has shown that such systems have become increasingly similar at a general level (Augestad, Bergsgaard & Hansen 2006; Green & Oakley 2001; Houlihan & Green 2008; Oakley & Green 2001). This book demonstrates how this kind of increased convergence may go hand in hand with increased divergence at a national and local level.

Major findings

At the organizational level of elite sport systems, there is not only growing divergence between the Nordic countries; it also happens in ways that run counter to what one might expect based on the general pattern of political and societal organization in the four countries. Norway is generally characterized by decentralization of authority and dislike for elites, but has ended up with the most centralized system and a high degree of legitimacy for elite sport. Denmark, where the state has been most reluctant to intervene in civil society and the economy, has ended up with the strongest role for the state. Finland, with the strongest tradition for centralization, has ended up with the most decentralized, fragmented system. Sweden, known for its ability to modernize and react to international trends in society and in the economy, preserves an overall system that tends to reproduce political cleavages.

Elias & Dunning (1986: 22–23) emphasized how modern sports developed in Britain as an autonomous sphere, with its own identity and rules, that to some extent was independent from society and general politics. He saw such tendencies as an expression of a general differentiation process, as part of modernization, in the context of general societal values and institutions. However, the fact that modern sports developed first in England was also a result of specific events, some of which were coincidental. What we observe in our Nordic comparison of modern elite sport is a different type of autonomy, but it seems to reflect a similar kind of conditionality. In line with Elias' argument, while some events may be viewed as necessary conditions for the developments that followed, one can hardly say that from the succession of earlier events that the later events had to happen.

Entrepreneurial initiatives, political alliances and conflicts within the sports movement, and between representatives of sport and national politicians, seem to play a major role. In this sense the observed differences add to our understanding of modern elite sport. This relates not only to the level of analysis; i.e. the abstract notion of elite sport organization versus the concrete organizational patterns. It also raises questions about the interaction between the dynamics of international trends versus space for national adaptation. Such adaptations may reflect path dependencies, but also lead to radical breaks that may change elite sport organization as well as its role and legitimacy in wider society and politics.

The four cases of successful sports highlight different types of institutionalization processes. In other words, they are not the outcome of rational grand designs. Ambitions, perceptions of opportunities, and requirements for success emerge and mature along the way. The case stories are about evolving systems, where important incidents and entrepreneurial initiatives play an important role. Despite strong international competitive pressures, these stories are not primarily about local adaptation of international standards and requirements. International competence was required to further develop local models. The main sources of influence came through the hiring of internationally recognized successful coaches, or through increased interaction with foreign federations and elite clubs. They represented holistic rather than specialized and scientific knowledge. Sustained success was secured by further developing local factors that could provide competitive advantages.

Our discussion shows that the Nordic countries despite many similarities have developed quite different national elite sport systems. The system concept does not imply an integrated, well-functioning arrangement. Neither does it mean that arrangements are necessarily stable structures. They often contain elements of dynamics and change, where interdependencies, intensity of interaction, mechanisms for decision-making and aggregation of individual actions vary considerably. Even within a highly competitive domain of elite sport, subject to strong pressures toward convergence, there is considerable space for local ingenuity in identifying and making most out of their local resources.

The research agenda
In the Nordic context there are few studies of elite sport. The present study addresses some key issues and introduces a comparative perspective that may also have wider implications. Internationally there are numerous studies of elite sport. So far the macro and policy levels have received most attention. Such studies produce valuable knowledge for policy makers, but will often be perceived as abstract and loosely coupled to the concerns of actors within the elite sport domain. There are few detailed studies of how national elite sport systems are organized. Even fewer provide insight in how they actually operate and support elite sport efforts. There is a lack of comparative studies between national systems and across different sports. Detailed process studies are hard to find. Both quantitative and qualitative studies are needed to develop and deepen our understanding of how current elite sport operate and develop.

Reference list

Agergaard, S. (2008), 'Elite athletes as migrants in Danish women's handball', *International Review for the Sociology of Sport*, 43/1: 5–19.

Åkesson, J. (2010), *Idrottens akademisering: kunskapsproduktion och kunskapsförmedling inom forskning och utbildning* (Örebro: Örebro universitet).

Alapuro, R. & Stenius, H. (1989), 'Kansanliikkeet loivat kansakunnan' [National movements created a nation], in R. Alapuro, I. Liikanen, K. Smeds, & H. Stenius (eds.), *Kansa liikkeessä* [*Nation on the move*] (Vaasa: Kirjayhtymä Oy).

Andersen, S.S. & Eliassen, K.A. (1993), *Making Policy in Europe* (London: Sage).

Andersen, S.S. (2009), Stor suksess gjennom små intelligente feil: Erfaringsbasert kunnskapsutvikling i toppidretten [Big success through small, intelligent failures: Experience-based knowledge development in top sport], *Tidsskrift for samfunnsforskning* 50: 427–461.

Andersen, T. (2005), *Håndballjentene. Et norsk idrettseventyr* (Oslo: Libretto Forlag).

Anderson, T. & Carlsson, B. (2009), 'Football in Scandinavia: a fusion of welfare policy and the market', *Soccer and Society*, 10/3–4: 299–316.

Andersson, G. & Karlsson, L. (2002), *Idrottarliv: en antologi* (Stockholm: En bok för alla).

Andersson, T. (2002), *Kung fotboll: den svenska fotbollens kulturhistoria från 1800-talets slut till 1950* (Eslöv: Symposion).

Aroponen, A.O. (2006), 'Suomen urheiluliiton organisaatio ja johtajat' [Organization and Leaders of the Finnish Athletes' Federation], in Seppo Martiskainen (ed.), *Suomi Voittoon – kansa liikkumaan* [*Finland to Win – Nation to Move*], 39–67. Suomen Yleisurheilun 100 vuotta [One Hundred Years in Finnish Athletics].

Augestad, P. & Bergsgard, N.A. (2007), *Toppidrettens formel: Olympiatoppen som alkymist* (Oslo: Novus Forlag).

Augestad, P. & Bergsgard, N.A. (2008), 'Norway', in Houlihan, B. and Green, M. (eds.), *Comparative Elite Sports Developments: Systems, Structures and Public Policy* (Amsterdam: Elsevier).

Augestad, P., Bergsgard, N.A. & Hansen, A. (2006), 'The institutionalization of an elite sport organization in Norway: The case of 'Olympiatoppen', *Sociology of Sport Journal*, 23/3: 293-313.

Bailey, R. (2007), 'Talent development and the luck problem', *Sport, Ethics and Philosophy*, 1/3: 367-377.

Bairner, A. (2010), 'What's Scandinavian about Scandinavian Sport?', *Sport in Society*, 13/4: 734-743.

Befring, E. (1997), 'The enrichment perspective: A special education approach to an inclusive school', *Remedial and Special Education*, no. 3: 182-87.

Bergsgard, N.A. & Norberg, J.R. (2010), 'Sport policy and politics – the Scandinavian way', *Sport in Society*, 13/4: 567-582.

Bergsgard, N.A. & Rommetvedt, H. (2006), 'Sport and Politics: The Case of Norway', *International Review for the Sociology of Sport*, 41: 7-27.

Bergsgard, N.A., Houlihan, B., Mangseth, P., Nødland, S.I., & Rommetvedt, H. (2007), *Sport Policy: A Comparative Analysis of Stability and Change* (Amsterdam: Butterworth-Heinemann).

Bernard, A.B. & Busse, M.R. (2004), 'Who wins the Olympic Games: Economic resources and medals totals', *Review of Economics and Statistics*, 86: 413-417.

Bernhus, O. (1988), *Håndballjentene* (Oslo: Hjemmets forlag).

Billing, P., Frantzen, M. & Peterson, T. (2004), 'Paradoxes of professionalization in Sweden: A club approach', *Soccer and Society*, 5/1: 82-99.

Bjerkrheim, S.G. & Nordberg, R. (1999), *God i håndball* (Oslo: Gyldendal Tiden).

Boelke, N. (2006), 'New insights in the nature of best practice in elite sport system management – exemplified with the organization of coach education', *New Studies in Athletics* 1/ 2007: 49-58.

Boelke, N. (2007), *Best practice of elite sport systems*, Working paper 2009.

Bøje, C. & Eichberg, H. (1994), *Idrættens tredje vej: Om idrætten i kulturpolitikken*, (Århus: Forlaget Klim).

Bøje, C. See after 'Boelke'.

Bonde, Hans (1988), 'Den hurtige mand', *Dansk Historisk Tidskrift*, 1.

Bourdieu, Pierre (1978), 'Sport and Social Class', *Social Science Information*, 6.

Buckley, W. (1967), *Sociology and Modern Systems Theory* (Englewood Cliffs, NJ: Prentice Hall).

Burns, T.R., Flam, H. & De Man, R. (1987), *The Shaping of Social Organizations: Social Rule Systems Theory with Applications* (London: Sage).

Campbell, D. T. (1975), 'Degrees of freedom and the case study', *Comparative Political Studies*, 8/2: 178-93.

Carlsson, B. & Lindfeldt, M. (2010), 'Legal and moral pluralism: Normative tensions in a Nordic sports model in transition', *Sport in Society*, 13/4: 718-733.

Carlsson, B. (2009), 'Insolvency and the domestic juridification of football in Sweden', *Soccer and Society*, 10/3-4: 477-494.

Carlstedt, J. (2010), Interview, 22 June.

De Bosscher, V. (2007), *Sports policy factors leading to international sporting success*, Dissertation presented in partial fulfillment of the requirements for the

degree of Doctor in Physical Education (Vrije Universiteit Brussel, Brussels: VUBPRESS).
De Bosscher, V., Bingham, J., Shibli, S., van Bottenburg, M. & De Knop, P. (2008), *The Global Sporting Arms Race. An International Comparative Study on Sports Policy Factors Leading to International Sporting Success* (Aachen: Meyer & Meyer).
De Bosscher, V., De Knop, P., & Heyndels, B. (2003), 'Comparing relative sporting success among nations: Create equal opportunities in sport', *Journal for Comparative Physical Education and Sport*, 3: 109–120.
De Bosscher, V., de Knop, P., & van Bottenburg, M. (2009), 'An analysis of homogeneity and heterogeneity of elite sports systems in six nations', *International Journal of Sports Marketing & Sponsorship*, 10: 111–131.
Den Butter, F.A.G. & van der Tag, C.M. (1995), 'Olympic medals as an indicator of social welfare', *Social Indicators Research*, 35: 27–37.
Digel, H. (2002), 'A comparison of competitive sport systems', *New Studies in Athletics*, 17/1: 37–49.
DiMaggio, P.J. & Powell, W.W. (1983), 'The iron Cage revisited: Institutional isomorphism and collective rationality in organizational fields', *American Sociological Review*, 48: 147–160.
Eichberg, H. & Loland, S. (2009), 'Sport and popular movements: Towards a philosophy of moving people', *Sport, Ethics and Philosophy*, 3/2: 121–138.
Eichberg, H. & Loland, S. (2010), 'Nordic sports – from social movements via emotional to bodily movement – and back again?', *Sport in Society*, 13/4: 676–693.
Elias, N. & Dunning, E. (1986), *Quest for Excitement. Sport and Leisure in the Civilizing Process* (Oxford: Blackwell).
Eliasson, A. (2009), 'The European football market, globalization and mobility among players', *Soccer and Society*, 10/3–4: 386–397.
Elmgreen, H. (2000), 'Det regnede pa Ordrupbanens første løbedag: Strejflys over Ordrupbanens historie gennem 112 ar', *Program: Ordrupbanens finalestævne søndag 3. september 2000*, 4–9 (Copenhagen: DBC).
Elmgreen, H. (2006a): 'DBC – en ganske særlig cykelklub.' *DBCs 125 ars jubilæumsstævne søndag 7. Maj 2006*, 4–7 (Copenhagen: DBC).
Elmgreen, H. (2006b): 'Fra Ordrup til Ballerup.' *DBCs 125 ars jubilæumsstævne søndag 7. Maj 2006*, 8–9 (Copenhagen: DBC).
Engström, L.-M. (1999), *Idrott som social markör* (Stockholm).
Enjolras, B. & Waldahl, R.H. (2007), 'Policy-making in sport: the Norwegian case', *International Review for the Sociology of Sport*, 42/2: 201–216.
Eriksson, S. (2006), *Vägen till elittränarskap?* [*The road to elite coaching?*] (Stockholm: Riksidrottsförbundet).
Eriksson, S. (2007), 'Idrottsgymnasiernas bidrag till elitdrotten?' [The contribution of upper secondary schools with sports profiles to Swedish elite sports?] *Svensk idrottsforskning*, 16: 54–56.
Esping-Andersen, G. (1990), *Three Worlds of Welfare Capitalism* (Oxford: Polity).

Fahlén, J. (2006), *Structures beyond the frameworks of the rink: On organization in Swedish ice hockey* (Umeå: Umeå universitet).
Fotheringham, W. (2008a), 'Revolution in the art and science of cycling that led to Olympic gold', *The Guardian*, 23 August: http://www.guardian.co.uk/sport/2008/aug/23/olympics2008.britisholympicteam
Fotheringham, W. (2008b): 'Revolutionaries'. *Observer Sport Magazine*, December, 53: http://www.guardian.co.uk/sport/2008/nov/23/olympicm-cycling-team
Gammelsæter, H. (2009), 'The organization of professional football in Scandinavia', *Soccer and Society*, 10/3-4: 305-323.
Gangdal, J. (2004), *Mika og den gode følelsen* (Oslo: Aschehoug).
George, A. & Bennett, A. (2005), *Case Studies and Theory Development in the Social Sciences* (Cambridge, MA: MIT Press).
Gerring, J. (2007), *Case Study Research: Principles and Practices* (Cambridge: Cambridge University Press)
Gjelstrup, G. & Sørensen, E. (2007), 'Introduction', in G. Gjelstrup & E. Sørensen (eds.), *Public Administration in Transition* (Copenhagen: DJØF Publishing), 21-37.
Goffman, E. (1959), *The Presentation of Self in Everyday Life* (Reading: Penguin Books).
Goksøyr, M. & Hanstad, D. V. (2005), *Fred er ei det beste: Festskrift for Hans B. Skaset* (Oslo: Gyldendal).
Goksøyr, M. (2011), Idrett for alle. Norges Idrettsforbund 150 år [Sport for all. Norwegian Confederation of Sport 150 Years] (Oslo: Aschehoug).
Goksøyr, M., Andersen, E. & Asdal, K. (1996), *Kropp, kultur og tippekamp: Statens idrettskontor, STUI og idrettsavdelingen 1946-1996* (Oslo: Universitetsforlaget).
Gotvassli, K.Å. (2005), *Et praksisbasert perspektiv på dynamiske læringsnettverk i toppidretten*. Ph.D.-avhandling (Steinkjer: Høgskolen i Nord-Trøndelag).
Green, M. & Houlihan, B. (2004), 'Advocacy coalitions and elite sport policy change in Canada and the United Kingdom', *International Review for the Sociology of Sport*, 39: 387-403.
Green, M. & Houlihan, B. (2005), *Elite Sport Development: Policy Learning and Political Priorities* (London: Routledge).
Green, M. & Oakley, B. (2001), 'Elite sport development systems and playing to win: Uniformity and diversity in international approaches', *Leisure Studies*, 20: 247-267.
Green, M. (2007), 'Olympic glory or grassroots development? Sport policy priorities in Australia, Canada and the United Kingdom, 1960 - 2006', *International Journal of the History of Sport*, 24: 921-953.
Green, M. (2009), 'Podium or participation? Analysing policy priorities under changing modes of sport governance in the United Kingdom', *International Journal of Sport Policy*, 1: 121-144.
Gynnild, A. (1993), *I steget - handball med Trine Haltvik* (Trondheim: Nordafjells).

Häkkinen, K. (2009), 'Pelaajasiirrot NHL:lään ja niihin liittyvät sopimukset' [Player transfers and contracts to the NHL], Turun yliopisto, Oikeustieteellisen tiedekunnan julkaisuja, Urheiluoikeuden sarja 24. Turku.

Hansen, H.F. (2008). 'Forvaltningspolitiske reformer: kontinuitet eller brud?', *Politik. Tidskriftet Politik*, 1.

Hansen, J. (1995a). 'Fusioner – Danske Gymnastik- og Idrætsforeninger – Danmarks Idræts-Forbund: Et historisk essay', In *Idrætshistorisk Årbog 1994* (Odense: Syddansk Universitetsforlag), 23–29.

Hansen, J. (1995b). 'Et samfund i opbrud', in Trangbæk, E., Hansen, J., Nielsen, N.K. (eds.), *Dansk Idrætsliv*, vol. 2, *Fritid og Velfærd* (København: Gyldendal), 104–110.

Hanstad, D.V. & Skille, E.Å. (2010), 'Does elite sport develop mass sport? A Norwegian case study', *Nordic Sport Studies Forum*, 1: 51–68.

Hanstad, D.V. (2002), *Seier'n er vår, men hvem har æren?* (Oslo: Schibsted).

Hanstad, D.V. (2006a), *Skal Norge søke vinterlekene 2018?* [*Shall Norway Apply for the 2019 Winter Olympics?*] (Oslo: Norges Idrettshøgskole/Norges Idrettsforbund og Olympiske Komité).

Hanstad, D.V. (2006b), 'The Norwegian model for elite sport', in *Olympic Winter Games Symposium, Turin, Italy 9 February 2006.*

Hardy, C. & Maguire, S. (2008), 'Institutional entrepreneurship', in Greenwood, R., Oliver, C., Sahlin, K. & Suddaby, R. (eds.), *The Sage Handbook of Organizational Institutionalism* (London: Sage).

Hayhurst, L., & Frisby, W. (2010), 'Inevitable tensions: Swiss and Canadian sport for development NGO perspectives on partnerships with high performance sport', *European Sport Management Quarterly*, 10: 75–96.

Häyrinen, R. & Laine, L. (1989), 'Suomi Urheilun Suurvaltana' [Finland as a superpower of sport]. Liikuntatieteellisen seuran julkaisuja 115. Gummerus; Helsinki

Hedal, M. (2006), *Sport på dansk tv - en analyse af samspillet mellem sport og dansk tv, 1993–2005* (Copenhagen: Idrættens Analyseinstitut): http://www.idan.dk/upload/sportp%C3%A5dansktv.pdf

Heikkala, J. (1993a), 'Discipline and excel: techniques of the self and body and the logic of competing', *Sociology of Sport Journal*, 10: 397–412.

Heikkala, J. (1993b), 'Modernity, morality and the logic of competing', *International Review for the Sociology of Sport*, 28/4: 355–369.

Heikkala, J. (1994), *Ajolähtö turvattomiin kotipesiin* [*Bases loaded for unsafe home bases*]

Heinilä, K. (1984), 'The totalisation process in international sport', in Ilmarinen, M. (ed.), *Sport and International Understanding* (Berlin: Springer-Verlag).

Heinilä, K. (1998), *Sport in Social Context by Kalevi Heinilä*, ed. Pauli Vuolle (Jyväskylä: University of Jyväskylä).

Heiskanen, H. (1997), 'Jääkiekon amatööriseurojen nykytila' [The current state of amateur ice-hockey clubs], Raportti, Yliopistopaino, Helsinki.

Hellberg, B. (2006) (ed.), *Svenska Tennisförbundet 100 år* (Stockholm).

Helle-Valle, J. (2008), 'Discourses on mass versus elite sport and pre-adolescent football in Norway', *International Review for the Sociology of Sport*, 43/4: 365–382.

Hentilä, S. (1982), *Suomen työläisurheilun historia I* [*History of Finnish Workers' Sports I*], Työväen urheiluliitto 1919–1944 [Finnish Workers' Sports Federation 1919–1944] (Hämeenlinna; Arvi A. Karisto Oy).

Hentilä, S. (1989), 'Urheilu, kansakunta ja luokat' [Sports, Nation and Classes], in R. Alapuro, I. Liikanen, K. Smeds & H. Stenius (eds.), *Kansa liikkeessä* [*Nation on the Move*] (Vaasa; Kirjayhtymä Oy), 213–235).

Hentilä, S. (1992), 'Väljä irtiotto työläisurheilun historiasta' [Loose Detachment from the History of Workers' Sports], in K. Olin, H. Itkonen, E. Ranto (eds.), *Liikunnan muutos, murros vai kaaos* [*Change, Turning Point or Chaos in Sports*] (Helsinki: TUL), 56–67).

Hodges, N.J., Starkes, J.L & MacMahon, C. (2006), 'Expert performance in sports: A cognitive perspective', in Ericsson, K. A., Harness, N., Feltovich, P. J. & Hoffman, R. R. (eds.), *The Cambridge Handbook of Expertise and Performance* (Cambridge: Cambridge University Press).

Holm, K. (1984), Tale ved Det Konservative Folkepartis April 1984 konference om sport, *Idrætsliv*, no. 4.

Holstein, J.A. and Gubrium, J. (2002), 'Active interviewing', in Weinberg, D. (ed.), *Qualitative Research Methods* (Oxford: Blackwell).

Horne, J. (2007), 'The four "knows" of sports mega-events', *Leisure Studies*, 26/1: 81–96.

Houlihan, B. & Green, M. (2008) (eds.), *Comparative Elite Sport Development: Systems, Structures and Public Policy* (Oxford: Butterworth-Heinemann).

Houlihan, B. (1997), *Sport, Policy and Politics: A Comparative Analysis* (London: Routledge).

Houlihan, B. (2009), 'Mechanisms of international influence on domestic elite sport policy', *International Journal of Sport Policy*, 1: 51–69.

Huippu-urheilu & Yhteiskunta [Elite Sports and Society] (1973), Jyväskylä Summer Festival / Sport Congress 1973, Kalevi Heinilä & Jukka Wuolio, eds. (Jyväskylä: Jyväskylän kesä ry).

Ibsen, B. & Seippel, Ø. (2010), 'Voluntary organized sport in Denmark and Norway', *Sport in Society*, 13/4: 593–610.

Ibsen, B. (1995), 'Det offentlige og idrætten', in Trangbæk, E., Hansen, J., Nielsen, N.K. (eds.), *Dansk Idrætsliv*, vol. 2, *Fritid og Velfærd* (København: Gyldendal), 111–130.

Ibsen, B., Hansen, J., Storm, R. (2010), 'Elite sport development in Denmark', In Houlihan, B. & Green, M. (eds.), *Routledge Handbook of Sport Development*, vol. 1 (London: Routledge), 381–393.Janson, A. (2004) (ed.), *Golf – den stora sporten* (Stockholm).

Jensen, J. (1983), 'Nu skal der for alvor satses på idrætseliten – Berører ikke breddeidrætten', *Dansk Idræt*, no. 24, December.

Jepsen, A.A. (2010), 'De gravede dybt og fandt', *Jyllandsposten*, 22 March.

Johnson, D.K.N. & Ali, A. (2000), 'Coming to play or coming to win: Participation and success at the Olympic Games', *Wellesley College Working Paper 2000-10*.
Johnson, D.K.N. & Ali, A. (2004), 'A tale of two seasons: participation and medal counts at the summer and winter Olympic Games', *Social Science Quarterly*, 85: 974-993.
Jones, R., Armour, K., & Potrac, P. (2004), *Sports Coaching Cultures: From Practice to Theory* (London: Routledge).
Jones, R.L. & Wallace, M. (2005), 'Another bad day at the training ground: Coping with ambiguity in the coaching context', *Sport, Education and Society*, 10/1: 119-134.
Jones, R.L. & Wallace, M. (2006), 'The coach as "orchestrator": More realistically managing the complex coaching context', in R. Jones (ed.), *The Sports Coach as Educator: Re-conceptualising Sports Coaching* (London: Routledge).
Jones, R.L. & Wallace, M. (2010), 'Talentudvikling i verdensklasse', *Cycling World*, no.1: 32-33.
Jørgensen, P. (2005), 'Danmarks Olympiske Komité – idrætspolitisk magtfaktor eller blot et historisk appendiks?', in: Hansen, M.M. & Trangbæk, E. (eds.), *Som ringe i vand. En antologi i anledning af Danmarks Olympiske Komités 100-års jubilæum* (København: Danmarks Idræts-Forbund), 14-31.J. R. (1984), 'Forslag til statsstøtte til den danske eliteidræt', *Firmaidræt*, no. 1, January.
Julin, L.A. (2002), 'Svensk elitidrott i internationell konkurrens' [Swedish elite sport in international competition], in Lindroth, J. & Norberg, J. R. (eds.), *Ett idrottssekel: Riksidrottsförbundet 1903-2003* (Stockholm: Informationsförlaget), 343-359.
Juppi, J. (1995), 'Suomen julkinen liikuntapolitiikka valtionhallinnon näkökulmasta vuosina 1917-1994' [Public sport policy in Finland from the viewpoint of state administration in 1917-1994]. *Studies in Sport, Physical Education and Health* 36. Jyväskylän yliopisto. See after 'Jones'.
Kaas, D., Kaggestad, J. & Kristiansen, H.T. (2007), *Fra ord til handling. Om prestasjonsutvikling i praksis* (Oslo: Cappelen Akademisk Forlag).
Kantola, H. (2007), *Valmennuksen jalanjäljet. 100 vuotta suomalaista urheiluvalmennusta* [*Footsteps of coaching. A Century of Finnish Sport Coaching*]. Gummerus; Jyväskylä.
Karhatsu, H. (2003), 'Suomalaisen joukkueurheiluyritysten menestystekijät' [Success factors of Finnish team sport companies] Helsingin kauppakorkeakoulu, markkinoinnin laitos, pro gradu –tutkielma. Julkaisematon lähde.
Kaspersen, L.B. (2008), *Danmark i verden* (København: Hans Reitzels Forlag).
Kauhala, H., Hannula, M. & Laine, M. (2003), *Pelaajien puolesta. Suomen jääkiekkoilijat ry:n 30-vuotishistoriikki* [*For the players. The History of the Finnish Ice-Hockey players Association*] Gummerus; Jyväskylä.
Kempas, M. (1986), *Pyrhä Ureilo: Senttejä ja sekuntteja, kamppailua ja ristiriitoja. Vaihtoehtoisen kehityksen tie suomalaisessa liikuntakulttuurissa* [*Sacred Sports: centimeters and seconds, struggle and conflict. Alternative development paths in the Finnish sports culture*]. Vaasa.

Kirkebøen, S.E. (1984), 'Rimejorde leder for "Prosjekt 88"'. *Aftenposten*, 27 November.

Kivinen, O. Mesikämmen, J. & Metsä-Tokila, T. (2000), 'Kylmä kiekkosota; kaksi mannerta, kaksi kulttuuria' [Cold hockey war; two continents, two cultures] Liikuntatieteellisen seuran julkaisu nro 151. Helsinki.

Knudsen, T. (2007), *Fra folkestyre til markedsdemokrati: Dansk demokratihistorie efter 1973*. 1st ed., vol. 2 (Copenhagen: Akademisk Forlag).

Kolehmainen, T. (1972), *Työläisurheilu Suomessa 1. Tie koiton talolle [Workers' Sports in Finland 1. Road to the Koitto Building]* (Helsinki: Otava).

Korsgaard, A. & Børsting, A. (2002), *Mod statslig involvering – En analyse af dansk idrætspolitik i perioden 1974–2000*. Thesis at the Institute of Sports Science and Clinical Biomechanics (Odense: University of Southern Denmark).

KPMG Consulting (2002), *Eliteidræt – et økonomisk øjebliksbillede på specialforbundenes udgifter til eliteidræt* (Brøndby: Danmarks Idræts-Forbund).

Kraatz, M.S. & Block, E.S. (2008), 'Organizational implications of institutional pluralism', in Greenwood, R., Oliver, C., Sahlin, K. & Suddaby, R. (eds.), *The Sage Handbook of Organizational Institutionalism* (London: Sage).

Kristensen, K.M. (2008), 'Hvor blev juniorerne af?', *Cycling World*, no. 2: 2–5.

Kulturministeriet (2003), *Dansk Eliteidræt – Udvikling og Fremtidspespektiver* (København).

Kulturministeriet (2004), Lov nr. 288 Lov om eliteidræt (København).

Kuper, S. & Szymanski, S. (2009), *Soccernomics: Why England Loses, Why Germany and Brazil Win, and Why the US, Japan, Australia, Turkey --and Even Iraq-- Are Destined to Become the Kings of the World's Most Popular Sport* (New York: Nation Books)

Kvale, S. (1996), *InterView: An Introduction to Qualitative Research Interviewing* (London: Sage).

Laine, L. (1984), *Vapaaehtoisten järjestöjen kehitys ruumiinkulttuurin alueella Suomessa v. 1856–1917, I [Development of Voluntary Organisations in the Field of Physical Culture in Finland in 1856–1917, I]*, Society for Research in Sport and Physical Education Publication no. 93 A (Lappeenranta: Etelä-Saimaan Kustannus Oy).

Laine, L. (2007), 'Sillanrakennusta ja tehovalmennusta' ['Bridge Building and Intensive Coaching'], in V. Tikander, O. Viita, M. Vilen & E. Paavola (eds.), *Sadan vuoden Olympiadi. Suomalaisen olympialiikkeen historia [Coaches and Conciliators. Centennial History of the Finnish Olympic Movement]* (Porvoo: WSOY), 174–228.

Lämsä, J. & Vuolle P. (1998), 'Globalization of top sport in Finland: Olympic success and international migration of athletes in 1966–1998, in *Proceedings of the Fourth Annual Congress of the European College of Sport Science*, Rome 14–17 July 1999, 171.

Lazonic, W. (1993), 'Industry clusters versus global webs: Organizational capabilities in the American Economy'. *Industrial and Corporate Change*, 2/1: 1–23.

Lee, N. & Lings, I. (2008), *Doing Business Research: A Guide to Theory and Practice* (London: Sage).
Liikuntagallup (2010a), 'Kansallinen liikuntatutkimus 2009–2010. Lapset ja Nuoret' [National Sport Gallup 2009–2010: Children and youths] SLU:n julkaisusarja 7/2010. SLU; Helsinki.
Lindfeldt, M. (2007), *Eliten é liten – men växer. Förändrade perspektiv på elitidrott.* Stockholm: Riksidrottsförbundet, FoU 2007: 11.
Lindroth, J. (1974), *Idrottens väg till folkrörelse. Studier i svensk idrottsrörelse till 1915* (Uppsala: Uppsala universitet).
Lindroth, J. (1998), 'Den moderna tävlingsidrottens intensifisering: Principiella synpunkter och praktiska exempel på försummad dimension' [The intensification of modern competitive sport: Principal standpoints and practical examples from a neglected dimension], *Idrott, historia och samhälle*, 4: 35–75.
Lippe, G.V.D. (1994), 'Handball, gender and sportification of body-cultures: 1900–1940', *International Review for the Sociology of Sport*, 29: 211–231.
Løvstrup, I. & Hansen, J. (2002), *Da eliteidrætten blev stueren* (Odense: Syddansk Universitetsforlag).
Lundkvist, S. (1979), *Folkrörelserna i det svenska samhället 1850–1920* (Uppsala: Uppsala universitet).
Lundström, T. & Wijkström, F. (1995), *Från röst till service? Den svenska ideella sektorn i förändring* (Sköndal: Sköndalsinstitutet).
Madsen, E. (1983), 'Eliten skal have sin egen organisation', *Dansk Idræt*, no. 16, August.
Maguire, S., Hardy, C. & Lawrence, T.B. (2004), 'Institutional entrepreneurship in institutional fields: HIV/AIDS treatment advocacy in Canada', *Academy of Management Journal*, 47: 657–679.
Mäkinen, J. (2010), *Urheilun tuki ja rakenteet Suomessa, Ruotsissa ja Norjassa.* [Differences in the organizational structures and public funding of sports in Finland, Norway and Sweden]. Kilpa- ja huippu-urheilun tutkimuskeskus. KIHUn julkaisusarja nro 17.
Mäkinen, J. (2011), *Idrottsorganisation och offentligt stöd – En jämförelse mellan Finland, Norge och Sverige.* Available at: http://www.idrottsforum.org/articles/makinen/makinen110126.html
March, J. & Olsen, J.P. (1989), *Rediscovering institutions: The organizational basis of politics* (New York: Free Press).
Margolinsky, A. (1984), 'Repræsentantskabet – Gamle grænser skal brydes ned', *Idrætsliv*, no. 2.
Maskell, P. (2001), 'Towards a knowledge-based theory of the geographical cluster', *Industrial and corporate change*, 10/4: 921–943.
Mattsson, K. (2010), Interview, 16 August.
Meckstroth, T.W. (1975), '"Most different" and "most similar" systems: A study in the logic of comparative inquiry'. *Comparative Political Studies*, 8/2: 132–157.

Meinander, H. (1999), *Tasavallan tiellä: Suomi Kansalaissodasta 2000-luvulle* [*On the Road to a Republic: Finland from the Civil War to the 21st Century*] (Helsinki: Schildts).
Mennander, A. & Mennander, P. (2004), 'Liigatähdet. Jääkiekon SM-liiga 30 vuotta, 1975—2005' [The league stars: FC-league 30 years, 1975–2005], Gummerus; Jyväskylä.
Mennander, A. (1997), *Hjallis – Hartwall Areena*. Otava; Keuruu.
Mennander, P. (2000), 'Katsotaanpa kaukaloon. Suomen jääkiekkoliiton kansainväliset suhteet ja maajoukkueen toiminta 1944–1959' [Let's watch the rink. The international relations and the national team of the Finnish Ice-Hockey Federation in 1944–1959] Jyväskylän yliopisto, historian laitos. Pro gradu –tutkielma (Julkaisematon lähde).
Merkel, U. (1999), 'Sport in divided societies – the case of the old, the new and the "re-united" Germany', in: J. Sugden & A. Bairner (eds.), *Sport in Divided Societies* (Aachen: Meyer & Meyer), 139–165.
Mesikämmen, J. (2002), 'Luonnonjäiltä areenoille, intohimosta leipäpuuksi: ammattilaistumisen avaimia suomalaisessa jääkiekossa' [From the lake to the ice stadium: professionalization in Finnish Ice-hockey], in H. Roiko-Jokela & E. Sironen (eds.). Lajien Synty. Suomen urheiluhitoriallisen seuran vuosikirja 2001–02. Atena kustannus oy; Jyväskylä, 103–120.
Meyer, J. W. & Rowan, B. (1977), 'Institutionalized organizations: Formal structure as myth and ceremony', *American Journal of Sociology*, no. 2: 340–363.
Micheletti, M. (1994), *Det civila samhället och staten: Medborgarsammanslutningarnas roll i svensk politik* (Stockholm: Fritze).
Ministeriet for kulturelle anliggender (1974), *Betænkning om idrætten og friluftslivet*, Betænkning nr. 709 (København).
Ministeriet for kulturelle anliggender (1983), *Betænkning om eliteidræt i Danmark*, Betænkning nr. 992 (København)
Morton, R.H. (2002), 'Who won the Sydney 2000 Olympics? An allometric approach', *The Statistican*, 51: 147–155.
Nielsen, K. & Storm, R.K. (2010), *Sparekniv og fremgang: Dansk eliteidræt med vind i sejlene:* www.idan.dk
Nielsen, K. (1996), 'Hvilke konsekvenser har eliteidræt på samfundsmæssigt niveau?', in E. Trangbæk (ed.), *Grænser for vækst i eliteidrætten* (København: Danmarks Idræts-Forbund & Center for Idrætsforskning), 109–119.
Nielsen, M.K. (2010), 'Tilliden til Team Danmark er væk', *Berlingske Tidende*, 21 April.
Niemi-Nikkola, K. (2004), 'Suomalainen valmennujärjestelmä' [Finnish Coaching System], in A. Mero, A. Nummela, K. Keskinen & K. Häkkinen (toim), *Urheiluvalmennus* [*Coaching in Sport*] (VK-Kustannus Oy), 387–397.NIF (1973), *Profesjonalisering i samfunnet og i idretten* (Oslo: Norges Idrettsforbund).
NIF (1979), *Vilkårene for toppidrett* (Oslo: Norges Idrettsforbund).

NIF (2005), *Olympiatoppen – en fremtidsrettet og inkluderende organisasjon med særforbund som premissleverenandør, 1. versjon* (Oslo: Norges Idrettsforbund og Olympiske Komité).

NIF (2006a), *Olympiatoppen – en fremtidsrettet og inkluderende organisasjon med særforbund som premissleverandør, 2. versjon* (Oslo: Norges Idrettsforbund og Olympiske Komité).

NIF (2006b), *Protokoll for Idrettsstyrets møte nr. 22 – 2004–2007, 4.april 2006* (Oslo: Norges Idrettsforbund og Olympiske Komite).

NIF (2007), *Idrettspolitisk dokument for tingperioden 2007 til 2011* (Oslo: Norges Idrettsforbund og Olympiske Komité).

NIF /NOK (1988), *Prosjekt 88: Sluttrapport* (Oslo: Norges Idrettsforbund og Norges Olympiske Komité).

Norberg, J.R. (1997), 'A mutual dependency: Nordic sport organizations and the state', *International Journal of the History of Sport*, 14/3: 115–135.

Norberg, J.R. (2002a), 'Idrottsrörelsens utbredning, anslutning och sammansättning', in Lindroth, J. & Norberg, J. R. (eds.), *Ett idrottsekel: Riksidrottsförbundet 1903–2003* (Stockholm: Informationsförlaget).

Norberg, J.R. (2002b), 'Idrottsrörelsen och staten', in Lindroth, J. & Norberg, J. R. (eds.), *Ett idrottsekel: Riksidrottsförbundet 1903–2003* (Stockholm: Informationsförlaget).

Norberg, J.R. (2004), *Idrottens väg till folkhemmet: Studier i statlig idrottspolitik 1913–1970* (Stockholm: Stockholms universitet).

Nordberg, R. (1997) (ed.), *Norsk håndball gjennom 60 år* (Oslo: Norges Håndballforbund).

Nordisk familjebok (1940), 'Friidrott', in *Nordisk familjeboks sportlexikon: uppslagsverk för sport, gymnastik och friluftsliv*, vol. 3 (Stockholm: Nordisk familjeboks förlag).

Nygren, H. (1980), *Jääkenttäsäätiö, Isbanestiftelsen 1954–1979* [*The Foundation of the Ice Stadium 1954–1979*] Mainosrengas Oy; Helsinki.

Oakley, B. & Green, M. (2001), 'The productions of Olympic champions: International perspectives on elite sport development systems', *European Journal of Sport Management*, 8/1: 83–105.

Olstad, F. (1987), *Norsk idretts historie: Forsvar, sport, klassekamp 1861–1939* (Oslo: Aschehoug).

Opetus- ja kulttuuriministeriö [Ministry of Education and Culture] (1994), *Huippu-urheilu 2000: Strategia huippu-urheilun kehittämiseksi* [*Elite sport 2000: the development strategy*], Opetusministeriön, Suomen Olympiakomitean ja Suomen Liikunta ja Urheilu ry:n asettaman työryhmän muistio.

Opetus- ja kulttuuriministeriö [Ministry of Education and Culture] (1998), *Huippu-urheilu 2000-luvulle: Strategiaohjelma huippu-urheilun kehittämiseksi.* [*Bringing the elite sport into the year 2000: the development strategy*], Suomen Olympiakomitean, opetusministeriön ja Suomen Liikunta ja Urheilu ry:n asettaman työryhmän muistio.

Opetus- ja kulttuuriministeriö [Ministry of Education and Culture] (2000), *Valmennuskeskusten kehitystyöryhmän muistio*. [*The memorandum of the working group on national training centers*], Opetusministeriön työryhmien muistioita 2000, 23, Tekijät: Puheenjohtaja: Mirja Virtala, Sihteeri: Jari Piirainen.

Opetus- ja kulttuuriministeriö [Ministry of Education and Culture] (2004a), *Huippu-urheilutyöryhmän muistio* [*The memorandum of the working group on top-level sports*], Opetusministeriön työryhmämuistioita ja selvityksiä 2004: 22. Tekijät: Puheenjohtaja: Kalevi Kivistö, sihteeri: Hannu Tolonen, Kari Niemi-Nikkola.

Opetus- ja kulttuuriministeriö [Ministry of Education and Culture] (2009), Ohjeet urheilijoille tarkoitettujen verottomien valtion valmennus- ja harjoitteluapurahojen hakemisesta ja myöntämisestä vuodeksi 2009 [*The directions to note regarding applications for the tax-free athlete grants for the year 2009*], available: http://www.minedu.fi/OPM/Liikunta/liikuntapolitiikka/avustukset/Urheilijoiden_valmennus-_ja_harjoitteluapuraha

Opetus- ja kulttuuriministeriö [Ministry of Education and Culture] (2010), 'Sanoista teoiksi': Huippu-urheilutyöryhmän ajatuksia suomalaisen huippu-urheilun kehittämiseksi [*From Word to Actions: The ideas of the working group to develop Finnish top-level sport*], Opetusministeriön työryhmämuistioita ja selvityksiä 2010: 13.

Ottesen, L., Skirstad, B., Pfister, G. & Habermann, U. (2010), 'Gender relations in Scandinavian sport organizations – a comparison of the situation and politics in Denmark, Norway and Sweden', *Sport in Society*, 13/4: 657–675.

Pedersen, M.E. (2008), 'Vi bruger hele vores liv pa at blive de bedste', *Cycling World*, no. 2: 30–32.

Petersen, R. (1952), *Oslo 1952 – De VI olympiske vinterleker* (Oslo: Aschehoug).

Peterson, T. (1993), *Den svengelska modellen* (Lund: Arkiv).

Peterson, T. (1989), *Leken som blev allvar: Halmstads Bollklubb mellan folkrörelse, stat och marknad* (Lund: Arkiv).

Porter, M.E. (1985), *Competitive Advantage: Creating and Sustaining Superior Performance* (New York: The Free Press).

Porter, M.E. (1990), *The Competitive Advantage of Nations* (London: MacMillan Press).

Potrac, P., Jones, R.L., & Armour, K.M. (2002), '"It's all about getting respect": The coaching behaviours of an expert English soccer coach', *Sport, Education and Society*, 7/2: 183–202.

Proposition 2008/09:126, *Statens stöd till idrotten*.

Proposition 2009/10:1, Utgiftsområde 17, *Kultur, medier, trossamfund och fritid*.

Puhakainen, J. & Suhonen, A. (1999), *Valmentaja ja filosofi* [*Coach and philosopher*], Elämänmakuinen kirja ihmisestä, urheilusta ja filosofiasta. Like, Juva.

Rasmussen, A. (1984), 'Perspektiver i nyåret'. *Dansk Ungdom og Idræt*, no. 1, 6 January.

Regeringens proposition 2008/09:126. (2009), *Statens stöd till idrotten* [*The government support to sport*] (Stockholm: Riksdagen).

Regeringsgrundlaget 2001 (2001), Section 'Bedre vilkår for idrætten': http://www.stm.dk/publikationer/regeringsgrundlag/reggrund01.htm#idrætten

Reinebo, P. (2010), Interview, 2010-06-07.

Riksidrottsförbundet (2005), *Idrottens föreningar, en studie om idrottsföreningarnas situation*, Stockholm: Riksidrottsförbundet, FoU 2005: 3.

Riksidrottsförbundet (2008), *Vägval för svensk idrott: Riksidrottsstyrelsens diskussionsunderlag*, retrieved 15 October 2010 from *www.rf.se*: http://www.rf.se/ImageVault/Images/id_980/scope_128/ImageVaultHandler.aspx

Riksidrottsförbundet (2009a), *Idrotten vill: idrottsrörelsens idéprogram, antagen av RF-stämman 2009*, Stockholm: Riksidrottsförbundet.

Riksidrottsförbundet (2009b), *RF:s Stadgar i lydelse efter RF-stämman 200*. Stockholm: Riksidrottsförbundet, 2 kap. 1 §.

Riksidrottsförbundet (2009c), *Så byggs den gemensamma elitsatsningen*, retrieved 15 October 2010 from *www.rf.se*: http://www.rf.se/Nyheter/2009/Januari-juni/Sabyggsdengemensammaelitsatsningen/

Riksidrottsförbundet (2009d), *En samlad elitsatsning, steg 2*, retrieved 15 October 2010 from *www.rf.se*: http://www.rf.se/ImageVault/Images/id_2627/ImageVaultHandler.aspx

Riksidrottsförbundet (2009e), *Förslag om en samlad elitsatsning*, retrieved 15 October 2010 from *www.rf.se*: http://www.rf.se/ImageVault/Images/id_2625/ImageVaultHandler.aspx

Riksidrottsförbundet (2010a), *Verksamhetsinriktning för Riksidrottsförbundet 2010-2011*, retrieved 15 October 2010 from *www.rf.se*: http://www.rf.se/ImageVault/Images/id_2529/ImageVaultHandler.aspx

Riksidrottsförbundet (2010b), *Utveckla eliten! Jobba tillsammans med RF:s elitstöd*, Stockholm: Riksidrottsförbundet.

Riksidrottsförbundet (2010c), *Riksidrottsförbundets verksamhetsberättelse med årsredovisning 2009*, Stockholm: Riksidrottsförbundet.

Ronglan, L.T. (1992), *Makt og avmakt blant særforbundene i Norge*, Hovedfagsoppgave i idrett (Oslo: Norges Idrettshøgskole).

Ronglan, L.T. (2000), *Gjennom sesongen: En sosiologisk studie av det norske kvinnelandslaget i håndball på og utenfor banen*. Ph.D.-avhandling (Oslo: Norges Idrettshøgskole).

Ronglan, L.T. (2011), 'Social interaction in coaching', in R. L. Jones, P. Potrac, C. Cushion & L. T. Ronglan (eds.), *The Sociology of Sports Coaching* (London: Routledge),151-165.

Røvik, K.A. (2007), *Trender og translasjoner* (Oslo: Universitetsforlaget).

Salo, U. (2006), 'Valmennustoiminta' [Coaching], in Martiskainen, S. (ed.), *Suomi Voittoon – kansa liikkumaan* [Finland to Win – Nation to Move], 205-249. Suomen Yleisurheilun 100 vuotta [One Hundred Years in Finnish Athletics].

Schelin, Bo (1985), *Den ojämlika idrotten – om idrottsstratifiering, idrottspreferens och val av idrott*. Doctoral dissertation in sociology (Lund: Lunds Universitet)

Schou-Andreassen, K.S. & Wadel, C. (1981), *Ledelse, teamarbeid og teamutvikling i fotball* (Flekkefjord: SEEK A/S).

Schulman, P.R. (1993), 'The negotiated order of organizational reliability', *Administration and Society,* 25: 353-373.
Seippel, Ø. (2010), 'Professionals and volunteers: on the future of a Scandinavian sport model', *Sport in Society,* 13/2: 199-211.
Silverman, D. (2005), *Doing qualitative research* (London: Sage).
Sitkin, S.B. (1992), 'Learning through failure: The strategy of small losses', *Research in Organizational Behaviour,* 14: 231-266.
Sjöblom, P. & Fahlén, J. (2010), 'The survival of the fittest: intensification, totalization and homogenization in Swedish competitive sport', *Sport in Society,* 13/4: 704-720.
Sjöblom, P. (2004), 'Sport for all? The "Sports city programme" in Norway', *Sport in Society,* 7/2: 192-210.
Sjöblom, P. (2006), *Den institutionaliserade tävlingsidrotten. kommuner, idrott och politik i Sverige under 1900-talet,* (Stockholm: Stockholms universitet).
Skille, E.Å. (2005), 'Individuality or cultural reproduction? Adolescents' sport participation in Norway: alternative versus conventional sports', *International Review for the Sociology of Sport,* 40/3: 307-320.
Skille, E.Å. (2009), 'Sport as social policy: A conceptual reflection about policy making and implementation through the case of the Norwegian sports city programme', *International Journal of Applied Sport Sciences,* 21/2: 1-15.
Skjerk, O. (1999), 'Team handball in Denmark 1898-1948: Civilisation or sportification?', in A. Krüger & E. Trangbæk (eds.), *The History of Physical Education and Sport from European Perspectives* (Copenhagen: CESH), 97-110.
Slagstad, R. (1998), *De nasjonale strateger* (Oslo: Pax).
Soares, J. (2007), 'Cold war, hot ice: International ice hockey 1947-1980. *Journal of Sport History,* 34/2, 207-230.
Sonera Next Generation ja Suomen Valmentajat [Finnish Coach Association] (2010), Valmentajakysely lajien välisestä yhteistyöstä [*Coach Survey: Horizontal cooperation among different sports*]. Available at: http://feed.ne.cision.com/wpyfs/00/00/00/00/00/12/4D/2B/wkr0005.pdf
Sørensen, E. (2007), 'Public Administration as Metagovernance', in G. Gjelstrup & E. Sørensen (eds.), *Public Administration in Transition* (Copenhagen: DJØF Publishers), 107-126.
Sørensen, E. See after 'SOU'.
SOU (1969) 1969: 29, *Idrott åt alla. Betänkande avgivet av Idrottsutredningen.*
SOU (2006) 2006: 23, *Nya skatteregler för idrotten.*
SOU (2008) 2008: 59, 'Föreningsfostran och tävlingsfostran. En utvärdering av statens stöd till idrotten', *Rapport från Idrottsstödsutredningen* (Stockholm: Fritze)
St.meld nr. 8 (1973-74) (1973), *Om organisering og finansiering av kulturarbeid* (Oslo: Kulturdepartementet).
Stamm, H. & Lamprecht, M. (2000), 'Der Schweizer Spitzensport im internationalen Vergleich: Eine empirische Analyse der Olympischen Spiele, 1964-1998', *Schriftenreiheder Gesellschaft zur Förderung der Sportwissenschaften an der ETH Zürich,* 21.

Starbuck, W.H. & Hedberg, L.T. (2006), 'How organizations learn from success and failure', in Starbuck, W. H. (ed.), *Organizational Realities: Studies of Strategizing and Organizing* (Oxford: Oxford University Press).
Starbuck, W.H. (2004), 'Why I stopped trying to understand the real world'. *Organization Studies* 25/7: 1233–1254.
Steen-Johnsen, K. & Hanstad, D.V. (2008), 'Change and power in complex democratic organizations: The case of Norwegian elite sport'. *European Sport Management Quarterly*, 8/2: 123–143.
Stensbøl, B. (2010), *Makten og æren i toppidrettens kulisser* (Oslo: Kagge Forlag).
Stewart, B., Nicholson, M., Smith A. & Westerbeek, H. (2004), *Australian Sport: Better by Design? The Evolution of Australian Sport Policy* (London: Routledge).
Støckel, J.T., Strandbu, Å., Solenes, O., Jørgensen, P. & Fransson, K. (2010), 'Sport for children and youth in the Scandinavian countries', *Sport in Society*, 13/4: 625–643.
Storm, R.K & Almlund, U. (2006), *Håndboldøkonomi.dk – fra forsamlingshus til forretning* (København: Idrættens Analyseinstitut).
Storm, R.K. & Nielsen, K. (2010a), 'In a peak fitness condition? The Danish elite sports model in international perspective: managerial efficiency and best practice in achieving international sporting success', *International Journal of Sport Management and Marketing*, 7: 104–118.
Storm, R.K. & Nielsen, K. (2010b), 'Dansk eliteidræts konkurrenceevne: Resultater, målemetoder og investeringer.' *Scandinavian Sport Studies Forum*, 1: 27–50.
Storm, R.K. (2008), *Team Danmarks støttekoncept. Evaluering af støttekonceptet for 2005 – 2008* (Copenhagen: Danish Institute for Sports Studies).
Storm, R.K. (2009), 'Danmarks position i det internationale elitesportskapløb – Post Beijing', *Forum for Idræt*, 1: 47–65.
Suomen Olympiakomitea [Finnish Olympic Committee] (1987), *Valmennuskeskusten perustamista koskeva muistio* [*The Memorandum Concerning the Establishment of National Training Centers*].
Suomen Olympiakomitea [Finnish Olympic Committee] (2006), *Suomen Olympiakomitean Valmennuksen toimintasuunnitelma 2007-2010* [*The Operation Plan for the Coaching of the Finnish Olympic Committee Years 2007-2010*].
Suomen Olympiakomitea [Finnish Olympic Committee] (2007), *Urheiluakatemiat osana suomalaista huippu-urheilujärjestelmää* [*Sport Academies as a Part of the Finnish Elite Sport System*].
Suomen Olympiakomitea [Finnish Olympic Committee] (2009), *Urheiluakatemioiden valtakunnallinen kehittämisohjelma 2010-2013* [*National Program for the Development of Sport Academies 2010-2013*].
Suomen Olympiayhdistys ry [Finnish Olympic Association] (2002), *Huippu-urheilu 2000-luvulla: Strategia suomalaisen huippu-urheilun kehittämiseksi 2002-2006*. [*Elite Sport in 2000: The Elite Sport Development Strategy for the Years 2002–2006*]. Suomen Olympiakomitean ja opetusministeriön kokoaman työryhmän muistio suomalaisen huippu-urheilun uudesta strategiasta.
Svenska dagbladet (2007a), *RF-basen kritisk till tidig gallring,* 2007–12–11.

Svenska dagbladet (2007b), *Idrottsministern: 'Jag vill veta hur de tänker'*, 2007-12-11.

Svenska fotbollförbundet (2009), *Analys av allsvenska klubbarnas ekonomi 2008* (Solna: Fotbollförbundet).

Sveriges Olympiska Kommitté (2009), Årsredovisning 2009, retrieved 15 October 2010 from *www.sok.se:* http://www.sok.se/download/18.33d4878b127b4538e2f80003326/SOK_Arsredovisning_2009_WEB.pdf

Sveriges Olympiska Kommitté (2010a), *Vad är SOK?* Retrieved 15 October 2010 from *www.sok.se:* http://www.sok.se/omsok.4.18ea16851076df6362280008256.html

Sveriges Olympiska Kommitté (2010b), *Olympiskt program*, retrieved 15 October 2010 from *www.sok.se:* http://www.sok.se/olympisktprogram.4.18ea16851076df6362280008264.html

Sylvén, S. & Karlsson, O. (2008), *OS: historia & statistik* (Stockholm: Norstedts).

Syrjäläinen, A. (2008), *Miksi siksi loikkariksi? Huippu-urheilijoiden loikkaukset TUL:sta SVUL:oon 1919-1939* [*Why One of Those Defectors? Defections of Elite Athletes from TUL to SVUL in 1919-1939*], University of Joensuu, Publications in Social Sciences, no. 89 (Joensuu: Joensuu University Press).

Taalesen, B. (1988), 'Vi må tenke nytt', *Aftenposten*, 27 February.

Team Danmark (2009), *Team Danmarks støttekoncept 2009-2012* (Brøndby: Team Danmark)

Thornton, P.H. & Occasio, W. (2008), 'Institutional logics'. In Greenwood, R., Oliver, C., Sahlin, K. & Suddaby, R. (eds.), *The Sage Handbook of Organizational Institutionalism* (London: Sage).

Thygesen, J.K. (1983), 'Statsstøtte til eliten', *Dansk Ungdom og Idræt*, no. 47, 16 December.

Tønnesson, S. (1986), *Norsk idretts historie: Folkehelse, trim, stjerner 1939-1986*. [*Public health, exercise, stars 1939-1986*] (Oslo: Aschehoug).

Tranckle, P. & Cushion, C. (2006), 'Rethinking giftedness and talent in sport', *Quest*, 58/2: 265-283.

Trondman, M. (2005), *Unga och föreningsidrotten: En studie om föreningsidrottens plats, betydelser och konsekvenser i ungas liv*, Stockholm: Ungdomsstyrelsen, 2005: 9.

Uebel, M. (2006), *Nya perspektiv på Riksidrottsgymnasierna – Vad flickor och pojkar värdesätter i RIG-verksamheten*, Stockholm: Riksidrottsförbundet, FoU 2006: 4.

Ulseth, O. (2006), 'Mindre bråk – færre gull', *Adresseavisen*, 25 February.

Vasara, E. (2004), *Valtion liikuntahallinnon historia* [*History of State Sports Administration*], Society for Research in Sport and Physical Education, Publication no. 157 (Tampere: Society for Research in Sport and Physical Education).

Vauhdikasta viihdettä (1985), *Jääkiekon SM-liiga 1975-1985* [*Energetic entertainment. FC-league 1975-1985*] Gummerus; Jyväskylä.

Wacklin, M. (2005), *Kirvesrinnat – Tapparan tarina* [*Kirvesrinnat – the story of Ice Hockey team Tappara*] Karisto; Hämeenlinna.

Wallin, B. (2003), *Idrotten till tjugohundra: en trettioårig utvecklingsperiod* (Farsta: SISU Idrottsböcker).

Wedlin, L. (2007), 'The role of rankings in codifying a business school template: Classification, diffusion and mediated isomorphism in organizational fields'. *European Management Review*, 4: 24–39.

Weick, K.E. & Sutcliffe, K.M. (2001), *Managing the Unexpected: Assuring High Performance in the Age of Complexity* (San Francisco: Jossey-Bass).

Weick, K.E. (2006), 'Faith, evidence and action: better guesses in an unknown world', *Organization Studies*, 27: 1723–36.

Wenger, E. (1998), *Communities of Practice: Learning, Meaning, and Identity* (Cambridge: Cambridge University Press).

Wijk, J. (2007), 'Det svenska "golf- och tennisundret": En parallell framgångshistoria – om tennisens och golfens elitutveckling samt en ansats till förklaringsmodell gällande orsaksfaktorer till Idrottsframgångar'. *Idrott, historia & samhälle.*

Wikberg, K. (2005), *Amatör eller professionist? Studier rörande amatörfrågan i svensk tävlingsidrott 1903–1967* (Stockholm: SISU idrottsböcker).

Yin, R.K. (1989), *Case study research: Design and methods* (London: Sage). See under 'A'

Presentation of authors

Svein S. Andersen is a professor of organization studies at the Norwegian Business School, BI and adjunct professor at the Centre for Training and Performance, Norwegian School of Sport Sciences. He has been director for Centre for EU Research, University of Oslo, and Chair of the Department of Leadership and Organizational Behaviour as well as Dean of Studies at the Norwegian Business School. He has a Ph.D. From Stanford University and has published a number of books and articles. During the last years he has focused on leadership and organization in Nordic elite sport.

Lars Tore Ronglan is an associate professor and senior researcher at the Centre for Training and Performance at the Norwegian School of Sport Sciences (NSSS). He is the former Head of Department of Coaching and Psychology at NSSS. In 2000, he completed his Ph.D. thesis; a sociological analysis of a performance group in elite team sport. Recently, he has published books and articles on leadership, learning and coaching in sport; e.g., co-edited 'The Sociology of Sports Coaching' (Routledge, 2011).

Josef Fahlén is an associate professor at the Department of Education, Umeå University. Fahlén's main research areas are sport policy and the organization and governance of the Swedish sport movement, focusing specifically on the concepts of stability and change.

Matti Goksøyr is a professor at the Department of Social and Cultural Studies at the Norwegian School of Sport Sciences, Oslo. Goksøyr is a sport historian, and his main research interests are sport and identity and the development of modern sports.

Jørn Hansen is a professor at the Institute of Sports Sciences and Clinical Biomechanics, University of Southern Denmark, Odense. His basic research areas are sports history and international sports politics; sports and public health.

Dag Vidar Hanstad is an associate professor and Head of Department of Social and Cultural Studies at the Norwegian School of Sport Sciences, Oslo. His research areas are elite sport and anti-doping.

Aage Hoffmann is a former schoolteacher and has a Ph.D. in history. His research interests are the history of Danish sports organizations, in particular the workers' sports federation.

Jari Lämsä has a master's degree in sport sociology and works as a researcher at KIHU – Research Institute for Olympic Sports in Finland. His research interest is the organization and workings of elite sport systems.

Jarmo Mäkinen is a researcher at KIHU – Research Institute for Olympic Sports in Finland. His research areas are the development and structure of Finnish organized sport.

Klaus Nielsen is a professor in institutional economics at Birkbeck College, University of London. His research interests are institutional theory, innovation, social capital, economics and the business of sport.

Johan R. Norberg is an associate professor in sports science at Malmö University. Norberg's research areas are sport history, sport politics and organizational developments and challenges within sport.

Paul Sjöblom is an assistant professor at the Department of History, Stockholm University. Sjöblom's academic disciplines are sport science and sport history, and his basic research areas are sport politics, sport cultures, and elite sport.

Rasmus K. Storm is a senior academic researcher at the Danish Institute for Sports Studies (Idan), and a Ph.D. scholar at the University of Southern Denmark. Storm is primarily engaged in elite sport and sports economy.

Johnny Wijk is a professor at the Department of History, University of Stockholm. His basic research area is politics in modern society during the twentieth century with special interest in the development of sports in society.

Index

Amateurism 19, 29, 69, 280
Autonomy 11, 13, 283–284

Central authority 11, 268, 277, 281
Coaching 17, 66, 92, 213
Coach education 73, 120–121
Convergence and divergence 17–18, 260–62
Crisis 18, 75, 104, 265

Danish Elite Law 54, 58–59

Elite sport culture 95, 250
Elite sport success 13, 14–16, 81
Elite sport system 13, 21–22, 33, 261
Entrepreneurial 27, 272, 284

Facilities 17, 89, 145, 180, 271
Funding 39, 57, 66, 215, 279

Institutional entrepreneurship 18, 261
Institutional stalemate 267
Institutional perspective 13–14, 24, 260, 269

Learning model 24, 251
Legitimacy 29, 68, 242, 279

Mass sport 20–21, 269–72
Methodology 21–23
Most similar systems 14, 22, 23, 260

National model 211, 244–47, 262, 265, 277
National sports Confederation
  Denmark (DIF) 46

Norway (NIF) 29
Sweden (RF) 64–65, 77, 193
Finland (SVUL, TUL) 85–86, 99, (SLU) 103
National Olympic Committees
  Denmark 46, 58
  Norway 29
  Sweden 67, 199–204
  Finland 93–94

Olympiatoppen 36, 237
Olympic results 14–16
Organizational model 13–14, 277
Overall organization Nordic sport 262

Professionalization 12, 67–71, 260

Specialization 76, 175, 223
Sport cluster 237, 244–247
Sports model 66–68
Sports movement 19, 65, 85,
State role 11–12, 20, 22, 278–79

Team Denmark 43, 57–58
Team culture 121
Team organization 121–122, 227, 274
Top down, bottom up 270, 272–273

Utilitarian 28, 260

Voluntary movement 19, 273, 278

Welfare state model 19, 44, 63–64, 235